Winnifred
E. Short
Memorial

J. Morehouse

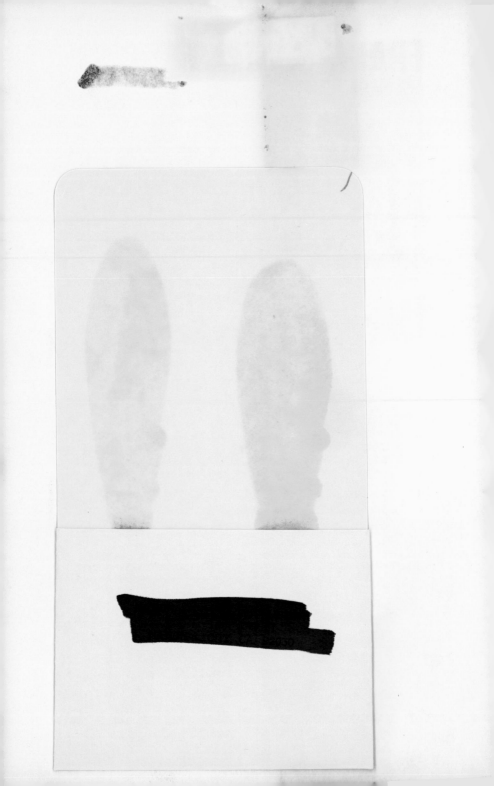

FRANK
THE FIRST YEAR

Other Books by Dave Anderson

Countdown to Super Bowl
Sugar Ray (with Ray Robinson)
Always on the Run
(with Larry Csonka and Jim Kiick)

FRANK

THE FIRST YEAR
FRANK ROBINSON
WITH
DAVE ANDERSON

Holt, Rinehart and Winston
New York

Published simultaneously in Canada by Holt, Rinehart
and Winston of Canada, Limited.

Library of Congress Cataloging in Publication Data
Robinson, Frank, 1935–
  Frank: the first year.
     1. Robinson, Frank, 1935–   2. Cleveland. Base-
ball club (American League) 3. Baseball managing–
Personal narratives. I. Anderson, Dave, II. Title.
GV865.R59A27   796.357'092'4 [B]   75-29787
ISBN 0-03-014951-7

First Edition

Printed in the United States of America

10 9 8 7 6 5 4 3 2 1

To Barbara, Kevin, and Nichelle;
to the memory of Jackie Robinson;
to Hiram Cuevas; to everyone
in the Cleveland Indians' organization;
to Ed Keating;
and to all the others who helped
make the first year possible.

1975 Cleveland Indians
(with 1974 records)

Player	B	T	HT	WT	Birthdate	1974 Club	HR	RBI	BA
					CATCHERS				
Ashby, Alan	S	R	6-2	190	7-8-51	Oklahoma City	2	24	.284
Ellis, John	R	R	6-2	215	8-21-48	Cleveland	10	64	.285
					INFIELDERS				
Bell, Buddy	R	R	6-2	185	8-27-51	Cleveland	7	46	.262
Brohamer, Jack	L	R	5-9	165	2-26-50	Cleveland	2	30	.270
Carty, Rico	R	R	6-2	190	9-1-40	Cleveland	1	16	.363
Crosby, Ed	L	R	6-2	180	5-26-49	Tulsa	0	7	.287
						Oklahoma City	0	8	.389
DaVanon, Jerry	R	R	5-11	175	8-21-45	Tulsa	8	34	.276
						St. Louis	0	4	.150
Duffy, Frank	R	R	6-1	180	10-14-46	Cleveland	8	48	.233
Hermoso, Angel	R	R	5-9	155	10-1-46	Cleveland	0	5	.221
Kuiper, Duane	L	R	6-0	175	6-19-50	Oklahoma City	3	53	.310
						Cleveland	0	4	.500
Lis, Joe	R	R	6-0	200	8-15-46	Minn.-Cleve.	6	19	.200
McCraw, Tom	L	L	6-0	190	11-21-40	Cal.-Cleve.	6	34	.294
Powell, John	L	R	6-4	250	8-17-41	Baltimore	12	45	.265
Robinson, Frank	R	R	6-1	194	8-31-35	Cal.-Cleve.	22	68	.245

vii

1975 Cleveland Indians
(with 1974 records)

OUTFIELDERS

Player	B	T	HT	WT	Birthdate	1974 Club	HR	RBI	BA
Berry, Ken	R	R	5-11	190	5-10-41	Milwaukee	1	24	.240
Gamble, Oscar	L	R	5-11	165	12-20-49	Cleveland	19	59	.291
Hendrick, George	R	R	6-3	195	10-18-49	Cleveland	19	67	.279
Lee, Leron	L	R	6-0	197	3-4-48	Cleveland	5	25	.233
Lowenstein, John	L	R	6-1	175	1-27-47	Cleveland	8	48	.242
Manning, Rick	L	R	6-1	180	9-2-54	Oklahoma City	5	36	.262
Smith, Tommy	L	R	6-3	215	8-1-48	Oklahoma City	10	67	.312
						Cleveland	0	0	.097
Spikes, Charlie	R	R	6-3	220	1-23-51	Cleveland	22	80	.271

PITCHERS

Player	B	T	HT	WT	Birthdate	1974 Club	W	L	ERA
Andersen, Larry	R	R	6-3	180	5-6-53	San Antonio	10	6	3.83
Arlin, Steve	R	R	6-3	200	9-25-45	S.D.-Cleve.	3	12	6.22
Beene, Fred	L	R	5-8	160	11-24-42	N.Y.-Cleve.	4	4	4.66
Bosman, Dick	R	R	6-3	200	2-17-44	Cleveland	7	5	4.11
Buskey, Tom	R	R	6-3	220	2-20-47	N.Y.-Cleve.	2	7	3.36
Eckersley, Dennis	R	R	6-2	190	10-3-54	San Antonio	14	3	3.40
Ellingsen, Bruce	L	L	6-0	170	4-26-49	Oklahoma City	3	4	5.34
Grossman, Bob	R	R	6-4	205	6-19-51	Cleveland	1	1	3.21
						San Antonio	9	11	5.14
Hood, Don	L	L	6-2	180	10-16-49	Baltimore	1	1	3.47
						Cleveland	4	3	4.88
Hilgendorf, Tom	S	L	6-1	190	3-10-42	Oklahoma City	17	7	2.52
Kern, Jim	R	R	6-5	185	3-15-49	Cleveland	0	1	4.80
Kline, Steve	R	R	6-3	200	10-6-47	N.Y.-Cleve.	5	10	4.64
Perry, Gaylord	R	R	6-4	215	9-15-38	Cleveland	21	13	2.51
Perry, Jim	S	R	6-4	205	10-30-36	Cleveland	17	12	2.96
Peterson, Fritz	S	L	6-0	208	2-8-42	N.Y.-Cleve.	9	14	4.39
Raich, Eric	R	R	6-4	230	11-1-51	San Antonio	5	4	2.68
						Oklahoma City	5	6	6.12
Wilcox, Milt	R	R	6-2	185	4-20-50	Cleveland	2	2	4.67

AMERICAN LEAGUE, 1974

EAST	W	L	Pct	GB
Baltimore	91	71	.562	—
New York	89	73	.549	2

WEST	W	L	Pct	GB
Oakland	90	72	.556	—

Prologue:
The First
Shall Not Be Last

Tucson

Shortly after I joined the Cleveland Indians for the last three weeks of the 1974 season, I realized this was a ball club in trouble. The dugout was virtually segregated. On one side was the manager, Ken Aspromonte, with almost all the white players. On the other side was Larry Doby, a black coach, with all the black players. I sat here and there, mostly in the middle. Any ball club that's split along racial lines like that had to be in trouble. The standings reflected my thinking. As late as August 22, the Indians had been in second place in the American League East but now they had dropped to fourth. With a winning streak, they would have had a chance to overtake the Baltimore Orioles or the New York Yankees for the divisional title. That's why they had acquired me—to spark a pennant drive. But in my three weeks, I never heard Ken Aspromonte or any of the coaches or the other players say, "We've still got a chance to win this thing, let's bust our ass." I mentioned it a few times but all I got was blank stares. They just let the team die. The Indians finished a flat fourth with a 77–85 won-lost record.

The next day the Indians announced that I was the new manager, the first black manager in major-league history.

By then I'd seen enough to know I had a tough job to bring the Indians back to life. The segregated dugout was only the beginning. Two weeks before the season ended we were playing a twi-night doubleheader against the Yankees in Shea Stadium when Gaylord Perry, who had been described as "the franchise" ever since he joined the Indians in 1972, lost the opener 5–4, on a ball that fell in the gap in right-center field. George Hendrick, the centerfielder, had no chance to get it. George has a casual style anyway and, I was told, he hadn't been playing all out because he had lost respect for the manager. He also had a pulled hamstring muscle that slowed him up even more. Whatever the reason, a Yankee runner scored from first base for the ball game. In the clubhouse between games, Gaylord was storming around.

"If a guy doesn't want to play," Gaylord growled, "he shouldn't be playing. The next time I pitch, I don't want him out there."

The next two times that Gaylord started, Aspromonte didn't

use George in center field. The third time, on the last day of the season, George went home before the game began because he knew he wouldn't be in the lineup.

Now, as I looked around the Shea Stadium clubhouse, I realized I was the only black player in there. The others, including George, apparently had expected Gaylord to be snarling and had stayed with Larry Doby in the dugout. Some came in later, but Doby and George waited until everybody else joined them in the dugout when the second game was about to start. Everybody but Gaylord, because he took a shower and left the ball park, as a starter usually does after working the first game of a doubleheader.

Within a week, Gaylord was complaining about me and my salary. I heard him on the TV news one night.

"I'm going to be tough contractwise next year," Gaylord said. "I want one dollar more than what Frank Robinson gets."

The next morning, in the Cleveland *Plain Dealer*, his quotes were along the same line—that he'd had three big years as the Indians' best pitcher, that he hadn't really been rewarded, that now that the front office was paying Frank Robinson nearly $175,000, they couldn't say they couldn't afford to pay him big money. That didn't bother me. But in the afternoon paper, the *Cleveland Press*, his quotes were stronger—that the Indians shouldn't be paying me for what I had accomplished with the Cincinnati Reds, the Baltimore Orioles, the Los Angeles Dodgers, and the California Angels, that they should pay me for what I could do now, that he had earned his money but he wondered if I had earned mine. These quotes annoyed me.

I took a copy of the *Press* with me to the ball park. I wanted to show Gaylord the quotes and ask him if they were accurate. I've occasionally had quotes come out stronger than I meant them.

In the clubhouse Gaylord was sitting on the stool in front of his locker. He's a big guy, bigger than me. He's 6-4 and about 215 and he likes to go a day or two without shaving to make him look meaner to batters. I picked up the copy of the *Press*, walked over, and offered it to him.

"Are these quotes straight?" I asked.

He didn't even look at the paper. He just snapped, "Yes," and that really set me off.

"I don't care how much you make next season," I said. "The important thing to me is not that I'm the highest-paid ballplayer on this club or any other club. The important thing to me is that I'm satisfied with what I'm making."

He just looked up at me, not saying a word, not even getting up off his stool.

"I don't want my name dragged through the papers," I said, my voice rising now. "I don't want my salary tossed around in the papers by someone else. I don't want you negotiating your contract through me. If you want to use my salary behind closed doors with Phil Seghi in trying to get more money, fine. Or if I can do anything for you behind closed doors, fine, I'll do it. But not in the papers."

"I'll do anything I want to do," Gaylord said slowly. "As long as I get my money."

It wasn't a shouting match. I was the only one shouting. Gaylord hadn't raised his voice.

"I'm looking out for the young kids on the ball club," Gaylord said. "If I don't stand up for them and speak up, they're not going to get the money they deserve. Me and the other pitchers have been here longer than you have. We deserve ours. And if I don't speak up, the kids aren't going to get theirs."

"Are you going to wait," I said, "until everybody has signed their contract and make sure they got what they want before you sign? You're not worried about these kids. You're worried about yourself. I'm telling you this time—don't use my name in the papers anymore. Next time I won't tell you."

By that, I meant that if it happened again, I'd fight him. But there wasn't anything close to a fight then. I read later that we "almost came to blows," but that was an exaggeration. The other players didn't even have to intervene. They just listened to me yell.

What broke it up was Ken Aspromonte standing in the middle of the clubhouse.

"Let's settle down, everybody," he said. "I want to have a meeting now." And that's when Ken told the players that he had resigned as manager, effective at the end of the season. Apparently he was aware of the whispers that I was going to be the next manager. When he asked the general manager, Phil Seghi, how he stood for next season and didn't get any assurance that he'd be back, he resigned. The newspapers had a big story now. Not only had Ken Aspromonte resigned but the next manager, meaning me, and the Indians' best pitcher had had a confrontation. Gaylord and I didn't talk at all the last few days of the season. But after the news conference when I was announced as manager, I stopped by Phil Seghi's office. Gaylord was there to talk contract. When he saw me, he looked up.

"Congratulations," he said.

"Thank you," I said. "And that thing last week, that was nothing personal. As far as I'm concerned, it's over. Again, if you can use my salary behind closed doors to help your salary, go ahead."

I wasn't shouting this time.

"I realize now that you had a lot of pressure on you then," he said. "Me talking about making one dollar more than you was just a phrase country boys use. I'm happy you're on the ball club because it means I can make more money now. I want you and Phil to know that I don't want to be traded. I'll be happy to pitch for you if I'm here next season."

"As far as I'm concerned," I said, "you will be here next season. I can't guarantee you won't be traded, because a trade could always develop. But we're not going to offer you around just to get rid of you."

We shook hands and that was it. We parted with no hard feelings. Nothing hanging over us. As the new manager, I wasn't about to get rid of my best pitcher, who had won 64 games and pitched more than 1,000 innings in the last three years.

As the new manager, my job is to get my team together, to get the best out of the players, and to win. Gaylord will help us win. He's always been a competitor, like I am. That's good enough for me. I don't blame him for wanting more money. I've always wanted more money. With a one-year contract as a manager who also will be the Indians' designated

hitter, I'll make more money this season than I ever have—
$180,000 plus a furnished apartment in Cleveland for my
wife, Barbara, and our two children, twelve-year-old Kevin
and nine-year-old Nichelle, round-trip airfare from Los Angeles for my family, and the use of a car that the Indians
will arrange for.

Ed Keating put that deal together for me. Ed is in charge
of the team-sports division of the International Management
Group, the firm operated by Mark McCormack, who made
Arnold Palmer a multimillionaire. Ed has been representing
me since 1972 and we're real close.

I don't think any one person is completely responsible for
me becoming the first black manager. But there are four people who each deserve a big share of the credit—Ted Bonda,
Phil Seghi, Ed Keating, and my wife, Barbara, not necessarily
in that order. As the Indians' executive vice-president, Ted
Bonda had to approve when Phil suggested me. Phil knew me
as far back as 1958 when he took over as the Reds' farm
director. But back in July, when the Angels hired Dick
Williams after I thought I might get that job if Bobby Winkles
was fired, I understand now that that was when Ed Keating,
who lives in Cleveland, began thinking about how he could
get me the Indians' job. When the ball club slipped out of
contention, Ed had his chance and he made the most of it.
He even negotiated with Ted and Phil for at least a week
before I knew much about it.

"I didn't tell you," Ed told me later, "because I didn't want
to get your hopes up in case the deal fell through."

It didn't fall through, because Ed had me in the right spot
at the right time. I also had the right credentials—five seasons
in the Puerto Rican Winter League as the manager of the
Santurce team. That's where Barbara comes in. When you're
a ballplayer, you're away from home half the time during the
season. And when I wanted to go to Puerto Rico to manage
to see if I liked it and if I could do it, I talked it over
with her.

"You go ahead," she said. "Don't worry about me and the
kids. We'll be all right." Not every wife would say that.

Along the way there have also been dozens of others who

helped me get where I am now—Jackie Robinson for one, just for what Jackie Robinson did; Hiram Cuevas for another, just for hiring me to manage his Santurce team. I've been a successful player. But other successful black players who have thought about managing weren't willing to go to the Puerto Rican Winter League to learn how to manage. I also learned about myself. I learned that when I'm angry at a ballplayer, wait until tomorrow when I've cooled off to talk to him. I learned not to expect a ballplayer to do what I've done as a hitter or an outfielder or a base runner, I learned to expect only what *he* can do. I learned about handling ballplayers, such as George Hendrick, my centerfielder now.

I don't know why George didn't respect Ken Aspromonte, but I know he respects me. He batted .362 to win the Puerto Rican Winter League batting title last year at Santurce where he played for me.

I'm very open with my players, maybe too open. But I've got to be that way to let them know where I stand and where they stand. At first I didn't talk much to George down there. I knew he had heard so many people nag him about his great potential, about how if he put out more he'd be a superstar. I knew that if I started talking about his potential, I'd bug him. Talk like that used to bug me. But one day George went to bat four times and never swung. I don't mean he never swung hard, I mean he never swung, period. Never took the bat off his shoulder. He looked at every pitch, even the good pitches. Just looked at them. And with men on base. The next day I took him aside.

"What was your thinking yesterday?" I asked. "I'm a hitter. I know you can get fooled the first time up, maybe the second time. But in four times up, you've got to take at least one swing."

"I just got fooled," he said. "Every time I thought inside, the pitch was outside. Every time I thought outside, the pitch was inside. I just kept guessing wrong on every pitch all day."

As we continued to talk, I got deeper into the thinking process of hitting—situations, what the pitcher is thinking, what the batter should be thinking, where the infielders are moving on the pitch, when the base runners should be running, things like that.

"You've got to have a positive attitude every time up," I said. "If you've got five hits, go for six."

"I never heard that before," he said. "Nobody ever talked to me about thinking like that every time you go up there."

"You've got to be kidding me?" I said.

"No," he said very seriously. "Nobody ever sat down and talked baseball to me like this before."

"I'll talk baseball anytime," I said.

I'm always ready to talk baseball. I'm a baseball man. As far back as 1961, when I was with the Reds, I realized that when my career as a player ended, I wanted to stay in baseball. Not in the front office. Not enough action there. I wanted to stay in the dugout as a manager. And by the time I was ready to be a manager, I believed baseball would be ready for a black manager. Not that I was thinking about being the *first* black manager. It turned out that way, but I would be just as happy being the third or the fifth black manager. Probably happier. I understand the social significance of being the *first*, but I don't like the idea of the manager appearing to be bigger than his ball club, the idea of the manager getting most of the attention. That's not fair to the ballplayers. I'm just hoping to blend into the scenery, but that will take time.

To be ready to be a manager, I've also analyzed the styles and the strategies of my own managers. I always wanted to know *why* they did what they did.

With the Orioles when Hank Bauer was the manager, Steve Barber was pitching against the Detroit Tigers in a scoreless game. But he was wild, as he often was. He had walked five or six batters. Around the seventh inning the Tigers had runners on second and third with two out. Al Kaline was the batter, Norm Cash was on deck. I assumed that Hank would order Barber, a lefthanded pitcher, to issue an intentional walk to Kaline, a righthanded batter, and then pitch to Cash, a lefthanded batter. But he let Barber pitch to Kaline, who made the third out. The next day I stopped in Hank's office.

"This isn't a second guess," I said. "But just for my own information, why didn't you put Kaline on?"

"Barber was wild enough by himself," Hank explained. "If we put Kaline on, now they got the bases loaded and there's no open base if he walks Cash—no margin for error. If you got a good control pitcher out there, you put him on. But not with a pitcher who's wild anyway."

I had learned something, as I learned from many of my managers in my travels. For better or for worse.

Birdie Tebbetts, my first manager with the Reds, was always talking to his players in the dugout, especially young players. The first time we were going to face Don Newcombe of the Brooklyn Dodgers my rookie year, Birdie put his arm around me.

"I want you to watch Big Newk tonight," Birdie told me in his fatherly way. "You'll be in the lineup the next time."

Fred Hutchinson was so tough that some of the Reds were afraid of him. I don't want my players afraid of me.

Hank Bauer was a good manager, but he also taught me that a manager should never say something that he doesn't mean. In a meeting once he snapped, "I'll be here when a lot of you guys are gone." We players just looked at each other because we knew that's not the way it works. The players stay and the manager goes, as Hank did the next season. Then the Orioles hired Earl Weaver, the most complete manager I've ever known. The way he used his bench, he involved all twenty-five guys in almost every game. And if we scored eleven runs, he wanted twelve runs. He was always on top of his players and on top of the game, always trying to paint the other manager into a corner.

When I was traded to the Dodgers, I thought Walter Alston would be the same way, on top of everything. But he wasn't.

Alston usually reacted very slowly to situations. He didn't take advantage of his personnel. The year I was there, he seemed to have two plans for every game—to use Manny Mota as a pinch hitter and to use Jim Brewer out of the bullpen, the way he used Mike Marshall out of the bullpen later. I felt when I went to the Angels that the Dodgers wouldn't win a pennant unless the players won it, which is what happened in 1974 when Steve Garvey, Jimmy Wynn, and Mike Marshall each had a big year.

Alston was the only manager I've known who would let a player call in sick. Maury Wills and Willie Davis often did it. The next day, neither of them ever bothered to tell the manager he was all right. Alston had to call them into his office to find out if they could play.

Alston had two sayings. One was "We don't have any superstars here, everybody's the same." That's bullshit. Some players have to be better than others. The other was "I don't care, I don't have to worry about a job, I've got enough shotgun shells." He likes to go hunting in the off-season. But if the manager doesn't care, the players won't care.

I'd always heard about the "Dodgers way to play baseball," how the organization stressed fundamentals. But the year I was there, Willie Davis hardly ever hit the cutoff man on a throw from center field. As far as I could see, nothing was ever said to him. In the dugout, Alston and the coaches would gripe when he missed the cutoff man. But after the inning, I never saw anybody mention it to him. I don't know why.

I do know that I'll mention mistakes like that to my players or I'll have my coaches mention them. I didn't keep any of Aspromonte's coaches, because I wanted to clear the air. In particular, I didn't keep Larry Doby because he had shown me he wasn't loyal to the manager. Doby was hoping to be the first black manager himself. But splitting the team racially wasn't the way to do it.

My third-base coach will be Dave Garcia, who managed El Paso to first place in the Texas League last year. Before that, he was the first-base coach of the San Diego Padres for four years. He was a minor-league infielder for nearly twenty years. He managed in the minors for fourteen years, winning four championships. He also managed in the Mexican Winter League, winning a championship there. Dave Garcia has been around. Anytime I'm not available, like if I'm ejected, he'll be in charge.

My first-base coach will be Tom McCraw, who also will

be a pinch hitter and a first baseman. He's a good hitting instructor and he knows the American League. He's been in it since 1963.

My pitching coach will be Harvey Haddix, who handled that job with the New York Mets, the Cincinnati Reds, and the Boston Red Sox before settling down on his Ohio farm the last three seasons. He's the same Harvey Haddix who pitched a perfect game for twelve innings for the Pittsburgh Pirates in 1960 before losing, 1–0, to the Milwaukee Braves in the thirteenth on an error, an intentional walk, and a hit.

My bullpen coach will be Jeff Torborg, a smart catcher with the Dodgers and Angels when I was there. He'll work with both the pitchers and the catchers. He's the only man to have caught both Sandy Koufax and Nolan Ryan in no-hit games.

And now, as my coaches and I wait for the start of spring training, Phil Seghi has finally completed a deal that he and I have been trying to make for several months. We've got Boog Powell, the big first baseman and an old buddy, and Don Hood, a lefthander I've always liked, from the Orioles for Dave Duncan, a catcher we didn't need. Phil likes the deal. I can tell from the way he's puffing on his pipe. I like the deal too. But mostly I like the idea that it's time to play baseball again. Up to now, I've been mostly talking baseball. During the winter the Indians had me on a promotional tour. They even had me narrate a concert of the Cleveland Orchestra, which was out of my league. But mostly I was on the dais at sports dinners. Barbara was with me at one in Chicago and when it was over, she asked me if I had heard what a man in the audience had grumbled while I was talking.

"No," I said. "What did he say?"

"Oh, never mind now," she said.

"Barbara, what did the man say?"

"He said, 'Sit down, nigger, you're going to finish last.' "

Not this nigger.

In the Desert

Tucson, Thursday, February 27

When my wake-up call rang at 7 o'clock, I got dressed and went to have breakfast with my coaches. I didn't think I would be nervous and I don't think I was. But in the reflection of the big windows near the Sheraton Pueblo lobby, I realized that I had forgotten to comb my hair. My first hour on the job and I wasn't even managing myself too well.

But the ball park relaxed me. I'm always comfortable at the ball park, any ball park. We train at Hi Corbett Field, a beautiful little minor-league ball park where the Tucson team of the Pacific Coast League plays. Behind the outfield fence are palm trees and fir trees. High beyond the grandstand are desert mountains that range in color from pink to purple, depending on the angle of the sun. Off our clubhouse I have a small white-walled office with a desk, a telephone, a locker, and my own shower. I had just finished putting on my uniform with number 20 on it when the writers drifted in—Russ Schneider of the *Plain Dealer*, Bob Sudyk of the *Press*, and Hank Kozloski of the *Lorain Journal*, a suburban newspaper. Schneider and Sudyk are very competitive. They don't even talk to each other. I've already told both of them that they're not going to get me between them. "If one of you ask me a question when the other isn't around, I'm going to answer it," I told them a few weeks ago. "But then I'm not going to run to the other guy and tell him I told you this or that." I had to establish rules for them, just like I've had to establish rules for my players. On my desk was a clipboard with sheets of white paper on which my rules had been mimeographed. Russ Schneider's first question was about the rules.

"Are you going to have a curfew?" he asked.

"We'll have one here in training camp, 2 o'clock," I said. "But not during the season."

"Not during the season?"

"Grown men having to be in by midnight, that's silly," I said. "Or even two and a half hours after a night game. If the bus gets to the hotel after 11 o'clock, that's 2 o'clock right there. Most guys are back by then anyway. Anybody who wants to break it finds a way to break it. If somebody abuses it, I'll clamp down on the individuals, yes, but I don't believe in taking away privileges from the rest of the ball-club. Out of twenty-five guys, you only have to worry about five or six."

"Were you ever fined," I was asked, "for breaking curfew?"

"No, and I was caught only one time. With the Angels last season, we were in Milwaukee on my thirty-ninth birthday and we lost, 6–5, after leading, 5–2. I decided not to do anything. I figured it was silly to go over to the Red Garter and drink just to drink, but John Roseboro called and asked me to go to dinner. We went downstairs in the hotel about 10:30 and the next thing we knew it was 1 o'clock. Back in my room, the red message light was blinking. I called the operator and she told me, 'You have a message from Mr. Dick Williams, he called at 12:15.' But I didn't want to call him then, he might be asleep. The next day I heard some of the players talking about how Williams had checked their rooms and I told them he had checked me too. 'He wouldn't call *you*,' they said. But he did. When he talked to me, he told me, 'I'm not going to fine you, we were only after two guys.' The two relief pitchers who had blown the game. But they were in. He could have fined me anywhere from $250 up."

"Maybe that got you traded," one of them said.

"Could be," I said. "I never thought of that."

"You don't seem to be under much pressure."

"Not today," I said. "It might happen on the 3rd [the first day with the full squad] or the 13th [the first exhibition game] or April 8th [the season opener], but not today."

"How good a team do you think you'll have?"

"We'll have a good exciting, entertaining ball club. Real-istically, you've got to feel like you can win. Otherwise you're shortchanging the players. But it's going to be a tough divi-sion. I always like Baltimore. I've been there and they still have the talent. You have to make them co-favorites with the Yankees right now."

I glanced at the pocket watch on my desk. "It's time for the meeting," I said and they drifted out.

We have twenty-seven players in camp now, almost all

pitchers and catchers. They were sitting on the red wooden benches in front of their lockers at 9:30 when I walked in to hold my first meeting. No big speech. I talked mostly about the routine until Monday, when the rest of the ball club would be here. As the other players were filing out toward the field for the workout, Buddy Bell came over. His father, Gus, and I were teammates on the Reds and Buddy used to be around the ball park, a cute towheaded kid. He's still got that whitish blond hair and he's my third baseman and a good one. But he's coming off knee surgery. He asked if he could run up and down the steps of the stadium and exercise his knee with weights instead of doing calisthenics. No problem. But he was concerned about his weight.

"I'm scared to get on that scale," he said.

Several weeks earlier I had sent each player a letter that included a weight he was to report at.

"You want me at 200," he said. "But I think my best weight is 205. I feel weak when I'm only 200."

"What are you now?"

"I don't know. I'm scared to get on there. I might weigh too much."

"You're not really supposed to weigh in until Monday anyway," I said. "If you want to see what it is now, go ahead. I won't look. Get it down to 205 and we'll go from there."

"Yes, sir," he said.

He's a big kid, he can carry the weight. And he's a good kid, the all-American boy, easy to manage. I'm not worried as much about his weight as I am about his knee. The less he weighs, the less strain he'll be putting on his knee.

Out on the field, the weather was perfect. Warm and dry, not a cloud in that big blue desert sky. I joined in the calisthenics but I didn't run the two laps around the field. I threw with the others to loosen up my arm a little, but I was the last to take batting practice. When the pitchers ran fifteen laps from foul line to foul line, I did seven. That was enough for the old man. I wasn't worried about myself. It was more important for me as the manager to get the other players in shape first.

As soon as I got back to my desk after the workout, Cy Buynak, our clubhouse man, was there with two Cokes and a cardboard cup with ice cubes in it. He filled the cup for me, the bubbles frothing up over the ice. "How about that?" I said out loud. It was the first time anybody ever poured a Coke for me at a ball park. I must be the manager.

Tucson, Friday, February 28

During batting practice I stayed in the outfield, going from player to player, asking their ideas on what we can do to make this a better ball club. Two things kept coming out— more work on fundamentals and a better attitude of rooting for each other. Gaylord Perry suggested that instead of the pitchers waiting until after the end of the workout to do their running from foul line to foul line, they should be permitted to do it as soon as they're pitching batting practice so that their arms don't stiffen up. He also mentioned that he likes to take infield grounders during batting practice. It sharpens his fielding.

"Let me check with the coaches on the running," I said, "but it sounds all right."

Fritz Peterson mentioned something else that I didn't have an immediate answer for. "I hope you play as much as possible," he told me. "How much do you plan to play?"

"I don't know," I said. "I can't give you x number of games or x number of at-bats."

"It's important for you to play. I know when I was pitching for the Yankees, it was always a tougher lineup for me if you were in it. Not only because of your bat, but also the intangibles."

"I'll play," I assured him, "as much as I feel like I should play or have to play."

I want to play. I want to get 3,000 hits and 600 homers. I've got 2,900 hits and 574 homers. But most of all, I want my ball club to win. After the workout, for the first time I had to tell a player that he had been traded. Phil Seghi had completed a deal that sent Milt Wilcox to the Chicago Cubs for Dave LaRoche, a swap of lefthanded pitchers.

"Good luck, Milt," I said. "I hope you do well there."

That was all. I know what it's like to be traded. Tell me quick. I never wanted to hear any bullshit.

Tucson, Saturday, March 1

I informed the pitchers of the change in running procedure that Gaylord had suggested. I just wish Gaylord was as concerned about the calisthenics. He just goes through the motions. But his brother, Jim, has a great attitude. He's working hard. I also talked to the young pitchers privately. After the deals for Hood and LaRoche, some people think the staff is set. Bob Sudyk of the *Press* was talking as if he was going to make a big story out of it. I didn't want our young pitchers thinking they didn't have a chance. I talked to Jim Kern, Dennis Eckersley, Larry Andersen, and Eric Raich. I reminded them not to believe whatever they read or heard about the staff.

"If you look good here," I told them, "you can make this ball club. Or it'll help you to be called up later on."

I also walked around in the outfield again, talking to players and getting an idea on who would make a good captain. The names of Frank Duffy and Johnny Ellis were mentioned the most. I like the idea of Duffy, but Jeff Torborg thought that Ellis would have enough trouble handling all the catching by himself without also having the responsibility of being captain. I was still thinking about it when it was the manager's turn to hit in batting practice.

"Has everybody else hit?" I asked Dave Garcia.

"Everybody except Gene Dusan," he said, referring to one of the nonroster catchers we have in camp. "You hit after him."

But then Duane Kuiper walked up. He's one of our young infielders. He wasn't due to be in uniform until Monday.

"When did you get in, Duane?" I asked.

"Just a few minutes ago," he told me.

Gene Dusan had finished hitting by now and I was about to go into the cage when I heard Dave Garcia yelling.

"All right, Duane," he said. "You hit next."

I slammed the bat down like I was angry and threw my helmet. "Why don't you guys who are running things get organized and let the players know what's going on? Here's a guy in camp five minutes and he's hitting ahead of me." I ran out toward the outfield and I could hear everybody laughing. That's one of the ways I am. People wonder if I'm going to change now that I'm a manager, but I'm not going to change.

Tucson, Sunday, March 2

I was hoping that things would get better with Gaylord but they haven't and they probably won't. He went through the motions in the calisthenics again. And he was fooling around again. He and Jim Kern usually pair off in the calisthenics. And fooling around, Gaylord accidentally spiked him. Nothing serious. But it could've been. His spikes cut through Jim's sanitary hose and left a three-inch scratch on his shin. I might have overlooked that but then Gaylord ignored the running rule. I've told the players that when they're moving any distance from one spot to another on the field, I want them running. For the pitchers throwing batting practice, that means after they warm up in the bullpen beyond our third-base dugout, they're supposed to run to the mound. When it was Gaylord's turn, he waltzed to the mound. I say "waltz" because it was even slower than a walk. Then he took his sweet time scraping the dirt off the rubber with his spikes, moving the ball container around, flipping the resin bag. He threw batting practice at his pace until Buddy Bell hit a ball off the protective screen in front of the mound. Gaylord took exception to that. His next pitch was at Buddy's head. I don't like throwing at anybody in batting practice, period, but Buddy has a bad knee. If the pitch had been closer, Buddy might have twisted his bad knee trying to get out of the way. It could have ruined Buddy for the year. It could have hurt the ball club. Buddy retaliated by tossing his bat toward the mound. Not really angrily but to let Gaylord know how he felt.

"Nice try, Buddy," somebody yelled. "Too bad you missed him."

Gaylord was stomping around, saying, "It's about time I moved on to another team anyway." He's been making little comments like that all the time. They're not really directed at anybody, but everybody can hear them. When he's running from foul line to foul line, he'll be mumbling, "What are we doing all this running for? We don't need all this." Another time he said, "I guess they'll be trading me for a couple more lefthanders." Our two new pitchers, Hood and LaRoche, are lefthanders. Gaylord even told one of the coaches today, "Why aren't any of the black players out here working out?" I don't know what color he considers Charlie Spikes because Charlie was working out today even though, as an outfielder, he doesn't have to be in uniform until tomorrow. But we don't have any black pitchers or black catchers.

The first few days I gave Gaylord the benefit of the doubt on all his little comments. But tomorrow I'll call him into my office before the 9:30 meeting to talk to him man to man and see what's on his mind. I'm not going to put up with the attitude that he has now. It'll be my first meeting with a player whose attitude I'm unhappy with.

Tucson, Monday, March 3

In my office I phoned Phil Seghi to let him know that I would be talking to Gaylord about his attitude. I didn't want one of the writers finding out about our meeting and hitting Phil with it cold when he got to the ball park. And when Gaylord came into my office, I let him know right away I meant business.

"Close the door," I said.

He did, then he sat down.

"Is there anything on your mind that's bothering you?" I said. "Anything you don't like? Anything you have to say to me about the way things are being run so far?"

"No," he said. "Anything bothering you?"

"Yes, there is. I don't like your overall attitude. I told the players the first day that I want them running anytime they're moving around. That means the pitcher running from the bullpen to the mound, or running off the mound to wherever they're going. You haven't done this yet and I even reminded everybody Saturday."

"What are you talking about?" he said.

"Like yesterday you warmed up in the bullpen to throw bp, but when we called for you, you were in the dugout. You took your time coming out. You not only walked, you strolled to the mound. You took your time throwing bp, then you took your time walking off the mound when you were through."

"Well," he said, "I forgot."

"How could you forget when this is only our fifth day and I told you the third day and everybody else is running on and off the mound. And in the calisthenics, you're just going through the motions and fooling around. Yesterday you even spiked Jim Kern."

"I was just trying to have some fun," he said, "to break the monotony."

"And the little comments you're making about how we're going to trade you for two lefthanders and how it's time for you to get away from this ball club anyway. Apparently you want to be traded."

"That's baseball talk," he said. "You know I pitch my 300 innings every year. You know I win my 20 games. You don't have anybody else to do that."

"You're right, I can't look out there and say we have somebody who is going to pitch 300 innings and win 20 games, but if you feel that's going to keep you here with a bad attitude, you're wrong. I'd rather have someone with a good attitude, maybe not as much ability as you have, but with a good attitude that's better for the ball club than the attitude you have. You know the players here respect you, they look up to you. If they see you doing certain things, they're going to wonder why Gaylord can get away with these things. That pulls a ball club apart."

"Well," he said, "if you're going to watch every little move I make . . ."

"I'm not watching *you*. It's my job to watch *everybody*. This is why I was able to see you not doing what you're supposed to do. Instead of getting better, you're getting worse. Yesterday was the last straw."

"If you feel that way, if you're going to be watching every little move I make, maybe it's best that you trade me."

"If *you* feel that way, then evidently you've been thinking about wanting to be traded. If that's your attitude, I'm not going to let anybody tear this ball club apart. There's a super attitude here and we're going to keep it that way. No one individual is bigger than this ball club."

He looked at me, then he said, "You have anything else to say?"

"No, I've said mine," I told him. "You have anything else to say."

"No," he said.

He got up and walked out of the office. End of confrontation.

I'm not the type that holds grudges. I just felt that I had something I had to say to Gaylord and I said it. That's the way I am. I don't believe in holding things within me. I want my players to be the same way. I told them that a few minutes later, in my first meeting with the full squad. I told them I wanted a positive attitude.

"No one individual is bigger than the ball club," I said. "Everybody will be treated the same."

I made sure I wasn't looking over where Gaylord was sitting when I said that. I didn't mean just him.

"I don't want umpire baiters. I don't want a crybaby ball club that will get a reputation for crying about every call that goes against us. Anytime you have a beef, have your say and that's it. I'll be out there to back you up. If it comes to the point where somebody has to get run out of the game, let the manager get run out, not the player. The players are more important than the manager. We've got the players here for an aggressive, smart, running ball club. We've got as good a ball club as any in the American League, as good as any in our division. I know you've read where Baltimore has made trades and that the Yankees should be the favorites. But that's on paper. On the field I think we match up as well as anyone.

We're going to be a dedicated ball club that's willing to sacrifice individual performance for the good of the team. We're going to have togetherness. That's the only way good ball clubs are successful. That doesn't include Oakland—they have super talent, they're in a league by themselves as far as not getting along among themselves and still winning. But the ball clubs I've been on that have been successful have always had a togetherness. I think that's necessary. I want us to have it here."

I told them my thoughts on a curfew, then I read them my list of rules:

No children or friends admitted to the clubhouse at any time unless they have a pass or the manager's permission. *Never* after a loss. No friends will be permitted in our clubhouse on the road anytime.

The ball club will not be responsible for lost or damaged garment bags carried on charter or commercial flights.

Alcoholic beverages will not be allowed when flying on the day of a game. At other times, the abuse of this privilege will result in the elimination of all alcoholic beverages for the offender on future flights, plus a $200 fine.

The dress code is that a sport coat is to be worn on all flights while traveling as a member of the team; a sport coat also is to be worn in the dining room of the team hotel.

Players will be expected to conduct themselves as gentlemen on and off the field, in hotels, planes and other means of transportation. Violators, as judged by the manager, will be subject to disciplinary action.

Missing a team flight is a $500 fine. The player also will pay his airfare to the next city.

No wives will be permitted on charter flights but they will be permitted to travel on commercial flights, with the permission of the manager.

Moustaches are fine, but no other facial hair will be permitted. Long hair and sideburns are also allowed as long as they are well groomed.

Everyone out for batting and infield practice. If injured, be on the field unless excused by the manager or a coach.

They seemed to accept those rules easily, especially the lack of a curfew during the season. I hope they're mature enough to handle it. And on the field in our first workout with the full squad, the attitude continued to be super. Gaylord didn't have to do much except shag in the outfield. After the workout, and after the writers had finished talking to me, I called Frank Duffy and George Hendrick into my office, one after the other, and told them I'd like them to be my co-captains. George was really surprised.

"Why me?" he said.

"I want you to run the outfield," I said.

"I'd love that."

Just the way he said it, I knew that he liked the idea. I think it will be good for George and good for the ball club. I didn't do it to try to get along with him or to try and pump any life in him. The centerfielder should run the outfield. And with George in on the meetings with me and the coaches, the players will know officially that he isn't just the centerfielder out there moving people around; he's the co-captain and he carries authority. Frank Duffy, maybe the most underrated shortstop in the big leagues, also reacted enthusiastically.

"It'll keep me on my toes," he said.

"You'll be in on the meetings," I said. "You'll know how we want to pitch opposing hitters and how we want to defense them. You can move people around without asking me or without the dugout doing it. You can also save me trips to the mound."

"I'd be honored," he said.

Now that's a good attitude. I left my office in a better mood than when I arrived.

Tucson, Tuesday, March 4

Soon after the workout started, Phil Seghi told me that Gaylord had been in to see him yesterday.

"Yesterday?" I said.

"After the workout."

"Why didn't you tell me yesterday instead of waiting until now?"

"I thought it could wait."

I found out later that Phil didn't tell me until he realized that Russ Schneider had found out about his meeting with Gaylord, and he wanted to tell me before Russ did. But he should've told me yesterday, just like I phoned him before I had Gaylord in my office.

"What did Gaylord say?"

"He thinks," Phil said, "that after what you said to him, he might be better off being traded."

"What did you tell him?"

"That you were the manager. But after the workout, why don't the three of us sit down in my office and talk this thing out."

"Good, it might be better with three people."

After the workout we gathered in Phil's office under the grandstand. But instead of demanding to be traded, Gaylord talked about how the foul-line-to-foul-line running wasn't really helping the pitchers. He preferred 60-yard sprints.

"If you took a poll," he said, "most of the pitchers would rather be running sprints."

"I'm not going to take a poll," I said. "This isn't a popularity contest. This isn't a quiz show. But we were going to start having the pitchers run sprints Thursday anyway. That's in Harvey's schedule. If you think the pitchers would be happier running sprints, we'll start them tomorrow instead of Thursday."

"No," he said, "if we're going to run sprints Thursday we can do the foul-line running one more day."

"No, we'll do it tomorrow," I said. "If it'll make you happier, we'll do it tomorrow. What else is on your mind?"

"What about my routine before I pitch?"

He was talking about when he might throw between starts. "I'd be crazy to change any pitcher's routine," I said, "but the overall conditioning is going to be the same for everybody."

"But why'd you get on me for not doing the calisthenics? I can't respect you for that."

"You mean to tell me," I said, "that you don't respect me because something was on my mind and I called you into my office and told you face-to-face behind closed doors? You don't respect me for that?"

"That's right, I don't."

"I thought you were a bigger man than that. I could've gotten on you in front of everybody about the calisthenics, but that's not the way I am. You're a veteran player. You've earned that respect from me and now you're telling me you don't respect me for giving you that respect. If you feel that way, Gaylord, you're not the man I thought you were."

"I guess I took it the wrong way."

We talked a few more minutes, with Phil helping to smooth out our differences, then Gaylord stood up and said, "This was a good meeting, I liked this." We shook hands.

"It was a good meeting," I said. "I'm glad we did it."

Walking out of Phil's office, I had a good feeling inside. I think Gaylord realizes now that I have the backing of the front office. I think he also realizes that I'm willing to listen and learn. I don't know if he realizes that I don't have anything against him personally, because I can't look inside another man. I can only look inside myself. And now I think Gaylord and I will have a very workable relationship, a very professional relationship. That's what it's all about.

Tucson, Wednesday, March 5

Until now, Gaylord was always in the back of the pack when we ran two laps around the ball park at the start of the workout. But today he was up front. And now that my meetings with Gaylord have been in the papers, Charles O. Finley phoned Phil about trying to get Gaylord in a trade. Phil asked him what the A's were willing to give up.

"Blue Moon Odom," Finley said.

"We'll take Vida Blue," said Phil, "and Reggie Jackson."

"Be serious," Finley said.

Phil knew Finley wouldn't consider that deal. But with Finley, anything is worth a try. You don't know which player he might be angry at that day.

"But you have a pitcher," Finley said, "who isn't happy there."

"If *you* went by that," Phil said, "you'd have to trade everybody."

Tucson, Thursday, March 6

You'd never know it by reading the papers but Gaylord isn't my only player. He's not even my only pitcher. The exhibition games begin next Thursday and when I got back to my suite in the Sheraton Pueblo after the workout, I began jotting down a rotation for the seventeen pitchers on the big yellow legal pad that I do my paperwork on. It has to be done now so that the pitchers will have a schedule to go by—throw batting practice, rest the next day, pitch in a game the day after. And for each day's workout, I have to list the hitters on the extra diamonds we use for bp across the street from the ball park. I'm not used to paperwork. When she types up the lists, Phil's secretary, Trudy Hargis, has to bail me out sometimes.

"Don't you have a player named Powell?" she asked today.

"Of course we have a player named Powell," I told her.

"Well," she said, "he's not on these lists you gave me."

It's times like that when managing can be embarrassing. It also can be dangerous. After dinner I was having a Tanqueray and tonic with my coaches and munching on peanuts when I chipped a tooth. Got to find a dentist in the morning. Fast.

Tucson, Friday, March 7

My ball club was working out but I was in a dentist's chair. Dr. Frederic Sowerby was shaking his head.

"You'll need a root canal job for that molar," he said. "I have to send you over to Dr. Leonard Weiner."

By the time I finally got to the ball park, Dave Garcia had everything running smoothly. No big deal that the manager wasn't there. They probably never even missed me. Tonight I went over to the KGUN-TV studios to tape the "Issues and Answers" show. I was introduced as a managerial "first"—

yeah, the first one to need root canal work his first week on the job.

Tucson, Saturday, March 8

When it rains in the desert, it looks like it'll never stop. Not to waste the day, we had a chalk talk in the clubhouse on cutoff positions on throws from the outfield. Frank Duffy has a stronger arm than any of our second basemen. On balls hit to center field I want him out there as the cutoff man. To left field, Duffy naturally would be the cutoff man. To right field, the second baseman naturally would be. But in center field where I've got a choice, I want my shortstop taking the relay.

The rain fooled us. It stopped. I even threw a little bp myself, a little too soon. My arm is killing me tonight. But when my arm gets in shape, I'll be able to throw as much as half an hour of bp three times a week. I've got something on the ball.

Tucson, Sunday, March 9

In our first intrasquad game, Maury Wills stole two bases. He's been in camp since last Monday as our baserunning instructor. He did the same thing for the Dodgers in other years. When the Dodgers found out he was going to work for us, their president, Peter O'Malley, wrote him a letter saying that Maury had betrayed them. Maury replied that nobody from the Dodgers had even contacted him and here it was January, so he took our offer. The Dodgers can be very possessive. After he leaves us, he has plenty of time to go to the Dodgers' camp but they don't want him now. He'll work with the Houston Astros and the San Diego Padres instead. And he'll be working with us all year through the magic of videotape. During his first lecture, Tom McCraw suggested that we put Maury on videotape.

"Then if we want to refresh a player on something during the season," Tom said, "we can play the tape."

Great idea. Phil agreed. Our public relations director,

Randy Adamack, got the University of Arizona to lend us a videotape machine. But as good as Maury's lectures and conversations were all week, the real thing today was even better. Here's a guy who's forty-two years old, who last played in 1972, and he stole two bases easier than any of my ballplayers could. He's not anywhere near as fast as he used to be, but that's the point—it's not the speed, it's knowing how to get a jump. Against lefthander Mike Baldwin, a nonroster pitcher we were looking at, he took a lead, checked the pitcher's motion on two pitches, and he was gone. He probably had the base stolen but the hitter fouled off the pitch.

To show how smart he is, he realized he got a good jump, but he also realized he wasn't as fast. On the next pitch he broke quicker and used a different slide, a hook slide away from the tag. Duane Kuiper took the throw. No chance.

In his lectures, Maury had told the players that when they're on first base against a lefthanded pitcher, to watch his head. If he's looking at the runner and starts his motion, he's going to the plate. But when he looks at the runner, looks to the plate, and then his leg comes up, he's going to try a pickoff. His head is the decoy. So when Baldwin looked over and then came up with his leg before looking at the plate, Maury knew. He took off.

On his other steal, Maury was leading off second base with righthander Bob Grossman pitching. Grossman looked back one time, then threw to the plate, but Maury stole third easily. I've known players who can hardly run when they put on spikes at spring training after an off-season of walking around in regular shoes. Here's a guy forty-two years old who steals two bases without hardly breaking a sweat. I just hope my ballplayers remember what Maury told them.

Tucson, Monday, March 10

I talked to some of the players to get their feelings on how they'd prefer to be used in the exhibition games. George Hendrick told me he'd like to play nine innings as often as possible during the early part, then slack off in the middle.

Jack Brohamer indicated he'd like to play second base the full nine innings two or three days in a row, then have a day off.

"That's fine with me," I said. "But the last week I want to put a team together to open the season with."

I didn't even ask Frank Duffy, because I want to make sure he gets a rest now and then. I'm told that last year he played every inning of every exhibition game and went into September before he had a rest. He was dog-tired by then.

Tucson, Tuesday, March 11

Another tough day. Cold and rainy. After some root canal work, I wasn't in much of a mood to do or say anything at the workout. Even when Phil told me that Tom Hilgendorf had been traded to the Philadelphia Phillies for a minor-league outfielder, Nellie Garcia, and cash, I just listened. From our reports, Hilgendorf was a lefthander who had trouble getting lefthanded hitters out. Now that we've acquired two new lefthanders in Hood and LaRoche, we felt Hilgendorf would have a tough time making the ball club. It's as simple as that. Phil also mentioned that the Red Sox keep calling him.

"They want Gaylord," he said.

"Who are they offering?" I asked.

"Moret, Griffin, and Carbo."

"No way," I said. "No way."

"That's what I told them."

Roger Moret is an unproven lefthander. Doug Griffin is a second baseman with a bad back. Bernie Carbo is a part-time outfielder. If the Red Sox want our best pitcher, they'll have to come up with a better offer than that.

Tucson, Wednesday, March 12

I went to Greyhound Park and bet a few dogs tonight, the first time I've relaxed since spring training started. It was nice to get away from the phone. But it cost me a few bucks. I don't know exactly how much because when I lose, I don't figure out how much. I only count it when I win. I'm not much of a gambler. I take Barbara up to Las Vegas once a year and play a little blackjack and a few slot machines. But that's all.

Tucson, Thursday, March 13

For the first exhibition game, Joe Garagiola had me wired for his TV show. Joe told me, "Do your thing, we'll bleep out anything that shouldn't be in there." Joe's easy to work with because he was a ballplayer himself. He's got a sense of humor that ballplayers appreciate. Just before I carried the lineup card out to the umpires, I was thinking about Jackie Robinson and all the people, black and white, who helped me in my lifetime, who made this thing happen. The dugout was jammed with ballplayers and writers and cameramen and technicians, but it was very quiet. Maybe they understood my moment of reflection. Whatever, there was hardly a sound. But those are the moments that Joe Garagiola waits for.

"Just think about it, Frank Robinson," he said solemnly in that crowded dugout. "Managing is a lonely job."

I broke up at that because managing has been anything but lonely for me. And there was that question from the writers again, "Are you nervous?" I told them no because I really wasn't nervous then. But once the game got under way, my heart was pounding a little faster than usual. I didn't want to foul up. I didn't want to forget anything. When we got a 3–0 lead on the San Francisco Giants, that settled me down. Gaylord wasn't as sharp as he will be, but his brother, Jim, was very impressive with good control. But the Giants tied it up in the ninth at 4–4 and in the tenth they got two on with two out. I brought in Dave LaRoche to pitch to Ed Goodson, a lefthanded hitter as far as I knew. But he stepped in right-handed. On the first pitch he doubled to right-center for two runs and we lost, 6–4.

I learned later that Goodson is experimenting on being a switch-hitter this season. Now they tell me.

Overall we played a good game. We didn't make any errors. And our big rookie righthander, Jim Kern, threw the ball well. I wasn't that disappointed in losing, I really wasn't. It was good to get the first game out of the way so the ball club can return to normalcy. Maybe the nicest thing that happened today was getting a phone call just before game time from the front-office staff in Cleveland wishing me luck. That was a nice gesture.

Yuma, Friday, March 14

Phil was fuming. Commissioner Bowie Kuhn had been quoted in the papers as saying, "I was sorry to see Seghi get into the confrontation between Gaylord and Frank. I thought he should have let them settle it themselves." Phil phoned the commissioner and told him it was none of his business, that it was a club matter. That's a switch. Usually the commissioner describes a controversy as a "club matter" in order to avoid getting involved. To me, Phil did the right thing when he called Gaylord and me into his office. And he did the right thing today in defending his role as mediator.

After the workout, two buses took us across the desert to Yuma, where we'll play the Padres tomorrow. I got on the first bus and sat in the front seat across from the driver. That seat is always reserved for the manager. But sitting there wasn't strange to me. I'd sat there in Puerto Rico on bus trips. What was strange was making the trip at all. The last few years I didn't make many long bus trips, especially for the early games. But now I've got to make all the bus trips and this was a long one—five hours to Yuma, down in the corner of Arizona by the California and Mexican borders. Halfway here, the bus driver suddenly pulled off into a little roadside place.

"What's going on?" I asked.

"I get a coffee break here."

Both drivers got out and had their coffee. In about ten minutes, we were moving again. The next time Marvin Miller negotiates a contract for the players, maybe he'll arrange for a coffee break in the fifth inning. Or at least before we go into extra innings.

Yuma, Saturday, March 15

We beat the Padres, 9–1, and it was nice to get that first win even if I'm not going all out to win ball games now. I've got to look at too many ballplayers, good and bad. I didn't like the behavior of Bob Grossman, one of our rookie pitchers. After he got out of a jam in the first inning, he stormed up and down the dugout because he had been wild. I don't want any of my ballplayers doing that.

"Sit down and relax and think about the next hitter," I told him. "That inning is gone. Forget about it."

I had my first scene with an umpire after a ball rolled under the players' bench next to the dugout. In these small ball parks the dugouts sometimes aren't big enough for all your players and an outside bench is needed. When the ball went under the bench, I complained to Doug Harvey, the National League umpire, that it was the same as going into the dugout.

"No," he said. "The ball's in play."

"To me, it's like part of the dugout."

"You should've thought about that before the game," he said. "You should've asked me about it then."

"You should've told me about it."

We went at it pretty good but finally I said, "Hey, this is only spring training, I'm just kidding, settle down." Umpires don't always appreciate a sense of humor. Especially my sense of humor. I like to needle people, but not everybody realizes I'm kidding. Like in the B game this morning the plate umpire was Bob Bavasi, the twenty-year-old son of Buzzy Bavasi, the Padres' president. I thought the kid missed a few pitches.

"No wonder you're not in the front office with your dad," I yelled. "You can't see."

He didn't realize I was kidding and neither did his father. "Do me a favor," Buzzy said to me not long after, "don't be so hard on him." I wasn't trying to be hard on him. I was just trying to have some fun. I hadn't been to a B game since 1956 when I joined the Reds as a rookie. Then it was an honor to play in a B game. And if I wasn't invited to sit around for the regular game in the afternoon, I felt insulted. But times have changed. Now some players feel that the B game is degrading.

Yuma, Sunday, March 16

Another umpire scene developed, this time with Paul Maltby, who is being inspected by the American League for future reference. I knew him from Puerto Rico and he's not ready. He was squeezing the strike zone. He was giving the Padres' fastball pitchers the low strike, but not our sinkerball pitchers. I got on him a little, yelling, "The only place those low fast-balls would be strikes would be in a bowling alley." He came over to our dugout on the run and stuck his face in mine.

"The next time you do that," I said, "I'll bite your nose off."

By then Paul Runge, the National League umpire at first base, had also come over. He threatened to eject me.

"It's spring training," I said. "What're you going to prove?"

They both cooled off. But umpires get uptight anytime, any-place. Maybe with better calls on balls and strikes we wouldn't have lost again, 4–2, our second defeat in three games. Not that I'm disturbed. I'm still looking at ballplayers. And the more I look at rookie outfielder Rick Manning, the more I like him. He's got good baseball instincts. He runs the bases good. He has a good arm. He swings the bat good. But what's really good about him is that he's only twenty years old. Rick Manning probably won't go to Cleveland with us, but remember the name.

Palm Springs, Monday, March 17

I trained here with the Angels the last two years, so the beau-tiful weather didn't surprise me. But the game wasn't too beautiful. We lost again, 5–3, which didn't bother me as much as two mistakes. George Hendrick hustled a double when his hot grounder ran up the second baseman's arm and trickled into short centerfield. But on a grounder to the shortstop, he was thrown out at third base. That's one of the things we've talked about—if you're on second base with less than two out, don't run on a grounder to the shortstop. The other mistake involved Johnny Ellis not calling for a pitchout with Mickey Rivers of the Angels on first base. Mickey likes to run. He took a big lead and we almost picked him off.

"Don't be afraid to call for a pitchout," I've told all our catchers. "It's better to call for one than not to call for one."

Sure enough, Mickey took off on the next pitch, John Doherty doubled down the rightfield line, and Rivers scored from first. Now if John had been alert and called for a pitchout, we might've gotten out of the inning.

I want my ball club to think and see. That's what winning ball clubs do.

I also want Dick Williams to pay me the $500 he promised me. When he took over the Angels midway through last season, he appointed me captain.

"It's worth $500," he said. "And if the ball club doesn't give you the $500, I'll give it to you out of my own pocket."

I never brought it up, but after I was traded I asked Harry Dalton, the Angels' general manager, about it. He told me it was against club policy to pay the captain extra money. But when I mentioned it to Dick at the winter meetings in New Orleans, he said, "Harry didn't give you that money yet? I'll give you the money, don't worry." When we were exchanging lineup cards with the umpires today, I brought it up again.

"Harry didn't give you that money yet?" he said.

He didn't say he'd give it to me this time. He didn't have to say he'd give it to me last year but when he did, I expected him to keep his word. I'll keep embarrassing him until I get it. But now we've got something else going. Dick told the Angels' writers today that he has the best four-man rotation in baseball with Nolan Ryan, Bill Singer, Frank Tanana, and Andy Hassler, and the Angels' writers trotted over to ask me about it.

"I'm not sure about my fourth starter," I said, "but I'll match my top three against his top three anytime."

I was thinking of the two Perrys and Fritz Peterson, who I discovered later have a combined lifetime record of 527–441 against 203–201 for Ryan, Singer, and Tanana.

"But what about potential?" one of the writers said.

"Potential doesn't win ball games. Nolan Ryan can be one of the best pitchers of all time but he's still feeling his way. Singer is a fine pitcher when he's healthy but he's coming off a bad back. Tanana won 14 games last year but he lost 19, and Hassler's a good prospect but we're not talking about the future, we're talking about now."

I'm not going to let anybody knock my ballplayers.

Palm Springs, Tuesday, March 18

More mistakes in fundamentals. We lost to the Angels again, 5–4, in ten innings, and their last two runs really disturbed me. With runners on second and first, Winston Llenas bunted hard on one hop to Ed Crosby at third base. He threw to Duane Kuiper at second for the force and Kuiper threw to first for the double play, except that Joe Lis wasn't there. He had charged the plate on the bunt. The tying run scored on those two mistakes—Joe Lis didn't stay back, Duane Kuiper didn't look before he threw. In the tenth they had men on first and second with none out. Danny Briggs bunted to Crosby again. Crosby looked at third, where shortstop Jerry DaVanon was covering, looked at second, then finally threw to first— wildly. The winning run scored.

Those plays are designed to get you out of an inning. Instead they got the Angels a ball game they didn't deserve.

And in the sixth George Hendrick hit a tremendous shot to right field and went into his home-run trot. But the ball didn't go out. He only got a double instead of maybe a triple.

"I thought sure it was going out," he told me later.

"That's what I thought. Just don't do it again."

I didn't want to make a big deal out of it, because George has been really hustling, but I did want him to know I was aware that he hadn't run hard. You always run hard until you're sure it's out of the ball park. And with George's reputation, the writers are watching him where they wouldn't be watching another player. Ken Berry, one of our outfielders, hit a windblown fly that fell safely in Yuma and he held up at first instead of trying for second. And today I thought Jerry DaVanon might've gone to third instead of stopping at second when his fly ball was lost in the sun. But those things happen— to everybody, not just George Hendrick.

George is human. If the writers are going to watch his every move, they're going to see little things that he doesn't do but they're the same little things that other ballplayers don't do. Just give George a chance to play baseball.

Tucson, Wednesday, March 19

No game, but we worked out, especially the manager. I took batting practice with everybody else and then took ten extra minutes by myself. It's time for me to start bearing down on getting ready. Ted Bonda also wants me to start bearing down to win some exhibition games. When he arrived today, he suggested that it "would be good for the ball club" if we won a few games, meaning it would be good for the ticket sales back in Cleveland.

"Do me a favor," he asked me in his quiet way. "Win three or four in a row."

"If you want us to win three or four in a row," I replied, "then we will."

Tucson, Thursday, March 20

We lost, 5–1, when the Angels jumped on Fritz Peterson for four quick runs. Sorry about that, Ted.

In my suite at the Sheraton Pueblo later, I met with the coaches to discuss trimming the roster. It wasn't easy. Rick Manning is really coming. I like him more and more every day. But if I keep him as a spare outfielder, he might not play enough. He might be better off at Oklahoma City playing every day. I've got to talk to Phil about the kid because he can really play. There's another twenty-year-old kid I really like—Dennis Eckersley, the rookie righthander. He's got a good sinker, a good slider, and the makeup of a burglar. If he continues the way he's going, there's no reason why he can't be with us April 8 in Cleveland for the opener. I wanted to get the roster down to twenty-five in my mind, but I couldn't.

"Call the commissioner," suggested Tom McCraw, "and get permission to have twenty-eight players."

I had to laugh at that. But when it comes to cutting the players, I won't be laughing.

Tucson, Friday, March 21

After the workout, the coaches and I sat down with Phil to go over the roster. Like me, he's reluctant to keep Rick Manning unless the kid is in the outfield every day, which isn't likely to happen. We've just got too many outfielders. But unlike me, Phil had other angles that a general manager is always conscious of in trimming the roster. Which players probably won't clear waivers, which players probably will clear. Which players have options left, which have no options left. And if you release a player unconditionally during spring training, anytime through the day before the season opens, he gets 30 days' salary. If you release a player after the season has begun but before May 15, he gets 60 days' salary. If you release a player on or after May 15, he gets his full season's salary.

Those are things that I never paid that much attention to until now, but they're things that the ball club has to take into consideration.

But the only thing on Russ Schneider's mind seems to be when we're going to trade Gaylord, maybe because it's on Gaylord's now that the Red Sox have asked about him. Haywood Sullivan of the Red Sox was here yesterday and I'm told that when Gaylord saw him, he yelled, "Here I am, Sully, take me." That's baseball talk.

"But right now," Phil told Russ today, "the Tigers are more interested in Gaylord than the Red Sox are."

The Tigers can't be too interested because Phil didn't even mention to me that the Tigers had phoned. Phil did tell me that the Texas Rangers are interested in Jim Perry, but we can't afford to let Jim go either. After all, the Perry brothers had a combined 38–25 record last year (21–13 for Gaylord, 17–12 for Jim) and we're hoping they'll do as well this season. We're not trying to trade Gaylord, no matter what he thinks. For the team photo today, Gaylord was lined up in the middle of the back row but the photographer moved him over to one end.

"I guess I'm gone," Gaylord said. "When you trade me, you can cut me out of the picture easy now."

No matter what Gaylord thinks, I want him in our picture. Big. Like a 20-game winner should be.

Sun City, Saturday, March 22

On the three-hour bus ride, the driver got lost. But he wouldn't admit it. He pulled off the road, saying, "I got to make a bathroom stop." When he came back, he said, "We went about ten blocks past the ball park." Too bad he found it. We lost again, 9–5, to the Milwaukee Brewers in this retirement community in the desert outside Phoenix—nice homes with neat lawns on curved streets. Many of the old folks use golf carts to get around. They can even park their golf carts behind the last row of seats in Sun City Stadium, where Hank Aaron showed me he can still hit. Gaylord got a pitch up and out over the plate and Hank Aaron hit it like Hank Aaron can hit it—on a line to left field for a single.

Hank Aaron isn't in Sun City to retire. I know Phil hopes Hank comes to Tucson tomorrow. For the crowd.

Tucson, Sunday, March 23

Hank Aaron showed up and so did 6,249 people, the biggest crowd at Hi Corbett Field in the 29 years the Indians have been training here. We won, 12–8, just like I told Ted Bonda we would when the manager got serious. We fell behind, 7–1, but for the first time I managed a game to win. I felt I owed it to the big crowd. I used pinch hitters and pinch runners for the first time. I even used Frank Robinson as a dh. I batted second. Rather than move George Hendrick from third to second, I put myself there. I knew I'd be more comfortable there than George would. I hit a fly ball to left and I walked. But we came back with 2 runs in the fifth, 2 in the sixth, 2 in the seventh, and 5 in the eighth. Jim Kern didn't help himself, giving up 7 runs in three innings, but Dennis Eckersley did a good job and Don Hood was fantastic. Bill Champion started for the Brewers and I watched him closely. Phil had told me the Brewers will trade Champion for John Lowenstein, even up.

"No way," I said. "Not even up."

Phil agreed. Champion is a good righthander who had an 11–4 record last year, but I don't feel he's better than anybody in our rotation. I also feel Lowenstein is very important to our ball club. He's a good hitter, he creates excitement with his base stealing, and he can play both the outfield and third base.

Tucson, Monday, March 24

Off-day, and I mean off. I had told the players, "If anybody shows up at the ball park, the fine is $1,000." I made it ridiculously high to impress them. Also to make sure that nobody would even come out for a treatment from Jim Warfield, our trainer. I wanted Jim and our clubhouse man, Cy Buynak, to have an off-day too. But the fine didn't apply to the manager. I watched the minor-leaguers work out, then I talked to Phil about his discussions with the Red Sox, who keep asking about Gaylord.

"I told them," Phil said, "if they want Gaylord, we've got to have Bill Lee and Roger Moret and a minor-leaguer. But they said no, that they wouldn't trade Lee."

I don't blame them. Bill Lee won 17 games in each of the last two seasons. He's flaky but he can pitch. That's why we'd take him. Because he can pitch. But the Red Sox want to keep him for the same reason.

Tucson, Tuesday, March 25

I wrote my name on the lineup card before I remembered I had to have the Padres' permission to use the dh. Their manager, Johnny McNamara, wouldn't give it because the Padres' president, Buzzy Bavasi, doesn't want the dh used because National League teams don't use it. But when the Padres played the Brewers in Yuma last week, they not only let Hank

Aaron be the dh, they advertised him. In other words, if the
Padres can use the dh to make a buck, it's all right; otherwise,
it's not. But we won anyway, 3–2, the way I like to win. In the
third Frank Duffy singled. On the hit-and-run, John Lowenstein
lined a single to right, with Duffy going to third. Oscar Gamble
singled for one run, with Lowenstein going to third. With a
1-and-2 count on George Hendrick, I flashed Oscar the steal
sign. George struck out but the catcher didn't throw because
Lowenstein, a good base runner, was on third. And then
Charlie Spikes singled for two runs that we made stand up.

This is the type of close game we have to win. This is why
we're working on baserunning, why I want aggressive base
runners, why we're going to have a running ball club. Running
led directly to those three runs. If you can run, if you can
steal, then you'll win your share of close games. And you have
to win close games to be in the race.

I told the players before the game that I would be making
more moves now, that I would be creating situations where
they can get used to me and where I can get used to seeing
them under game conditions. I also have an opportunity to
get used to seeing Barbara and the kids. With the kids in
school, Barbara stayed in our Bel Air home. But now the kids
are on their Easter vacation, so everybody flew over from Los
Angeles tonight. I picked them up at the airport. Barbara and
Nichelle, who we call Nini, moved in with me but Kevin and
a friend of his, Hank Weinstein, are rooming together down
the hall. I went down to check on them about midnight and
they were drinking Cokes they had ordered from room service.
Kevin had signed the tab.

"How much were they?" I asked.

"Couple of bucks," he replied.

"There's a Coke machine downstairs for 30 cents," I said.
"Get your Cokes there."

Tucson, Wednesday, March 26

It snowed in the desert today. Snow that turned to sleet and
rain and washed out our game with the Padres, our B game

too. Next year I don't want to have as many open dates on the exhibition schedule. I told Barbara that tonight and she laughed.

"Next year?" she said. "You've only got a one-year contract."

I know, but I have confidence in myself. I can't go around saying, ". . . if I'm here next year." That's a negative thought. I don't have negative thoughts. I'm not assuming anything but I'm thinking I'm going to be the manager next year. Not the dh, just the manager.

We went to Greyhound Park tonight. The feature race was The Frank Robinson Special, but I didn't bet the winner.

Phoenix, Thursday, March 27

We bussed up to play the Giants and we won again, 8–6. That's three in a row, Ted. But as good as the win was, the nicest part of the trip was when Bobby Mattick stopped by to congratulate me on becoming manager. He was the Reds' scout who signed me in 1953 when I was seventeen years old. He's now a special-assignment scout for the Montreal Expos.

Bobby Mattick helped me when it meant the most. I was living in Oakland and playing for McClymonds High School and the Bill Ervin American Legion Post 237 team. The coach of both teams was George Powles, the man who really got me into baseball—not only playing baseball but *thinking* it. Contrary to what many people believe, I hadn't really been inspired by Jackie Robinson being the first black player in the major leagues. I was only eleven when that happened and it didn't make much impact on me because I wasn't that interested in major-league ball then. To me, the Pacific Coast League meant baseball and I wasn't even all that aware that there had been no blacks in that league. Color had never been a big issue in our house. That's the way my mother was. I was born in Silsbee, Texas, not far from Beaumont, the last of her ten children. My father remained in Texas when my mother took me and two of my brothers, Sylvester and Johnny, to California, where some of my other brothers and sisters were living.

Our neighborhood in Oakland was a mixture of blacks, whites, Mexicans, and Orientals, but we all got along.

The first ballplayers I remember were on the Oakland Oaks teams that Casey Stengel managed in 1947 and 1948—Billy Martin, George Metkovich, Les Scarsella, Lloyd Christopher, and Chick Hafey.

I used to ride my bike over to the Emeryville section of Oakland where the ball park was and sneak in by climbing the steel girders outside the old wooden fence and dropping down underneath the bleachers.

I never missed the San Diego teams that had Luke Easter, Max West, Jack Graham, Minnie Minoso, Suitcase Simpson— they could hit.

By the time I was fourteen I had made the Ervin Post team that had won the American Legion national championship the year before. That's when I first met Bobby Mattick. He was scouting for the Chicago White Sox then, but he had moved to the Reds' organization by the time I graduated from McClymonds. Other scouts talked to me, but Bobby Mattick had the inside track because he had always impressed me as a nice man. He was nice to me and, more important, he was nice to my mother.

He took her out to dinner, he brought a turkey to the house for Thanksgiving—nothing extravagant but always thoughtful.

He had been a shortstop with the Reds and he would hit grounders to me. I was a third baseman then. That was a big deal, fielding grounders from a major-league scout. When he got down to talking about signing me, he not only explained the bonus rule but he also told me how the Reds were willing to start me out in Class C, which was important. The other team that was really after me was the White Sox, but they were talking about starting me in Class D, which I felt wasn't any better than the high school or American Legion ball I was playing.

In those years, if you got a bonus of more than $4,000, you had to start and stay in the majors for two years, like Sandy Koufax did.

"You don't want to go to the majors and sit on the bench,"

Bobby told me. "You're not ready for the majors yet. You're not ready for the high minors either. We'll give you a $3,000 bonus and start you in Class C at $400 a month. And the Reds don't have a big farm system. You won't get lost in it. If you show you can play, you'll move up fast."

The money might not sound like much now, but it wasn't bad then.

Tucson, Friday, March 28

We won our fourth in a row, 9–8, over the Oakland A's, but not easily. Going into the ninth we were leading, 7–3, and I brought in Tom Buskey to lock it up. But the A's got two runs off him, then Dave LaRoche wild-pitched another run in. I brought in Dennis Eckersley and he walked both Sal Bando and Reggie Jackson, then gave up a two-run triple to Joe Rudi to put the A's ahead, 8–7. In our half of the ninth, John Lowenstein got a bases-loaded single for our winning runs, but I'm getting concerned with our relief pitching. The bullpen people we're counting on aren't doing the job. Even so, I think this kid Eckersley is a pitcher. He wasn't really wild, he was only missing the plate by an inch or so in or out, not high or low. And he doesn't get upset out there. He's all business. After the game Harvey Haddix and I talked to him.

"You're trying to be too fine with your pitches," I told him. "With your stuff, just get the ball over the plate."

For only twenty years old, he's really mature. He listened calmly, he accepted advice. Some kids will say, well, this is the way I do it, or I don't think that will work for me. But this kid not only has the ability, he's got the proper attitude. If more kids only realized how important the proper attitude is.

Tucson, Saturday, March 29

No game today, just a workout. Barbara and Nini came over to the ball park but Kevin and his friend Hank stayed at the Sheraton Pueblo to play tennis and go swimming. Kevin isn't into baseball much. After dinner tonight I took Nini into the

Gaucho Lounge at our hotel to hear Mudcat Grant sing. Mudcat used to pitch for the Indians and the Twins, where he won 21 games in 1965 when they won the American League pennant, and for a few other teams. But now he and Harry Jones are the TV announcers on the Indians' games. He's also a singer and he arranged to appear in the hotel lounge here during spring training. Mudcat introduced Nini and dedicated his show to her.

"I want you to know," he told the audience, "that I can still get her daddy out."

"If you could still get me out," I said, laughing, "you'd still be pitching."

I had a Tanqueray and tonic and Nini had a Coke and a big time. But all through Mudcat's show, I kept thinking about the players I've got to cut tomorrow. And now I'm still thinking about it as I sit on the couch in my suite, staring at the TV set without really knowing what's on. Thinking about cutting players has affected me because I know I'm dealing with a player's career. What makes it extra hard on me is that I was never cut. I made the Reds my first shot with them. I was never sent *back* to the minors, like I'm going to send players back tomorrow. No matter what I tell them, it's not going to sound right to them.

Tucson, Sunday, March 30

We lost to the Brewers, 6–0, but for once I wished they had scored 60 runs or even 600 runs. That way I could've delayed facing the six players we decided to cut—Bruce Ellingsen, Jim Strickland, Eric Raich, Tommy Smith, Jerry DaVanon, and Rob Belloir. But sooner or later, I knew I had to face them in my office, one by one. Ellingsen really made it tough. He's a 25-year-old lefthander who had a 1–1 record with the Indians last year as a relief pitcher, but Don Hood and Dave LaRoche had moved ahead of him in our thinking. He wouldn't accept that. He kept talking about how he couldn't understand it, how he wanted to talk to Phil, how he thought he would be considered for the fourth starter, how he figured he hadn't worked that much because he thought I would get around to using him.

"And now you're telling me," he said, "that I didn't make the club because I was wild. I can't believe it."

"We could talk forever," I finally told him, "but that wouldn't change anything. Talk to Phil if you want to."

DaVanon also couldn't accept it. He's a shortstop we signed as a free agent on my recommendation last month. I thought he might be our utility infielder. I had managed him at Santurce and he had been up with the Cardinals, Orioles, and Padres as well as the Angels, where I played with him two years ago. But in camp he just hasn't done the job defensively. He hasn't even seemed alert. But he was alert now.

"I don't want to go to Oklahoma City," he said. "I'd rather play in California where I live."

"I can understand that and we'll try to put you there. But there's no way I can promise that."

Tommy Smith was another tough cut. He's had two big years as a Triple A outfielder at Oklahoma City—.312 last year, .342 the year before. He's twenty-six, an age when a good player resents staying in the minors. He had an option left, meaning we could send him back to Oklahoma City without waivers. I mentioned that to him, hoping that honesty would be the best policy. But he asked me the question I knew he would ask me, the question I had no answer for.

"What," he said, "do I have to do to make the major leagues that I haven't done?"

"Don't go down there with a bad attitude," I said. "Go down there with the attitude that you're going to force us to bring you up."

"You will," he said.

"I hope so," I said.

Eric Raich is a big righthander, a good prospect. He's only twenty-three and I assured him he's got a future with the Indians but there's no room on the staff for him now. He was very gracious about it. Rob Belloir also took it well. He's a shortstop who was here on a look-see. And Jim Strickland, a non-roster lefthander, accepted it. He was so nice, he sounded as if he was trying to make me feel better. Maybe he sensed my discomfort. As long as I'm a manager, I don't think I'll ever get to where cutting a player won't bother me. Players are very competitive people. In his heart, each player thinks he's good enough to make the ball club. If he didn't, he wouldn't be in camp. When you tell him he's been cut, you're really cutting that competitive heart. When it was over, I came back to my suite and just drifted through the evening. In a way I'm glad that Barbara and the kids went home before today's game. I really don't want to be with anybody. I didn't think it would affect me this much. Barbara likes to say that my emotions are "toned at one level," never up or down. But tonight I'm down.

And on Friday, six more players have to be told by the manager that they've been cut.

Tucson, Monday, March 31

Dennis Eckersley and Rick Manning are making it difficult to keep them off the 25-man roster. We beat the Cubs, 2–0, with Eckersley pitching three hitless innings and Manning knocking in both runs with a bases-loaded single. We've now won five of our last six but I'm worried about Frank Duffy's rib-cage pull. It hurt more today than it did yesterday when he got it on a swing. He wanted to stay in at shortstop.

"No, no," I said. "Go in and have it checked."

If he aggravated it on a throw, he could be out a month. That hurts the whole ball club. As it is, he'll only be out a few days. I hope. This ball club needs Frank Duffy at shortstop.

Bel Air, Tuesday, April 1

I loafed around our Bel Air home with Barbara and the kids. That's not an April Fool joke. I flew over last night to pick up some cold-weather clothes. The first few weeks of the season, baseball in Cleveland and the East is not the summer game. I left Dave Garcia in charge against the University of Arizona team. We lost, 6–5, but it's not anything to be ashamed of. Those college kids beat the Oakland A's, 14–8, about a week ago. Before missing the game, I checked with Phil if it was all right.

"Either that or miss the Yuma trip," he said.

"No, the Yuma trip's important," I told him.

Everybody assumed I would cop out of the Yuma trip on Thursday—5 hours across the desert by bus to play the Padres and 5 hours back the same day. But if I go to Yuma, none of the players can complain about having to go.

Tucson, Wednesday, April 2

Gaylord's ready. He shut out the A's for seven innings on two hits and we won, 11–3, for a 7–7 record. The program is starting to pay off. Our people are running, taking the extra base. And our pitching looks like it will be better this year. If not, I won't go all year with the pitchers who were here last year. I'm not afraid to reach down to Oklahoma City and bring somebody up. We're going to play better than .500 ball. We're going to surprise a lot of people. I'm really getting excited about this ball club. I just hope they're not distracted. Like today Dick Bosman, our player rep and one of our best pitchers, had a long meeting about uniforms and parking spaces. The ballplayers don't like the idea of the all-red uniforms that Ted Bonda has ordered for opening day. The ballplayers have seen a sample of a dark blue top that can be worn with white pants. They like the dark blue tops so much, they're willing to buy them. About $60 each. Ted Bonda didn't like the impression that the ballplayers were insulting the ball club by offering to buy the dark blue tops.

"That's not it," I told him. "All they're saying is, we want the blue tops so bad, we're *willing* to buy them."

The blue tops have been ordered and Ted is working on the Cleveland Stadium parking problem. In the past, each player got two spaces in the lot behind third base. But the Indians don't control the parking area, the Stadium Corporation does. This year the stadium has 102 new loges with two parking spaces allotted for each loge as part of the deal. The parking spaces are the ones the players used to have. Now the players have to park out behind left field in an unpaved area. They're really bitching about it.

I'm the manager but I'm on the players' side in this. I'm still a player too.

Yuma, Thursday, April 3

Up at 5 for the long bus ride to Yuma with a desert dawn. We lost to the Padres, 2–0, but the trip was worth it. Jim Kern pitched six innings, giving up only one run on three hits. He walked five but he wasn't that wild and he struck out four. Dennis Eckersley pitched the other two innings, giving up one run on one hit. He walked two but he struck out three. Those two kids have convinced me they deserve to go to Cleveland with us Sunday, but tomorrow I'll have to convince Phil.

Tucson, Friday, April 4

In the morning the coaches and I met with Phil in his office to cut the squad. When we got around to Kern and Eckersley, the general manager didn't want to keep them both.

"Not unless I can make a deal for Fred Beene," he said. "Let me make some calls."

No deal was available. But things worked out. Beenie aggravated a back injury in our 4–3 victory over the A's and we put him on the 21-day disabled list along with Angel Hermoso, the little second baseman with bad knees. That gave us room for both Kern and Eckersley to go with the two Perrys, Fritz, Bosman, Hood, LaRoche, and Buskey—nine pitchers. It also meant that we only had to cut four players instead of six. We decided to send Rick Manning to Oklahoma City, where he would be playing the outfield every day. Duane Kuiper, the young second baseman, also went there along with Joe Lis, a first baseman who will double as a coach. Mike Baldwin also had to go since we already had three left-handers on the staff. They all understood except Kuiper, and his complaint was money. According to his contract, if he's in the minors, he gets less money.

"I can't live," he told me, "off $1,200 a month down there."

"Talk to Phil about it," I said. "Maybe he'll renegotiate."

He nodded, shook hands, and left my office calmly. But when he left Phil's office later, he wasn't too calm.

"This is where you can get me," he snapped, tossing a piece of paper on Trudy Hargis's desk. "I'll be at this number."

The number had a 312 area code—that's Chicago, where Kuiper lives. But in his office Phil wasn't worried. He was puffing on his pipe as if nothing had happened.

"He won't go home," Phil said. "He'll report."

I don't think today's cuts affected me as much as last Sunday's had. Probably because it worked out that we could keep Jim Kern and Dennis Eckersley.

Mesa, Saturday, April 5

We bused up to Mesa where the A's train and we won, 11–6, to finish our exhibition schedule with a 9–8 record. We fly to Cleveland tomorrow. Of our last 10 games, we won 8. Ted Bonda is probably happier about it than I am. Because beginning Tuesday, when we open against the Yankees, I know we won't have it this easy.

We won't have T. J. O'Hays around either. Through the years I've heard managers talk about strangers bugging them for a tryout and now I know. During the winter in Puerto Rico, where I fulfilled a commitment to Hiram Cuevas to manage Santurce for the sixth year, I got a long-distance call from a guy who identified himself as T. J. O'Hays.

"I got a slide I want to show you," he said.

"Is that all you can do is slide?" I asked him.

"That's all I have to do," he said. "I'm only twenty-nine. I can be your pinch runner. I want to show you a slide that even if the fielder has the ball waiting on the runner, there's no way he can make the tag."

"What does the runner do—disappear?"

"Let me show you at spring training?"

"But the ball club has to invite you."

"I'll pay all my own expenses," he said.

"All right, if you pay your expenses."

I forgot about that conversation until last night when my phone rang. T. J. O'Hays.

"I'll see you in Mesa tomorrow," he announced.

"See me about what?" I said. "Who is this?"

"About the slide. I called you in Puerto Rico," he said, and then I remembered. "I showed the slide to the A's today, I showed it to Finley, he's some kind of kook. But that Reggie Jackson is a class guy. You ask Reggie about me, he'll tell you I'm all right. I'll see you in Mesa tomorrow."

Soon after we got in our clubhouse under Rendezvous Park where the A's train, a stranger walked in and put his little bag on a bench. He had longish blond straggly hair but if he's twenty-nine, then I'm twenty-nine too. All the coaches and the ballplayers were wondering who he was when he walked over to me.

"T. J. O'Hays," he said. "I called you about the slide."

"Well, yeah," I said. "But we don't have a uniform."

I was hoping that he wouldn't say that he had his own in his little bag.

"I'll get one from the A's," he said. "From Reggie."

I was on the field when he strolled out wearing a pair of A's pants, a windbreaker over his shirt, and carrying his little bag. He had on a pair of spikes that were patched up with protective metal on each side that made them look like football high-tops for a knight in armor. Then he taped a big sponge over his pants on each hip.

"I'm ready," he said.

We walked down toward the rightfield corner beyond our dugout. I threw a loose base on the grass.

"Stay at the base," he said.

He trotted away, then he turned and ran at me as if I was covering the bag. Suddenly he did a flip in the air with a Kung Fu kick and he landed on the base with one foot, whomp.

"See that?" he said.

"Yeah, I saw it."

"No way a fielder is going to stay at the base," he said. "He's going to see that foot coming down and he's going to flinch and I'm safe. And if I see him starting to flinch, I slide straight in."

"Yeah, it's different."

"I could teach your players that in 15 minutes."

"But they might get hurt."

"Not when they learn how to do it," he said.

"What about *until* they learn?"

"I can pitch too," he said, ignoring my question and pulling out of his little bag a big rock that must have weighed 2 pounds. "Give me a little time to warm up with my rock."

He went over near the screen and threw the rock about 10 feet. Back and forth. Maybe fifty times.

"I'm ready," he announced. "That rock really builds up your arm. You should have your pitchers use it. It shortens the tendons in your arm."

"How long would it take to teach the pitchers to use it?"

"About two weeks. If they pay attention. About two weeks."

Then he picked up a ball to really warm up. I had Jeff catching him. He threw a couple of pitches, but then he winced and grabbed his arm.

"Adhesions," he said. "This never happened to me before."

"You better go in and have the trainer check your arm."

He came out about 15 minutes later. He was dressed in his jeans and he was shaking his head.

"This never happened before," he said.

"Just when you had your big chance."

"I didn't show you my catcher's mitt." He reached into that bag again and pulled out a catcher's glove with a dial on the back. "You hit the pocket and the dial registers the speed of the pitch. You have to calculate. Like with Nolan Ryan's fastball, you know it's 100 miles an hour. If this registers 50 on his fastball, then you know that's equal to 100 miles an hour."

"But his fastball isn't always 100 miles an hour."

"It isn't?" he said. "Well, then, you'd have to calculate different. But there must be something I can do with your ball club. I'll do anything. I need the money."

"I'm sorry," I said.

I really was. I had started out laughing at T. J. O'Hays, but by now I was feeling sorry for him. As he trudged off the field with his little bag, I wished I could transplant his enthusiasm into a few of my ballplayers.

Cleveland, Sunday, April 6

As we checked out of the Sheraton Pueblo, it occurred to me that I hadn't gone to the swimming pool or played tennis at the hotel the whole six weeks of spring training. But then I hadn't even brought my swim trunks or my tennis racket. I'm not a swimmer but I'll sit around a pool. I like to play tennis. I just figured I'd be too busy, and I was. Other people go to Arizona for a winter vacation but a manager doesn't. And tonight we arrived in Cleveland for Tuesday's opener.

"The temperature," the pilot announced, "is 28 degrees."

Exactly the way I remember Cleveland early in the season. But what warmed us up was the turnout of about 250 people at Hopkins Airport. That's a big reception for a team that hasn't been a winner. Maybe the fans have the same feeling that I do—that this team will be a winner. From the airport the ballplayers who live here scattered to their homes or apartments. The others checked into the Keg and Quarter but I'm in the Hollenden House where all the visiting teams stay.

It's important that I don't stay at the same place here as my players do. I don't want them to think I'm spying on them.

Cleveland, Monday, April 7

As a dress rehearsal for tomorrow's opener against the Yankees, we put on our all-red uniforms for the first time. They're not as bad as everybody had feared. I had a short meeting, then Dick Bosman explained that the parking problem had been solved. Since all the loge boxes aren't constructed yet, Ted Bonda arranged for the players to use the parking spaces allotted to the incomplete loges. And after the workout, the writers, some from out of town, descended on the office of the first black manager. I gave them my lineup—Oscar Gamble in left field, the manager as the dh, George Hendrick in center, Charlie Spikes in right, Boog Powell at first base, Johnny Ellis catching, Buddy Bell at third, Jack Brohamer at second, and Ed Crosby at short with Gaylord pitching. Then the questions began.

"Where," one asked, "do you think you'll finish?"

"I've been saying all spring that I consider the Orioles and the Yankees to be the co-favorites in our division and that we should be considered right behind them. I know we'll play at least .500 ball and if we don't play better than .500 ball, I'll be disappointed."

In the *Plain Dealer* today, Russ Schneider picked us to finish third. Bob Sudyk of the *Press* picked us fourth.

"It doesn't matter where the so-called experts pick us," I said. "Third isn't too bad, even fourth isn't too bad, considering the division, but I really disagree with anybody who picks us fifth or sixth. I don't think there's any way this ball club will finish fifth or sixth unless we don't play anywhere near our potential."

And then I told them something that I have been thinking about, something I knew would surprise them.

"If I'm fortunate enough to be a major-league manager for five years," I said, "that will be enough for me."

I don't think they believed me. But in five years Kevin will be seventeen and Nini will be fourteen and I'd like to spend a few summers with them instead of with a ball club. Just live a normal family life in the summer—go on a vacation, go to the beach, go play tennis, go anyplace. Ballplayers never do that. But at least Barbara and the kids will be here with me for tomorrow's opener. I picked them up at the airport tonight in the blue Riviera that Quay Buick has loaned me for the season. Just having them here will help me relax and also add to the excitement. I'm enjoying the excitement.

Tomorrow's game at Cleveland Stadium will be the first time a black man will manage a major-league team. Once something is done it can never be repeated or recaptured. What happens tomorrow will be history.

The Home-Run
Hitter and
the Manager

Cleveland, Tuesday, April 8

I woke up about 6, but I went back to sleep off and on until about 8, then I got up and got dressed quietly because I didn't want to wake up Barbara and the kids. On leaving, I touched Barbara's shoulder and kissed her. She opened her eyes, whispered "Good luck," and closed her eyes. That's the way we are. Like me, Barbara and the kids don't get too excited about things, at least outwardly. Even today, I wouldn't expect them to be any other way.

At the newsstand in the Hollenden House coffee shop, the *Plain Dealer* had a color drawing of me on page 1. Not the first page of the sports section, page 1 of the paper. I enjoyed seeing myself on page 1 but at the same time, it was no big deal. I ordered what I've been having for breakfast most of the spring—three eggs scrambled medium with toast and coffee. At another table were Doc Medich and Pat Dobson, two Yankee pitchers, and I nodded to them. I knew I'd be seeing Medich later. On the mound.

I drove the few blocks to the ball park and even then, almost five hours before the game would start, a few dozen fans were waiting outside, shuffling their feet in the cold. Of all the major-league ball parks, Cleveland Stadium might be the coldest. It's an old concrete fortress down on the Lake Erie shore. Whitecaps are usually on the lake from a breeze or a strong wind. When it's cold, as it was today, that breeze makes it even colder. I was glad I had on a turtleneck. But even in the cold, when the fans recognized me as I crossed the parking lot to the office entrance, they yelled and waved and wished me luck. I waved back, then went upstairs to Phil's office. We were talking when he puffed on his pipe and looked at me.

"Why don't you hit a homer the first time up?" he said.

"Sure, sure," I replied.

He laughed with me, then I went downstairs to the clubhouse. I put on my all-red uniform and soon some writers arrived.

"Nervous?" somebody asked.

"Excited, but not nervous."

I didn't go out on the field until it was almost time for the regulars to take batting practice. By then, most of the writers and photographers were around the batting cage. After bp, I went back to my office but when I went back through the tunnel to the dugout for the pregame ceremonies, the drama of the day hit me. Rachel Robinson, Jackie's widow, was out near home plate. Ted Bonda had invited her to throw out the first ball. I kept waiting for somebody to bring Mrs. Robinson over to the dugout but nobody did. I didn't think it was my place to go on the field and shake hands with her. I'd met her before at a dinner in New York where she told me she was proud I was the first black manager and she knew that Jackie would be proud. It wasn't a question of me meeting her. But it would have been nice for the other players to meet her. I think they would've enjoyed that. But then the pregame ceremonies began. Over the public address system, the other players were introduced one by one. I couldn't believe the cheers and the enthusiasm of the crowd. And then I heard:

". . . and the new manager of the Indians . . ."

I didn't hear the rest of it. I hurried up out of the dugout and jogged toward home plate. I couldn't believe the ovation. I've had a few big ovations in my career but this was the biggest and the best. I just stood there enjoying it and up in the glass-enclosed loge, Barbara and the kids were standing and clapping. By now even I was excited inside. During the national anthem I had butterflies in my stomach but that's normal for me. Then the game began. After his first pitch, Gaylord tossed the ball toward our dugout with a little wave. He wanted me to have the first ball of my first game. It hadn't occurred to me to ask for that ball. It was a nice thing for Gaylord to do. When he stranded two Yankee base runners that inning, it was even nicer.

As the dh batting second, I spit my gum away and moved out to the on-deck circle as Oscar Gamble led off. By now, the sun had taken some of the chill out of the air. The temperature, I learned later, had been 36 degrees at game time. But kneeling there, I had a red rubber hot water bottle between my hands to keep them warm as Oscar lifted a foul pop to Graig Nettles, the Yankees' third baseman.

Walking up to the plate, I got another big ovation. Nearly

58,000 people were in the ball park and when there are that many people cheering, it really gets your adrenalin flowing. You want to run through a wall for them. Or hit a baseball over a wall. But for some reason I wasn't mentally ready to hit. Doc Medich got two quick strikes on me. I thought the first pitch was low, a breaking ball. When the plate umpire, Nestor Chylak, called it a strike, I didn't say anything but I looked at him. The second pitch was a fastball on the outside part of the plate, a good pitch to hit, but I just couldn't pull the trigger.

On the next pitch, Medich made a mistake. Not so much with the pitch as with his motion. He dropped down sidearm.

I thought, *Wow, he's trying to show you up*. It was like somebody had turned on a switch inside me. My brain and reflexes suddenly were working. The sidearm pitch was a curveball inside. I swung and fouled it off, a high hopper down the third-base line. Not a hard foul, but I felt better. He threw another curveball low and away, hoping I'd reach for it. I didn't. Ball one. Then a fastball inside that missed. Ball two. I felt I was really on top of him now. I was locked in, I was concentrating. On the next pitch, he came over the top, an overhand fastball. I knew it was a fastball by the rotation of the ball and the angle. With almost every pitcher, the fastball will come straight out of his hand. But on the curveball, his hand will arch as he snaps it. No way a pitcher can throw a curveball without arching his hand. That's what makes the slider tough to read. When a pitcher has a good slider, his delivery is almost the same as it is for a fastball but there's a little spin that you seldom pick up. If this 2-and-2 pitch had been a slider, it probably would've fooled me. In my mind, I usually decide to swing at a pitch when it's out near the cut of the grass. If you wait any longer, it's by you. Even though this fastball looked like it would be low and away, I reached out and hit it. I knew I hit it good because I was able to pull it. Usually a hitter is asking for trouble by trying to pull a pitch that's low and away. But not this time.

Running to first base, I didn't know if I'd hit the ball high enough. I saw the Yankees' leftfielder, Lou Piniella, go back to the fence and jump for it. But rounding first base, I saw that he hadn't come down with it. I knew it was a home run. But the drama of the home run really didn't occur to me right away. Not even the roar of the crowd penetrated.

Nearing third base, I saw Dave Garcia grinning and jumping and I realized, *Wow, wonders never cease.* Approaching home plate, I heard the crowd for the first time. I don't know why, but that's normal for me. I'm in a trance until I see home plate. George Hendrick was waiting for me with his palms up. I slapped his hands as I crossed the plate, then I took my helmet off and waved it to Barbara and the kids up in the loge. I waved to nearly 58,000 people who were on their feet cheering and yelling in an ovation even louder and wilder than the one during the introductions. My team and my teammates came out of the dugout to greet me, with Gaylord leading them, and they surrounded me and pounded me.

I was living my biggest moment in baseball. But that's all it was then, a moment. When the cheering subsided, when my team and my teammates went back to where they had been sitting in the dugout, when the ball I had hit for my 575th home run had been brought back to me, I took off my hard hat and put on my soft hat. I was no longer Frank Robinson the home-run hitter. I was Frank Robinson the manager.

As quickly as the Yankees' second, I returned to reality. Chris Chambliss put them ahead, 2–1, with a double to right-center on a low fastball. We had talked about pitching Chambliss up and in or up and away, but Gaylord got his fastball down. Thurman Munson then singled to make it 3–1 and the thrill of the home run was gone. But we got another run in the second and Boog hit a homer in the fourth to tie it up. Then we got two in the sixth for a 5–3 lead on a walk to George Hendrick, his steal, Boog's double, and Jack Brohamer's single that knocked Medich out. But in the ninth Ron Blomberg got a broken-bat single. With one out I thought about bringing in Dave LaRoche to pitch to Chambliss, a lefthanded pitcher for a lefthanded hitter, but I left Gaylord in. Chambliss pulled a long fly to right field. I thought, *Oh no, it's gone, a tie game, I should've brought LaRoche in*, but Charley Spikes went back to the wall and caught it. Two out. I hurried out to the mound to remind Gaylord not to give Munson anything he could pull for a home run.

"Keep the ball away from him," I said. "With good stuff."

"Yeah," he agreed. "I know what you mean. I'll get him."

Trotting back to the dugout, I realized that the big crowd was on its feet, waving Indian pennants and roaring and rooting for the final out. Munson probably couldn't hear himself think. He fouled off a few pitches, then hit a comeback bouncer to Gaylord and we had won, 5–3. In the roar, I hopped out of the dugout to congratulate Gaylord and we shook hands, then we put our arms around each other's shoulders. I did it instinctively and genuinely, without thinking about our previous problems or about the trade rumors. At that moment all I was thinking about was winning the season opener, winning my first game as manager.

The home run now meant more to me than it had earlier. In the clubhouse, I walked from locker to locker, shaking hands with all the players, not just the ones who had been in the game.

I went into my office and put my three souvenir balls in my desk, each in a different drawer so I would remember which was which—the first ball, the home-run ball, the ball for the last out. In my 19 previous seasons, I'd only saved five balls— for my 300th homer, my 400th homer, my 1,000th run batted in, my 2,500th hit, and my 545th homer that put me ahead of Harmon Killebrew in the all-time list. And now I had three balls in one day. Dozens of writers and radio-TV people had crowded into my bluish gray cement-block office that only seats six visitors. They kept me cornered for almost an hour.

"Right now," I told them at one point, "I feel better than I have after anything I've ever done in this game. The crowd sent chills up my spine. But if I could have asked God for a good kind of day, I never would have asked for something like this and expected it to happen."

My son, Kevin, had come down and was standing next to me. That was a nice feeling. I was sorry that Barbara and Nini couldn't have come into the clubhouse but, like Kevin, they had a historic memory they can cherish always. Not every father can give his family that. It also was a nice feeling to have done well with Rachel Robinson watching. But most people were more thrilled about me hitting the home run than they were about us winning the ball game—the opposite of what I was thrilled about.

It was a tremendous day for me, a day I'll always remember, the biggest day of my life in baseball.

I celebrated later with a quick Tanqueray and tonic with Ed Keating at the Theatrical, a lively bar and restaurant behind the Hollenden House, then Barbara and I had dinner with the Seghis at Lanning's Restaurant. By the time my prime rib was served, I already was thinking ahead to our next game, at Milwaukee on Friday, but they kept talking about today's game, about today's home run, about how Phil had suggested I hit the home run. Through it all, I tried to play it cool.

"I don't know what you're so excited about," I told them. "It was just another opening day."

I was joking of course. I knew what they were excited about. I knew better than anybody else.

Cleveland, Wednesday, April 9

Off-day. In the morning I took Barbara and the kids to the airport, then I went to the ball park for an informal workout. I also talked to Ted Bonda about a new parking problem—a player has to pay for a parking space for his wife. That's wrong. Ted agreed. After yesterday, I think he would have agreed if I had asked for his job.

Cleveland, Thursday, April 10

Another off-day. I went to the annual Kiwanis Club luncheon and got another big ovation. This town is really excited. Even the Hall of Fame at Cooperstown is excited. They want my opening-day lineup card and my home-run bat. They're a little late for the lineup card. I left it taped to the dugout wall. Somebody somewhere has it by now. But the official scorer, Russ Schneider, will send them his copy.

Milwaukee, Friday, April 11

Until today, I thought sure that we'd be the first team to win all 162 games. But we can't now. We lost to Bill Champion of the Brewers, 6–2, in Hank Aaron's return to Milwaukee.

Jim Perry's control was rusty, but what bothered me was Jack Brohamer messing up the rundown on a double steal. Instead of chasing Sixto Lezcano back to first base hard for the third out, Jack let a rookie set the tempo of the rundown. That let Darrell Porter, who was on third, jockey down the line. Jack then tried to nail Porter off third but he had a difficult throw and he threw wide. That's a play we worked on during spring training, but the first time it comes up, we blow it. And it helped cost us the ball game because both runners scored on Pedro Garcia's double off Dick Bosman for a 5–1 lead.

Hank Aaron had driven in their first run in the third with a groundout. He got a single later. He looks like he's trying to pull everything. We want to keep the ball away from him and down. We want to off-speed him as much as possible. That way, when he swings the bat, he supplies all the power. He can still swing that bat.

I want my pitchers to realize that Hank Aaron is not the average 41-year-old hitter. The man who broke Babe Ruth's home-run record naturally got a big ovation in the pregame ceremonies. The fans here remember when he played in County Stadium before the Braves moved to Atlanta, and they serenaded him with "Welcome Home, Henry" to the tune of "Hello Dolly." Until then the reception for me was just as loud, which surprised me. His ovation should've been louder. But he got me with the song.

I was the dh again but I didn't swing the bat well. I felt sluggish. I don't know why.

I strolled over to the Red Garter tonight, one of my favorite spots as a ballplayer. But when I saw some of my ballplayers in there, I left. As the manager, I'm better off in the hotel bars around the league instead of spots like Duff's in downtown Minneapolis or Play Street on New York's Upper East Side. That's one price of being the manager.

Milwaukee, Saturday, April 12

We lost again, 6–5, after the Brewers had jumped on Fritz Peterson for four runs in the first and another in the second. Every ball that Fritz was hurt on was up. He can't pitch up, because he doesn't have overpowering stuff. Even so, we had a chance to tie it in the ninth after George Hendrick led off with a homer into the leftfield bleachers. Charlie Spikes ran the count to 3 and 2, then fouled a pitch over near the Brewers' dugout. Their catcher, Charley Moore, wasn't that close to the ball when a fan reached out waist-high and deflected it. Nick Bremigan, the plate umpire, called Spikes out on the interference and I had my first bad scene with an umpire.

"The fielder has to be in a position to make the catch," I argued.

But in Bremigan's judgment, Moore was in position to make the catch. I kept arguing but he said, "That's it, let's go, it's a judgment call." That phrase "judgment call" really annoys me. Even if their judgment is wrong, the call stands. What made it worse was that Jerry Neudecker, the second-base umpire, came in and twice pushed me away from Bremigan.

"Don't ever do that to me again," I told him. "Keep your hands off me."

I got into it with Neudecker then but that didn't change Bremigan's call. Not that the call lost the game for us. We left eleven runners on base. That's what lost the game.

Milwaukee, Sunday, April 13

In the umpires' room at County Stadium, about a dozen players attended a religious service that Buddy Bell had organized. He's a member of the Fellowship of Christian Athletes and he arranged for another member, Mike McCoy of the Green Bay Packers, to conduct the service. Buddy had asked my permission and I was all for it but I didn't go. I don't go to church much anymore. As a kid I went every Sunday morning, but once I got into baseball I stopped. Methodist services are usually at 10 or 11 in the morning and I had to be at the ball park then. But you can be a good Christian without going to church, just as you can go to church without being a good Christian.

The dugout was quiet before the game. No reporters, no microphones, no photographers. After two straight losses, I guess I was no story. Which was nice, except that I'd rather be winning and be a story.

Afterward the reporters, the microphones, and the photographers returned because we won, 3–1. Pete Broberg had us shut out going into the ninth but John Lowenstein led off with a homer and Oscar Gamble walked. Del Crandall, the Brewers' manager, came out to change pitchers and motioned for a righthander. But after Ed Rodriguez rode the cart in, Crandall told the umpires he wanted Tom Murphy instead. Instead of motioning for a righthander, Del should've told the umpires explicitly, "I want Rodriguez" or "I want Murphy." Del obviously was stalling to give Murphy more time to warm up. Del knows that Murphy always walks in instead of riding the cart. I complained to the umpires about it, but they told me it was their fault.

"No, it's Crandall's fault," I told them. "Rodriguez took the cart in, he should be in the game."

As it turned out, Crandall and the umpires did me a favor. Murphy gave up a single to George Hendrick and a two-out double to Johnny Ellis for the winning runs. Gaylord then shut the door in the bottom of the ninth for his 200th victory. He got Hank Aaron on a called third strike for the third time. I never saw Hank look at a third strike three times in one game before. I can't even remember him ever doing it twice.

"I threw him everything," Gaylord told the writers later. "Well, almost everything."

Gaylord doesn't throw his spitball as such anymore. But he throws his greaseball occasionally. Just the thought that he might throw them bothers the hitters. Something was bothering Hank Aaron because he seemed very confused. Gaylord has changed since he left the National League after the 1971 season. He was more of a power pitcher with the Giants, he relied more on the illegal pitch than he does now. He's smarter now. He seemed to be one pitch ahead of Hank all day. He's 2–0 already, showing that another year on his birth certificate hasn't made any difference, that he's still a real pro. I wish I had eight other pitchers like him.

I also wish Oscar Gamble hadn't pulled a hamstring rounding second in the ninth. It's always a slow healing injury.

"You shouldn't have gone to the service this morning," I kidded him. "The Man Up Above knows you didn't belong there. You can't fool The Man Up Above, especially you. And now He's punishing you."

Oscar laughed and I laughed. But only on the outside. We'll miss Oscar's bat.

Cleveland, Monday, April 14

Off-day, no workout. I wanted to give the players a full day to get settled in their houses or apartments. The manager is still in the Hollenden House but Phil's secretary, Trudy Hargis, and Randy Adamack's secretary, Rosemary (Posey) O'Connor, are searching for a furnished apartment for me. But for now, the loneliness of a hotel room doesn't bother me. I'm the loner type. I roomed mostly with Vada Pinson during my years with the Reds, but ever since I was traded to the Orioles before the 1966 season, I've mostly roomed alone.

Cleveland, Tuesday, April 15

Another off-day, the second of four in a row. We don't play until Friday when the Brewers come in. According to the original American League schedule, we were to play the Tigers today and tomorrow, but Phil moved those two games to later in the season along with a game against the Yankees that was originally scheduled to be played last Thursday.

"The weather's always bad in Cleveland in April," Phil told me when the change was made. "We'll play them later on when it's warmer."

Phil turned out to be a prophet, at least today. It rained. It even snowed occasionally, canceling an intrasquad game I had planned. The pitchers were able to throw under the stands at the ball park. The rest of the ball club worked out at

Cleveland State University's field house. But this four-day lay-off concerns me. We can lose our competitive edge. I'd rather have the team scheduled to play. If the weather's bad, post-pone the game. But don't assume the weather will be bad. I think Phil also took into consideration that the attendance might not be too big at this time of year. It won't happen next season.

It also rained and snowed on the new silver Mercedes 450 SEL that I got today. I never thought I'd put this much money in a car.

We had an Eldorado, rose-mist with a white top, but it got to be too expensive. Every time it went into the shop, the bill was anywhere from $100 to $300.

"Let's get a Mercedes," Barbara kept saying. "You know I've always wanted one."

I surrendered. Hiram Cuevas had one in Puerto Rico and Ed Keating has one here. I liked the ride, the feel, the handle. It holds the road at 80 mph. Just driving it around today, I'm enjoying it even more than my first car, a '53 black-and-white Olds 88 that I bought with my bonus money after the Reds signed me. I'm enjoying the Mercedes so much, I might not even let Barbara drive it when she and the kids get here in June after school ends. I don't want to risk any scratches.

Cleveland, Wednesday, April 16

We could have played today if the schedule hadn't been changed. We had a good workout at the stadium. Frank Duffy looks like he'll be able to play Friday, nearly three weeks after he pulled his rib cage. That injury always takes longer to heal than appears at first. Ed Crosby's done a good job at short in Duffy's absence. But most people don't realize that Frank is one of the American League's outstanding short-stops. Defensively, he doesn't have to take a backseat to any-body. He doesn't have quite as strong an arm as Mark Belanger or Bert Campaneris or Toby Harrah, but he makes all the plays. Now if he only could hit for a higher average, but Tom McCraw is working with him on that.

Cleveland, Thursday, April 17

Another off-day, another workout, then the entire team attended the Shrine Club luncheon. All the players showed up. That surprised some people. But in the Players Association agreement, each team has to make two group appearances. This was a designated appearance.

We could've played today too.

Cleveland, Friday, April 18

The four off-days let me come back with Gaylord against the Brewers again. Baseball isn't like cards. You don't save an ace, you use it. But he wasn't the same Gaylord as last Sunday and we lost to Pete Broberg, 5–1, on homers by Darrell Porter, Johnny Briggs, and Hank Aaron—Aaron's first American League homer, his 734th in the major leagues. The most amazing thing about Hank is that, at forty-one, his wrists are still quick. He still gets the ball into the air with power. Most hitters, as they get older, don't pop that ball. Their reflexes are slower and they hit a lot of grounders because they're topping the ball.

But if you make a mistake with Hank, as Gaylord did today, the ball is in the air and it's gone.

Hank is still able to pull the ball, he's still swinging for home runs. When he was younger, he used to hit a lot of balls to right field. As the Reds' leftfielder then, I used to play him in left-center, with the centerfielder over in right-center. When he realized he had a chance to break Babe Ruth's record, he changed his stance. He didn't change his swing or his grip. But he opened his stance a little to make it easier to pull the ball for home runs. He's also taken care of himself physically, especially during the off-season. Most players don't realize it, but that's when it counts the most.

We also lost Boog for maybe a week. He got hit by a pitch on the right elbow. It's bruised and badly swollen.

I stopped in the Theatrical later for a drink with Birdie Tebbetts, my first big-league manager. Birdie scouts both major leagues for the Yankees now and he'd been at today's game. Phil had brought him down to the clubhouse to see me, but Birdie didn't like that.

"I told Phil not to bring me down here," Birdie said. "I don't belong in here."

That's typical of him. But over a drink, he was talking the way only Birdie can.

"Don't let what people say to you influence your judgment," he told me. "Make up your mind on players from what you see. And don't second-guess yourself. Know what you want to do before you do it. Don't make any hasty decisions. And always try to stay ahead of the game. In the seventh inning be thinking about what you might have to do in the eighth or ninth. Especially with your pitchers. Even if you don't use a guy, you're better off getting him up and having him ready. If he's not ready, sometimes it's too late to get him up."

I'm aware of those things but I appreciated him taking the time to emphasize them. I also appreciated something else.

"I just hope," Birdie said, "that you have players who are as much a pleasure for you to manage as you were for me to manage."

I hope so too.

Cleveland, Saturday, April 19

We lost, 3–0, to Bill Champion's two-hitter. I'm convinced the four off-days have affected our hitting. Frank Robinson the dh even was taken out for a pinch hitter by Frank Robinson the manager. The dh wasn't swinging the bat. No timing, no rhythm. He had flied out, grounded out, and struck out. He was 0 for 8 since the home run in the opener. So the manager sent up Rico Carty in the eighth. I think it's the first time somebody has hit for me since early in my rookie year when Birdie Tebbetts sent up Bob Thurman and I slammed my bat in the rack. Birdie glared at me.

"Are you mad," Birdie said quietly, "because I took you out of the game for a hitter?"

"No," I said. "I'm mad because you had to take me out because I'm not hitting."

"Good," said Birdie, "because I just want you to know who's managing this team."

That memory came back to me today, but not when I took myself out for a pinch hitter. I thought of it after Jim Perry's scene when I took him out for a relief pitcher. He had pitched well but we were losing, 1–0, going into the ninth. With one out, George Scott homered and Don Money doubled. I made up my mind to take Jim out and bring Tom Buskey in. To give Buskey more time to warm up, I ordered Jim to walk Darrell Porter intentionally to set up a double-play situation. After the walk, I sent Harvey Haddix out to the mound. But when Harvey asked for the ball, Jim kicked the dirt. I had told the players the first day at spring training that I didn't want them to show up me or my coaches, and we wouldn't show them up. Then when Jim got to the dugout, he grabbed his jacket and stalked off to the clubhouse. After the game I asked Harvey to tell Jim that I wanted to see him in my office.

"He's washing his hands," Harvey reported back. "But he said he'll come right in."

But he didn't come right in. After ten minutes, he still hadn't come in. I was really burning now. If a manager calls for me, I'm there. As quickly as possible.

"Harvey, tell him not to bother," I said. "I'm too upset. I'll probably say something I shouldn't. I'll see him tomorrow."

Moments later Jeff Torborg, the bullpen coach, told me that Jim was out by his locker, dressed and talking to the writers. "Jim said he can't come back now," Jeff said, "because the writers are talking to him." I glanced over at Harvey.

"Make sure," I said, "you get a paper in the morning."

Cleveland, Sunday, April 20

For breakfast I had scrambled eggs, toast, coffee, and Jim Perry's quotes in Russ Schneider's column in the *Plain Dealer*:

> I'm no rookie and I think I at least deserve the privilege of being asked if I still feel good, and if I'm still throwing the ball well. And if I had been asked, I would've told him I felt

good. I'm out there busting my back and here comes Harvey to tell me I'm out of the game. At this rate, Harvey will be hated by all the pitchers by the time the season is over. Every time he comes out, you know you're gone, without any questions about how you feel. They ought to know I'd be honest with them if they ask me. I'll tell them if I still have good stuff or not. I think I at least deserve the privilege of being asked. I've been around long enough to know myself, and for them to know me. You can't take it out on a pitcher in a game like this one.

At the ball park I asked Harvey to tell Jim that I wanted to see him. This time he arrived promptly. Harvey stayed with us. Anytime that I talk to a pitcher I want the pitching coach there.

I told Jim that I won't have anybody kicking dirt like he did yesterday, that I won't have players showing up me or my coaches or his teammates. Jim said that he wasn't upset with me or Harvey, that he was disgusted with himself. But then I asked him about why he didn't come into my office yesterday after Harvey told him I wanted to see him.

"I was shaving," Jim said.

"I don't care what you were doing," I said. "If you're in the shower, you come out of the shower and tell Harvey that you'll be right there. You never made any effort to come in to see me."

Then we got into his quote in the paper about how Harvey will be hated by the pitchers.

"Anytime that I send Harvey out there to take you out," I said, "I've made up my mind to take you out. I'm not sending him out there to ask you how you feel. I'm not going to put a muzzle on you about talking to the newspapermen. You can say what you want to say. But you're going to have some bad ball games and the newspapermen are going to come to talk to me. If you're going to rip me and my coaches when you have a decent ball game, then when they come to me after you have a bad ball game, I can do the same thing. If you want our protection, we want the same respect."

"I understand," he said.

That was it. We went out and won the last game of the weekend series with the Brewers, 7–4. We're 3–4 now—not too bad for a team that's not hitting with men on base. Fritz Peterson pitched super until he got tired in the eighth. We had a 7–1 lead then, but he didn't kick the dirt when I went out to bring in Dennis Eckersley to pitch to Hank Aaron with the bases loaded. I wanted to be there to talk to the kid.

"Now this is Aaron," I reminded him.

"I don't care," he said. "I'll get him out."

That's why I love this kid. Not even Hank Aaron awes him. But as tough as he is, he got flustered. When he got a sign from Johnny Ellis, he went into his windup quickly, but Ellis gave him another sign. The kid should have continued in his motion. But in the middle of his windup, he stopped and dropped the ball. That's a balk. The umpire, Nestor Chylak, walked out in front of the plate and waved his arms.

"No, no," Nestor yelled. "No, no, no."

Of all the American League umpires, I respect Nestor Chylak the most, but I had to talk to him now.

"You mean no balk?" I said.

"Of course it's a balk," he said.

"But you said, 'No, no, no.' "

"Look," he said, "if I can't call that, I might as well get out of this game."

"I didn't say it wasn't a balk. I'm just talking about what you were saying."

But now Nestor was glaring at me.

"I always respected you as a player, Frank," he said. "But since you became a manager, I don't respect you because you're always nitpicking."

That made me hot.

"I've got a job to do," I told him, "and if I'm not out here when I'm supposed to be out here, you wouldn't respect me at all. I'll be out here every time I feel I have a beef. I've always respected you as a man and as an umpire and don't ever say you don't respect me."

Nestor is always talking when he's umpiring. But after that he didn't say a word. Maybe he realized he had been out of line.

After the balk, Dennis Eckersley settled down. He threw a fastball that Hank fouled off. Then he threw a fastball inside that Hank hit into the upper deck, but foul—one of those classic Aaron shots, but foul. The kid threw another fastball inside that broke Hank's bat as he grounded to third. But back in the dugout, all Dennis talked about was the long foul off his best fastball.

"Wow," he said. "He can still get around on it, can't he?"

But the kid got him out. Hank Aaron had completed his rookie season with the Milwaukee Braves in 1954 before the kid was born.

Cleveland, Monday, April 21

Another off-day. At the workout I talked to Charlie Spikes about swinging at bad balls and about how the Brewers pitched him in a pattern. Their pitchers started him off with hard stuff. If they got behind, they threw breaking balls. But you can only talk about this so much. The hitter has to be aware of it himself. We'll keep reminding Charlie until it becomes automatic to him. Hopefully some of it will have sunk in by tomorrow when we're in Detroit to begin a ten-day road trip.

Detroit, Tuesday, April 22

We lost a tough one, 6–2. What made it tough was that Gaylord pitched a fine game. He gave up 12 hits but maybe 9 were handle hits. I can only remember 3 solid hits. We were ahead, 2–0, with two on and two out in the fifth when Ron LeFlore lifted a little fly ball to center field. I thought George Hendrick got a late start. Maybe the sun bothered him. He ran hard but the ball hit the heel of his glove and bounced away for what I considered a two-base error. The official scorer called it a hit, a hometown gift that wasn't fair to Gaylord because it meant both runs were earned. Gary Sutherland then bounced a single to center and Willie Horton hit a home run. That meant all five runs that inning were earned.

The dugout was quiet. Maybe some of the players were waiting to see if Gaylord would blow up at George, like he did late last season. Except that George had run hard this time. He should've caught it, but he didn't, that's all. Gaylord apparently realized that, because he gave no indication that he was teed off.

But some Tiger fans behind our dugout got on George pretty hard. No profanity, but I thought they were carrying it too far. About an inning later Leron Lee stood up and yelled something at them. I told Leron to sit down and walked over near them. I told them I appreciated they were rooting for the Tigers, but I thought they were getting on George too hard.

"We're not swearing," one said.

"I didn't say you were," I replied calmly.

"We paid our money," another said.

"I didn't say you couldn't get on a player. All I'm saying is, you're on him pretty hard and if you want to keep it up, I have no control over what my players may say to you. They may say something you might not want to hear."

The fans were quieter after that.

Detroit, Wednesday, April 23

We won, 4–3, with Jim Perry pitching in rain, cold, and wind into the sixth inning. When home runs by Gary Sutherland and Bill Freehan made it 4–2, I sent Harvey to take him out. No scene this time. Don Hood finished that inning. After a rain delay, Tom Buskey pitched the last three innings. George Hendrick knocked in what proved to be the winning run with a double in the fifth. But the writers more or less ignored it. Yesterday when he messed up that fly ball, that was all they wanted to talk about. They were all over him. I don't like the way they jump on him when he does something negative, but ignore him when he does something positive.

Baltimore, Thursday, April 24

Another off-day, the fourth one we've had after a winning game. That makes it difficult to maintain momentum. But it was a good feeling to return to Baltimore, where I had my best years. Winning years. That's what it's all about. At the

Lord Baltimore all the desk people and the bellmen gave me a big hello. There has always been a togetherness here with the players, the front office, and the fans that I think comes down from Jerry Hoffberger, the Orioles' owner.

That's why the Orioles win. That's why Baltimore will always be a home to me.

I had dinner tonight with Linda and Gordon Schwartz, who lived across the street from us for three years when Barbara and the kids and I stayed here during my Oriole years. We were the first black family in that neighborhood. We had trouble finding somebody willing to let us move in. But a big blond stripper owned the house we rented and our real estate man, Mel Sherman, convinced her and some of the neighbors to let us move in.

"You look like nice folks," she said. "You got a deal."

We became friendly right away with the Schwartzes and also with Marci and Buzzy Kolodney. I'm having dinner with the Kolodneys tomorrow.

Baltimore, Friday, April 25

First the bad news—we got rained out and we've got a twi-night doubleheader tomorrow. Now the good news—the rape charge here against Oscar Gamble has been dismissed. I had just joined the Indians last year when the case developed. It wasn't any of my business, so I didn't inquire about it. That's the way I am. And even when I became the manager, it never dawned on me to learn the details. Phil phoned me last night to tell me that somebody from the Maryland state attorney's office would be talking to me. I was hoping he wouldn't expect me to know all about the case. I was in the coffee shop when he introduced himself, Stephen Tully, and we walked out into the lobby.

"The case has been dropped," he said. "She refused to testify."

That's great. But some people will always associate Oscar with the charge. That's not fair to him. But some ballplayers aren't fair to themselves. I'm not referring to Oscar because I don't know how his problem developed, but I do know that some ballplayers don't realize how they can be trapped in a bad situation. If a girl phones and wants to come up to his room, he should tell her, "Wait a minute, I'll meet you in the lobby." At least check her out first. Otherwise, the ballplayer is asking for trouble.

Baltimore, Saturday, April 26

We almost won two. Almost. Gaylord was tremendous in the opener, winning, 3–0, on a five-hitter. Jack Brohamer hit a homer in the third. Ken Berry doubled with two out in the sixth and I thought sure that Earl Weaver would walk me intentionally. I know he hates for me to do anything against the Orioles and I had doubled my previous time up. But he let Ross Grimsley pitch to me. I hit a screwball up and out over the plate into center field, and on Paul Blair's throw home I kept going for second. I figured it might be close on Berry at the plate and I was trying to make Lee May cut the throw off to get me at second. But he didn't. The ball hit the back of the mound and kicked straight up. Berry scored, I got to second, then I scored on Rico Carty's double. Beautiful.

In the second game Dick Bosman was leading, 2–1, going into the ninth. With two out, he had two strikes on Ken Singleton but Singleton singled. He had two strikes on Elrod Hendricks but Elrod singled. First and third, Earl Weaver sent up Jim Northrup to pinch-hit.

I knew that Earl was trying to paint me into a corner, like he's done to other managers. He was hoping that I'd bring in Dave LaRoche, a lefthander, to pitch to Northrup, and if I did, he'd switch to Tommy Davis as his pinch hitter. I fooled him. I brought in Tom Buskey instead, knowing that a right-handed pitcher would keep Tommy Davis in the dugout. Tommy is a tougher out than Northrup, no matter who the pitcher is. I also figured that Buskey was a better bet to keep the ball on the ground with his sinker. He did. Northrup hit a high hopper to third. I thought, *We won two.* But the ball flattened out and went under Buddy Bell's glove. Tie game. The next hitter was Al Brumby, who's supposed to be pitched up and away, but Buskey got a fastball down. Base hit. We lost, 3–2. Had we swept, it would've put us over the .500 mark for the first time, not counting opening day.

But now I'm just hoping that losing the second game the way we did doesn't make us flat tomorrow. I've seen that happen.

Baltimore, Sunday, April 27

Just as I feared, we were flat. Al Brumby led off the Orioles' first with a double and went to third when Ken Berry let the ball get away. But it looked like Jim Perry might pitch his way out. He got Ken Singleton on a short fly, then Tommy Davis hit a short fly to Charlie Spikes in right field. Charlie had no problem coming in, but all of a sudden he shied away. The ball hit him on the arm for a two-base error. He called time and trotted in toward the dugout, signaling for his sunglasses. I couldn't believe it. The sun had been out all day.

"That's three hitters too late," I told him. "You should've had 'em on when the game started."

Charlie told the writers later that the sun had been in a different position before the game. Of course it had. The sun moves. He should've had his sunglasses on anyway. All you do is flip them up or down. He wasn't thinking. And this is a game of thinking. Instead of us maybe getting out of the inning, the Orioles went on to score three runs, and with Jim Palmer pitching a strong seven-hitter, we lost, 6–1. After the game I closed the clubhouse door and chewed out my ball club for the first time. I didn't point the finger at any one individual. The pitchers have been terrific, but I reminded the hitters and the fielders that they're not putting out enough, not thinking enough.

Sometimes the umpires don't seem to be putting out enough, or thinking enough. Like in the fifth inning when Elrod Hendricks of the Orioles got thrown out at the plate and threw his helmet. Throwing equipment is an automatic $100 fine and a warning the first time a player does it in a game, ejection the second time. I wanted to establish that Elrod had thrown his helmet so that if he did it again, he'd be ejected and maybe his absence would help us win the ball game. I knew the plate umpire, Nick Bremigan, had his back turned, so I went out to Jim McKean at first base. McKean had seen it and I asked him to invoke the fine.

"I can't," McKean said.

"Why can't you?" I said.

"Only the umpire-in-chief can fine him."

"You mean the plate umpire?"

"No, the umpire-in-chief of the crew, Neudecker."

"I think you're wrong," I said.

"Jerry's the only one," he said.

I walked over to Jerry Neudecker at second base. He told me he hadn't seen Elrod throw his helmet but that any umpire in the crew can invoke the fine.

"Then go and tell McKean that," I said.

"I'm not going anywhere," Neudecker said.

"Why not? McKean saw it, you didn't. He said you're the only one who can have him fined, but you say any umpire can have him fined. Go tell McKean that."

"I'm not going anywhere," he said stubbornly. "And why do you want to take $100 from Hendricks?"

"It's not the $100," I said. "The rule says the first time you're warned and fined $100, the second time you're ejected. I'm trying to protect my team. If you warn him now and he does it again, he's out of the game. If you don't warn him now and he does it again, he's still in the game."

I walked back to where McKean was.

"Jerry said," I told him, "that any umpire can fine him."

"No," he said. "I can't fine him."

Talk about passing the buck. After the game, outside the umpires' room, I tried to get it straight with Neudecker in case it came up again. But he was just as stubborn as before. In disgust, I took my cap off and slammed it down.

"You won't listen," I told him. "You just won't listen."

"If you're going to act that way," he said, "I'm leaving."

By that time John Stevens, American League umpire consultant, had come down from the stands. He told me that, in his opinion, Hendricks had thrown his helmet because he had come up short of the plate on his slide and he was angry at himself. That's mind reading. All he should be concerned with is Elrod throwing his helmet. But at least John had an opinion. And if McKean had told me that, all right, but he didn't. McKean and Neudecker kept passing the buck. Umpires have to hustle as much as ballplayers have to hustle. Those umpires weren't hustling.

New York, Monday, April 28

About a dozen teenagers were waiting for autographs in the New York Sheraton lobby when I came down for breakfast. But they're not ordinary autograph hunters. They're professionals. They wait in packs of three or four. When they see you, they surround you. Each kid has a stack of magazine covers or color photos for you to autograph, as many as ten of the same one. They don't want one autograph, they want as many as you'll give them. It's been like this in New York, and only New York, for the twenty years I've been coming here. If these kids go to school, they're playing hooky because they're around the lobby almost all day. The same kids are around over a span of three or four seasons. But there's a gradual turnover. The young ones are the most persistent.

"Frank, Frank," one of them was saying as I walked toward the coffee shop. "Frank, please."

I told him, "Later, get me later," and behind me I heard one of the older kids say, "Let him go." He's the veteran. And just like there are more autograph hunters in the hotel lobby in New York than anywhere else, there are more newsmen at the ball park. Especially tonight because this was the first appearance in New York of the first black manager. Reporters in New York seem to be more conscious of "first black" situations than reporters in other cities. If they had been on our bus to the ball park, they probably would have been shocked to see the first black manager sitting halfway back instead of in the front seat. I know the Cleveland writers were shocked. Russ Schneider asked me why.

"I just felt like it," I said. "I told you guys I'd be sitting in different seats on the bus. Coming in from JFK last night, I sat in the back."

In my Shea Stadium office before tonight's game, there were eight writers and two radiomen to greet the first black manager. We were talking baseball when Bill White, the Yankees' black announcer who also does spots on the "Today" show, stopped by to tell me that my time on tomorrow's show had been moved up an hour to 7 o'clock.

"I accept," I said, "then they change the time."

I was kidding him, but I'm not sure that he realized that.

"Why'd they send *you* to tell me?" I asked.

He knew I was kidding then, and he laughed. Moments later I was wrapping my left wrist with white adhesive tape when one of the writers asked me why.

"In case I have to move an outfielder," I said, "this is so they can see my hand."

But after the game, I wasn't in the mood to be funny. We lost, 6–1, our third in a row. Fritz Peterson only got one man out in the first as the Yankees got four quick runs. But most of the New York writers seemed more concerned with why I had Ken Berry running, with us behind, 5–0, in the fifth. Berry was on first, Frank Duffy on third, and Johnny Ellis was up with two out. The count was 1 and 1 and the Yankees weren't holding Berry on. I was hoping that if Rudy May threw a strike, Ellis would get a base hit and Berry might be able to score from first; if Ellis didn't swing, maybe Berry would steal second to put two runners in scoring position. But the move didn't work. Berry got a bad jump and he was tagged out in a rundown. I didn't think much about it after that, but in my office, that's about all the writers wanted to talk about.

"Ellis might've hit a home run," one of the writers said. "Like he did in the seventh."

"I don't manage on might've," I said. "I didn't stop Ellis from swinging when Berry ran."

According to the book some managers use, Berry should not have been running, but I don't always manage by the book. Any manager who does never surprises the other team. On the way back to the bus later Russ Schneider was walking with me.

"I heard your thinking," he said, "but aren't you afraid of being second-guessed?"

"Russ, if I was afraid of being second-guessed," I said firmly, "I wouldn't be here."

On the ride back to the New York Sheraton I sat in the first seat in the bus, the manager's seat. Then a message at the hotel assured me that my problems would soon be over. T. J. O'Hays had phoned.

"Am alive and well," the message said. "Arm almost better. Will call tomorrow."

New York, Tuesday, April 29

Up early to be at the "Today" show studio by 7 o'clock. Back at the hotel T. J. O'Hays phoned to tell me, "My arm is coming along but give me a few more weeks." In the afternoon I was honored with the first Image Award of the Edwin Gould Services for Children at a Park Avenue reception in the Seagram Building. Walking in, I heard a familiar voice behind me say, "Hiya, Slim." I turned and Roy Campanella was sitting in his wheelchair, smiling at me. Roy later told the 300 guests, "Being an old catcher, I always thought I was a manager." He probably was. Rachel Robinson also spoke.

"I hope you will all be around," Jackie's widow told the guests, "when things get rough."

In my thank-you speech, I recalled her words and added, "I'll tell you, things are rough right now." But at Shea Stadium tonight, things got better. After being used for only one-third of an inning since spring training, Don Hood pitched a four-hitter and we won, 3–1. He could be the starter we need. I had intended to play left field because Ken Berry spiked himself last night in that rundown. I took bp, then I went out to left field to see if I could make a hard throw if I had to. After a few easy throws, I realized that a hard throw probably would tear the muscles in the back of my arm. That happened in 1968 when I rejoined the Orioles after the mumps. I hadn't worked out, made one throw, and wrecked my arm. I was out two or three weeks. I didn't want to risk that again. I put Leron Lee in left field instead. When we won, our Kangaroo Kourt was called to order for the first time. Anybody with the ball club can be brought up on a gag charge for a $1 fine that goes into a kitty. To make sure it's strictly a fun thing, it's conducted only after a winning game. It's a carryover from my years with the Orioles when I was in charge of it. But the manager can't be in charge. The players voted Oscar Gamble the "Judge" of our court. He's got the proper sense of humor. He's also got a wild Afro, but it doesn't interfere with his play. We had a few laughs in the Kangaroo Kourt, especially when Leron Lee brought me up.

"I want the manager fined," Leron said, "for taking up my batting practice time."

Boston, Wednesday, April 30

Gaylord is now 14–1 lifetime against the Red Sox. No wonder they keep asking about him. He pitched a five-hitter with nine strikeouts and we won, 8–1, the closest we've had to a laugher so far. I enjoyed it so much, I tried to have a laugh with the umpires, but I don't think they understood my sense of humor. Late in the game Johnny Ellis called for a curveball but Gaylord thought he had signaled for a fastball. The pitch sailed past John's glove and hit Joe Brinkman flush in the mask. He wasn't hurt but he was stunned. In the dugout I turned toward Larry McCoy, the third-base umpire.

"I told them to do that," I yelled. "He's been missing too many pitches."

I was joking but I think Larry took me seriously. When he glared at me, I yelled, "I was just kidding," but I'm not so sure he believed me. I hope the umpires don't turn on me and my ball club for that. I was joking. No way I would ever tell my players to hurt an umpire. Not even Clif Keane would accuse me of that. Clif has covered the Red Sox for the Boston *Globe* since Paul Revere was a rookie. He's one of my favorite sportswriters. Maybe because his sense of humor is even more insulting than mine. In recent years he used to tell me, "I see you're still trying to knife your way in as a manager." But in the dugout before tonight's game, he was fairly quiet, for Clif.

"I'll bet 20,000 blacks are coming tonight," he said, "just to see you manage."

But the whole crowd was under 10,000.

Boston, Thursday, May 1

We lost, 7–6, after the Red Sox jumped on Jim Perry for a 5–0 lead in less than two innings. He was getting the ball up again. We have a 4–5 record on the road trip, a big disappointment to me. Another disappointment was that I couldn't bat in the ninth. We had the tying run on third and the potential winning run on first, but I sent Leron Lee up to hit for me. When he struck out, the writers questioned the manager for taking out the dh, but I had jammed my left shoulder diving back to first base in the second when Bill Lee picked me off. I got a single that drove in a run in the third, but by the ninth my shoulder had stiffened to where I couldn't raise my left arm high enough to hold the bat properly.

I'm really concerned about my shoulder. It's bothered me off and on for the last five years. But every year it takes longer to get better. Cortisone is the only thing that helps. I hope I don't need a shot.

I'm also concerned about Charlie Spikes's concentration. He not only forgot his sunglasses last Sunday but he's continually missing the cutoff man with his throws. He threw high in Baltimore and New York and again tonight. I had Tom McCraw tell him that the next time it happens, it's a $100 fine.

Cleveland, Friday, May 2

My left shoulder was stiff and sore when I woke up, but at least I woke up in an apartment instead of a hotel room. Trudy and Posey somehow discovered a vacancy in Lakewood at Marine Towers East—living room, dining room, modern kitchen, two bedrooms, two baths, and a nice view of Lake

Erie from a glass-walled room with a bar off the living room. It's on the eighth floor, halfway to the penthouse. There's a swimming pool downstairs and a putting green. I'm told I'm the first black tenant.

After we flew back from Boston last night, I moved in. Slowly. I don't recommend carrying luggage as proper therapy for a sore shoulder.

On the way to the ball park, I stopped for a cortisone shot from Dr. Earl Brightman, the Indians' orthopedist. I had to turn away when the needle went in or I'd have passed out. By the time tonight's game was over, my shoulder didn't feel any better, but I did. We won, 4–3, with our dh, Rico Carty, hitting a homer and knocking in the winning run in the eighth with a loop single. My twenty-year-old relief pitcher, Dennis Eckersley, got his first major-league victory. It won't be his last.

Cleveland, Saturday, May 3

My shoulder kept me awake most of the night. I went to bed about 2 but I didn't fall asleep until about 5 because of the pain. It was like a toothache. To work, the cortisone has to hit the right spot. I think it missed. But we pulled out a real good one over the Orioles, 6–1, a tremendous game to win.

Ross Grimsley had us handcuffed going into the seventh, but Buddy Bell led off with a double. I inserted myself as a pinch hitter for Jack Brohamer because even with my bad shoulder, I thought I could at least hit a ball to the right side of the infield that would move Buddy to third. On the second pitch, I hit a screwball up the middle for a single that scored Buddy with the tying run and I kept on going to second on the throw. Ken Berry got a ground single when Grimsley never left the mound to cover first, and I went to third. Frank Duffy looped a ball into center field that Paul Blair came hard for. I tagged up, but the tipoff that Blair wasn't going to catch the ball was that he put both hands out in front of him as a decoy. I took off and he didn't make a good throw to the plate. We kept going for a big six-run inning. Fritz Peterson went all the way, a good five-hitter. I got a bigger thrill out of this than opening day because it was more important. We're 9–9 now, only 2½ games out of first place.

I also won about $30 on Foolish Pleasure in the Kentucky Derby clubhouse pool. Maybe my luck has changed, but my shoulder hasn't. I needed another cortisone shot after the game.

Cleveland, Sunday, May 4

My shoulder felt better. The cortisone must've hit the spot this time. I would've been the dh today if the Orioles had used a lefthanded pitcher, but they didn't. We split, losing 11–1 and winning 4–3 in eleven innings.

Gaylord got bombed out. He also got too smart. We had been pitching Al Brumby outside with good success. Gaylord went outside with two pitches but then he and John Ellis wanted to get smart and come inside. They did. The ball landed about 400 feet away over the centerfield fence for a three-run homer. We've got to eliminate mental mistakes like that. The pitchers have to pitch hitters with the pattern we've discussed in the clubhouse. We have to lay the bunt down properly. We have to hit the cutoff man. Charlie Spikes missed the cutoff man again. Between games, I fined him $100, as I warned him I would. My first fine.

"I understand," Charlie told me. "I deserve it."

I wish Charlie would get more upset sometimes. He's too easygoing. In the second game, we won despite another mental mistake. Don Hood had been told that Dave Duncan was not to get a fastball. Throw him breaking balls and keep the ball away. For some reason Alan Ashby called for a fastball and Hood didn't shake him off. Duncan hit it over the centerfield fence for a 3–3 tie in the seventh. But we won for Tom Buskey in the eleventh when John Lowenstein slid hard into Bobby Grich, breaking up a double play that would've ended the inning, and George Hendrick got his fourth single. The victory kept us at .500 with three out of four from the Orioles this weekend. I remember when I was with the Orioles, we used to come to Cleveland figuring on sweeping the series. This time we almost swept them.

Back in the apartment I got the hiccups about 9:30 and they didn't stop until I went to bed. Every 30 seconds. I've had hiccups before, but never like this. I always got rid of them before by holding my breath or taking a drink of water. I don't know why it took so long this time. Maybe it's managing.

Cleveland, Monday, May 5

We lost to the Red Sox, 7–5, as Jim Perry got knocked out in the fifth. He's now 1–5 with a 6.82 earned-run average, 37 hits, and 14 walks in only 30 innings. He's not getting the ball down, where he has to get it. By next Sunday, when his turn comes up again, I might start somebody else. Before tonight's game, I had a sit-down with Russ Schneider and Bob Sudyk over Charlie Spikes's fine. Sudyk found out about it and wrote it for the *Press*, the afternoon paper. Schneider thought I should've announced it yesterday; that way, he would've had it in the *Plain Dealer* this morning, before Sudyk did.

"Anytime I fine a player," I explained, "it's between me and the player."

In a brief meeting with the players, I told them that if any-body wants to tell a writer that he's been fined, that's his business, but I don't think it's fair to tell a writer about an-other player being fined or anything else about another player that doesn't concern him. I don't know who told Sudyk, but it's typical of the way he and Schneider compete against each other. Like with me after a game, they'll come in and Schneider will ask questions but Sudyk won't. Sudyk just keeps his little notes. But as soon as Schneider leaves, Sudyk pursues his angle.

"I just need a couple of things," he'll say.

But after Bob leaves, Schneider somtimes comes back to see me.

"Anything I should know?" Russ will say.

"Ask me a question," I always tell him.

But the next day, if Sudyk has something special like the

Spikes's fine, Russ will wonder why I didn't tell him. Like when I had my meeting with Jim Perry two weeks ago, Schneider asked me what I told him.

"If I wanted you to know what I said," I told him, "I'd have had you in the meeting."

I told Russ a few things, but later Sudyk probed a little deeper. The next day, when Russ saw what Bob had written, he was annoyed.

"I thought that was off the record," he said.

I wish they would talk to each other. It might make life easier for them. And for me.

Cleveland, Tuesday, May 6

Jim Kern made up my mind for me tonight on next Sunday's starter. He shut out the Red Sox for 6⅔ innings, but it was the last 6⅔. Dick Bosman had been bombed for four runs. That was enough for Bill Lee, who stopped us, 4–1, on a six-hitter. We're just not hitting. And we're getting our good pitching from Kern and Dennis Eckersley and Dave LaRoche and Tom Buskey when it's too late. That's why Jim Kern is in the rotation now and Jim Perry is out of it.

Cleveland, Wednesday, May 7

At the ball park I went up to Phil Seghi's office to check with him like I always do. When he saw me, he asked if I had been downstairs yet.

"No," I said.

"Sit down."

I didn't know what to think. Maybe the clubhouse had collapsed. Maybe some players had been in a fight.

"Hood jammed his thumb in the infield."

From the start of spring training, I told the pitchers that I preferred them not to take grounders in the infield during batting practice. That's not their job. Pitching is. But ballplayers have a tendency to con you. The pitchers argue that it helps them field their position. But pitchers don't see the ball for 120 feet like most infielders do. They see it for 60 feet—if they're lucky. I went downstairs and talked to Hood to see if he thought he could start against the White Sox on Saturday night. He thinks he can. But in the clubhouse I told all the pitchers, "From now on, you take ground balls in the infield at your own risk. If you miss a turn because of an injury taking ground balls, you'll be docked a day's pay." I think I convinced even Gaylord not to take ground balls anymore. With his salary, he has more to lose than any of the pitchers.

We were swept by the Red Sox, 4–2, the last of the three-game series and dropped 3 games under the .500 mark. We're batting .241 as a team. In my mind, I think our hitters are still suffering from those four consecutive off-days two weeks ago, but I can't tell the writers that because I don't want to give the hitters a crutch.

Cleveland, Thursday, May 8

Off-day, but not for the manager. This was a decision day that most fans don't know about. But the older players do. Waivers must be asked today on a player if he's to clear by May 15, because if he's kept after that date and then released, he must be paid his full salary for the season. Phil and I decided to put outfielders Leron Lee and Ken Berry on waivers. Phil also told me that Charley Finley had phoned. The owner of the A's is interested in Jim Perry, which sounds like a deal that might develop. I know I'm not too interested in Jim Perry now.

Cleveland, Friday, May 9

Before tonight's 2–0 loss to the White Sox, I had a talk with Jim Perry to tell him that he's coming out of the rotation and going to the bullpen.

"I'm not a relief pitcher," he said.

"I know you're not, and I'm not saying this is permanent," I explained. "But we're going to start Kern in Sunday's game. I'm not a believer in letting a pitcher go out there and keep getting beat. Not for his own confidence and not for the ball club's confidence. Maybe somebody else will be just as bad, but I've got to give him the chance."

Jim wasn't happy and I'm sure he told Gaylord about it, but Gaylord didn't let it affect his pitching.

Gaylord had a no-hitter through five innings, but in the eighth Pat Kelly hit a two-run homer. That's all Jim Kaat needed. Kaat was quick-pitching the first two innings, pitching before the hitter was set in the batter's box. Bill Kunkel, the plate umpire, slowed him down after that but it didn't make much difference. We only got six hits. We've lost four in a row.

Cleveland, Saturday, May 10

We lost again, 8–3, for five in a row. Even with his jammed thumb, Don Hood pitched well through four innings. We were ahead, 2–1, in the fifth when he got a little wild. Harvey went out to remind him how to pitch to Buddy Bradford, the White Sox's rightfielder. We had gone over how Bradford is a low fastball hitter with power. Harvey reminded Hood that Bradford is not a good breaking-ball hitter.

"If you throw a fastball," Harvey told him, "be sure you keep it up."

Hood went to 3 and 0, then got a strike over. But on 3 and 1, he threw his fastball low. Bradford hit it about 425 feet over the centerfield fence for three runs. But then Bill Kunkel, the third-base umpire, did something that really annoyed me. Our bullpen in Cleveland Stadium is down behind third base, so we can see the pitchers easily from our first-base dugout. When we signaled for Buskey to come in and take over from Hood, Kunkel waved down there, but Buskey ignored him and threw a few extra pitches. Finally, as Buskey walked by third base on his way to the mound, I noticed Kunkel talking to him.

"He warned me," Buskey told me later, "that the next time I did that, they'd deduct the pitches I threw down there from the warm-up pitches on the mound. And then he said, 'The next time I'm behind the plate, I'm going to stick it to you.' "

I'll confront Bill Kunkel with that tomorrow. But our hitting is bothering me more than our pitching and the umpires. Buddy Bell, Charlie Spikes, and Johnny Ellis have come up with a total of over 150 runners on base and have driven in only 15—Ellis 9, Bell and Spikes 3 each. Away from the ball park, I've stayed to myself lately. In a losing streak, the manager shouldn't go where the fans are. Some fans will try to tell you what you're doing wrong. They mean well and they can be nice about it. But they don't always accept your answers. I know what we're not doing. We're not hitting.

Cleveland, Sunday, May 11

During the pregame meeting with the umpires, I got Bill Kunkel's eye.

"One of my players told me something I can't believe," I said. "Buskey said you told him last night that the next time you're behind the plate when he's pitching, you're going to stick it to him."

"You know I'd never say that," Kunkel said. "He must've misunderstood me."

I didn't say anything. I just wanted him to know that I knew what he told Buskey last night. And then we beat the White Sox, 4–3, on two wild throws in the eleventh. We're still not hitting but at least we got lucky. Jim Kern showed me he should stay in rotation. He went nine strong innings. With a little more luck, he could've had a 2–0 shutout. But he had thrown 155 pitches. I brought in Buskey again and the White Sox went ahead in the eleventh for what looked like our sixth straight loss. But then Rico walked and Charlie Spikes bunted him over, one of the few bunts we've gotten down. Buddy Bell flied out, with Rico going to third. Chuck Tanner, the White Sox manager, went against the book. He ordered his lefthanded reliever, Terry Forster, to walk Johnny Ellis intentionally, putting the potential winning run on first. Ed Crosby, who had replaced Jack Brohamer at second base, was up next, a lefthanded hitter. Tanner knew I was out of righthanded pinch hitters. Not even the manager was available. Batting for Brohamer in the seventh, I had singled in the tying run after Rico's homer. Now, in the eleventh, I had to send up Tom McCraw, another lefthanded hitter, to bat for Crosby, and he nubbed a grounder down the third-base line. Forster made a good play, but as he turned to throw to first, he slipped. His throw was low and bounced down the rightfield line. Rico scored and Ellis had reached third base when Bob Collucio, the rightfielder, retrieved the ball. Instead of running the ball back in, Collucio threw to the plate. When the ball bounced away, Ellis scored. You'd have thought we won the World Series the way the players jumped out of the dugout to celebrate. This gift might turn the ball club around.

But the frustration involved in managing detracted from the victory somewhat.

Like in the ninth, after Ellis led off with a single. Crosby was up next. I had told him earlier, "If John gets on, you're bunting on the first pitch." He squared away but fouled it off. He looked down at the third-base coach and Dave Garcia flashed him the bunt sign again. But on the next pitch, he swung. He missed, but he had swung.

I didn't see what I saw, I thought. *No, I didn't see that. He didn't really swing.*

To begin with, Ed Crosby is not a power hitter. One of the reasons he's with us is to bunt a runner over. The runner on first base represented the winning run in the ninth inning with nobody out. I could not believe that Ed Crosby would think he was swinging away in that situation. With two strikes now, he eventually flied out. When he came back to the dugout, I told him he had missed the bunt sign.

"I didn't see it," he said.

He better see it the next time or it will cost him. Or anybody else. We've missed about 15 signs in only 26 games. Talking with the writers later, one asked if I was going to fine Crosby for missing that bunt sign.

"No, but let's say it's our last free one," I said. "We've been missing too many signs."

Back at the apartment I made a Mother's Day call to Barbara and the kids. I had wired Barbara and my mother each a dozen red roses. Forgetting to do that would have been worse than if I had missed the bunt sign.

Cleveland, Monday, May 12

Off-day, with no workout. Let the players relax before a six-game road trip to Minnesota and Chicago that starts tomorrow. I've decided to go with a four-man rotation—Gaylord, Fritz, Don Hood, and Jim Kern, with Jim Perry and Dick Bosman in the bullpen. Phil told me today that the A's are asking about Bosman now. Charley Finley still wants Jim Perry but he wants another pitcher too. Phil also mentioned that the Rangers are asking about Jim again. I like Bosman but I don't think he's got the stuff to be in the rotation consistently. He's a good pitcher to have on your staff and a good person to have on your team. He'll be my spot starter when the spot develops.

Two Trades
and a Tirade

Minnesota, Tuesday, May 13

Before tonight's game I informed the players that there was a $100 fine for missing a sign. In the second inning Johnny Ellis missed the hit-and-run sign. But other than that, we played heads-up baseball against the Twins and won, 3–2. Buddy Bell hit a homer in the fifth for the decisive run, but Jack Brohamer made the big play in the third—a drag-bunt double. Rod Carew came in for the bunt but Charlie Spikes, running from first, was in his way. Carew couldn't make up his mind where to go, and the ball rolled past him to the outfield grass. In the confusion, nobody covered second and Brohamer got a double on a bunt that traveled maybe 120 feet. I was surprised at Carew's indecision because the fielder has the right of way, not the runner. If he had collided with Spikes, he could've claimed interference. Frank Duffy then doubled for two runs.

Fritz Peterson continued to be a Jekyll-Hyde, pitching well into the seventh. Dennis Eckersley finished with three hitless innings. That kid is amazing. He hasn't given up an earned run in 14 innings over 8 appearances.

With two wins in a row, the Kangaroo Kourt was in session again. I got fined for taking Bob Short's limousine into town instead of the team bus when we arrived at the airport. Short, who used to own the Washington Senators and the Texas Rangers, lives here. He had phoned Phil to say that his private limousine would be at the airport for us. When we saw it parked behind our bus, Phil and I got in. Russ Schneider looked in but he didn't want to ride in the jump seat. Bob Sudyk didn't mind.

"Frank Robinson, Phil Seghi, and Bob Sudyk are fined $1," Oscar announced, "for taking the limo."

But then I got Russ Schneider fined $1 by the Kangaroo Kourt for *not* taking the limousine.

Minnesota, Wednesday, May 14

This ball club has me baffled. We can't put a real winning streak together. For the fourth time, we had a chance to win three in a row and we lost. Jim Hughes, a rookie righthander, shut us out, 3–0, on four hits. We can't seem to hit pitchers we haven't seen before. Gaylord had a five-hitter, but two of those hits were home runs. He's given up nine homers, an alarming number. He also went to sleep with Rod Carew on third base. Carew stole home seven times in 1969, he's always a threat. When he's on third, most pitchers take their stretch, but Gaylord took his full windup. That's daring Carew, and he stole home cleanly for the Twins' first run. Next time up, Gaylord threw a slider up and in. Carew thought Gaylord was throwing at him. On the next pitch, Carew swung and let his bat go past the mound. He and Gaylord yelled at each other but the first-base umpire, Nestor Chylak, stepped in to quiet them down.

To me, Nestor should've warned Carew about throwing his bat. When the batter lets his bat go after a close pitch, the umpire knows it didn't just slip. Or he should know.

Minnesota, Thursday, May 15

We've now lost seven of our last nine. We keep making mistakes there's no excuse for. We were down, 6–2, and we came back to tie it up, but the Twins won in the ninth, 7–6, on two mistakes. Jim Perry, in long relief of Don Hood, walked the first batter. That was the first mistake. That's something a pitcher is not supposed to do in a tie game. When the Twins bunted him over, I ordered an intentional walk, then I brought in Dave LaRoche and he struck out Tony Oliva on four pitches for the second out. But LaRoche made the second mistake. On a 1-and-1 pitch, Rod Carew singled to center. Carew is the best pure hitter in baseball. He's won four American League batting titles, three in a row, and he'll probably win another one this season. I don't mind Carew beating my ball club with a base hit on a good pitch. But as soon as Carew connected, I turned to Harvey Haddix.

"What the hell kind of pitch was that?"

"It looked like a hanging slider to me," Harvey said.

"I don't think so, but I'll find out."

Johnny Ellis also must have been concerned, if not embarrassed. He came to me later, apologizing for the pitch. I asked him what it was.

"Forkball," he said.

"What?" I exploded.

Dave LaRoche's forkball is his least effective pitch. He's a fastball pitcher with a good slider. But with the winning run on second base and Rod Carew up, Dave LaRoche threw a forkball.

"We thought we'd trick him," Ellis said.

"You don't often trick Rod Carew with a pitcher's best pitch, much less his worst pitch," I said. "I've told you how I want the catcher to take charge out there. I can't believe you'd call for that pitch where a hit means the ball game. You should know better than that."

LaRoche also has been around long enough to know better. He had no excuse except the trick theory.

"The worst thing a pitcher can do is try to trick a hitter," I told him. "Go after a hitter with your best stuff. Especially a hitter like Rod Carew."

Hopefully, they won't make that mistake again. Hopefully.

Chicago, Friday, May 16

Another loss, 3–2, and another disappointment because we were leading, 2–0, going into the ninth. But when Jim Kern walked the first batter, I took him out. He had a three-hit shutout going but he had thrown 142 pitches. I wanted a fresh arm. The bullpen hasn't let me down too often, but they did tonight. Tom Buskey gave up three straight singles for one run without getting anybody out. With the bases loaded, Dave LaRoche struck out Bill Stein on a fastball, not a forkball. But with Buddy Bradford up, I brought in Dennis Eckersley and, for the first time, the kid didn't have it. He hit Bradford, forcing in the tying run. Then he walked Jorge Orta, forcing in the winning run. It was my fault for using him. He had the flu earlier in the week.

But taking out Jim Kern with a 2–0 lead won't keep me awake. I believe in making moves too soon rather than too late. We'll win more games that way than we'll lose.

Chicago, Saturday, May 17

I'll probably be fined and suspended for what happened to-night. I pushed umpire Jerry Neudecker during an argument. Even though he provoked me, I know the American League office won't let a manager get away with that. We lost to the White Sox, 10–1, and we were behind, 8–0, in the sixth when the incident occurred. But no matter what the score is, if I think an umpire made a mistake, I'm going out there to pro-tect my ball club.

Jorge Orta hit a line drive off the rightfield wall, but the ball came off at a right angle because a fan touched it. I not only saw a fan touch it, but a fan had to touch it. I've played out there often enough to know that. You can throw a ball off that wall forever and it won't come off at a right angle. When the ball bounced away from Charlie Spikes, Orta rounded second and went to third. I waited for the umpires to wave him back to second. When a fan touches that type of hit, it's a ground-rule double. But when Orta stayed at third, I walked out to Neudecker.

"Jerry," I said calmly, "didn't you see the fan touch the ball?"

"I saw him reach over," he said. "I didn't see him touch the ball."

"Then why," I asked calmly, "did the ball go at the an-gle it did?"

"I don't know," he answered, annoyed at me, "and I don't care."

He had the same stubborn attitude he had in Baltimore when Elrod Hendricks threw his helmet, and in Milwaukee when he pushed me twice after Nick Bremigan, the plate um-pire, had called Charlie Spikes out on fan interference with a foul ball.

"Why don't you ask Art Frantz at second base?" I said. "Maybe he had a better angle than you did."

He glared and replied, "I don't have to ask anybody." By now I wasn't talking calmly. We were arguing face to face, so close that he took his cap off. I didn't want to hit him with the peak of my cap, so I took my cap off. And now we really were face to face. Suddenly he bumped me with his chest. Then he stepped back.

"Did you bump me?" he yelled.

"I haven't even moved forward. How'm I going to bump you?"

"You bumped me," he yelled.

We were both yelling now, and I must have cursed him because he threw me out of the game. That's when I really got hot. He walked down the foul line away from me but I walked around him. I wanted to get my money's worth. Suddenly he deliberately thrust his chest out and bumped me twice. That's when I pushed him with both hands. He had a startled, frightened look on his face. I guess he thought I was going to attack him. No way I was going to do that. But by now some of my ballplayers were out there to break it up and Rico Carty grabbed me from behind. My arms were free but he had his big arms wrapped around my chest.

"Rico, let me go," I gasped. "Let me go."

It probably sounded like I wanted to go after Neudecker, but I was just trying to keep Rico from breaking my ribs. Things finally cooled down, but on my way to the dugout I turned toward Neudecker again.

"If you think I bumped you this time," I yelled, "next time I'll knock you on your ass."

Of all the American League umpires, Jerry Neudecker has the shortest fuse. As soon as anybody disputes him, he gets indignant and stubborn, like he's given an order that can't be questioned. It's not just me. Other managers tell me the same thing. He used to be in the Air Force, maybe that's when he got that way. Until this year, I never had much trouble with him but already I've had three bad scenes. On calls, he's usually a capable umpire. But if he's disputed, he flies off the handle. To me, that's not a good umpire. But he won't be fined or suspended. I will. Except that I'm going to appeal whatever disciplinary action is taken against me by Lee MacPhail, the American League president. I talked over the idea of an appeal with Phil and my coaches tonight over a few drinks at the Little Corporal after the game. They agreed that the umpires are on me and my ball club, whatever their reason is. I told Phil about Bill Kunkel last week, how Kunkel threatened to "stick it to" Tom Buskey the next time he was behind the plate and how Kunkel told me the next day that Buskey must have misunderstood him.

"Did Kunkel tell you that?" Dave Garcia said. "After Buskey came in that night, Kunkel told me the same thing."

Chicago, Sunday, May 18

My wake-up call rang at 9, but I was still laying in bed at the Executive House when the phone rang again at 5 after. Lee MacPhail wanted to hear my version. After he heard it, he told me that it was about the same as Jerry Neudecker's report.

"I'm fining you $250," he said, "and suspending you for three days."

"Why do I have to be suspended when I thought he was the aggressor?"

We talked some more and eventually he mentioned how the league office can't allow this type of behavior.

"I'd like to appeal it then."

"You can do that," he agreed.

"What'll happen," I asked, "if I win the appeal?"

"You get your fine back."

"What good will that do? I'll have lost three days with my ball club. That's more important to me than the $250 fine. Three days not only as a manager but also as a player."

"I'll tell you what," he said. "I'll postpone the suspension until I can have a hearing."

"That's fair enough," I said, "but I want to make sure I can play until the hearing is held."

"You can play," he said. "I'll get word to the umpires that you can play until the hearing."

I was still the manager and still a player. When we arrived at White Sox Park today, I canceled batting practice and had a rap session about why we have lost nine of our last eleven games. This is something I've always thought a manager should do when his ball club is going bad. Not a chew-out, a talk-out. I talked mostly about how we're not hitting with runners in scoring position, how a hitter should be prepared.

"But how," asked Frank Duffy, "do you prepare yourself to hit with men on base?"

"You should know what the pitcher's best pitches are," I said. "You should know yourself as a hitter. You should know what he's been throwing in that particular game and what he's got you out on in previous situations. Put all those things in the back of your mind in a little computer while you're in the on-deck circle. Walking up to hit, go over them. Then lock yourself into the situation. Concentrate."

Maybe the rap session helped. We won, 7–6. I knew that with Wilbur Wood pitching for them, batting practice wouldn't make that much difference.

Gaylord got his fifth win but he struggled. I took him out in the sixth, the earliest he's departed this season. With the tying run at second in the ninth, Dennis Eckersley struck out Bill Melton on three fastballs for the final out. The kid is cool. And the plate umpire was Jerry Neudecker—but my one time up as the dh, I didn't talk to him and he didn't talk to me.

At the Kangaroo Kourt later, the players remembered what happened last night and voted me the recipient of the red toilet seat—the Red-Ass Award.

Cleveland, Monday, May 19

Home for a week, but we lost to my old ball club, the Angels, 12–5, our worst-played game. We've now lost ten of our last thirteen and we've dropped into last place. I'm beginning to wonder if somebody else might do a better job managing this team. It's a ball club with a losing attitude. One problem is, the Indians haven't won the World Series since 1948, they haven't won a pennant since 1954 when they got wiped out in the World Series by the New York Giants in four straight, they haven't even had a .500 season since 1968 when they finished third with an 86–75 record. Hardly any of our players have been on winning teams.

The only ones who've been on a World Series winner are Boog and myself, on the 1966 and 1970 Orioles, and George Hendrick on the 1972 Oakland A's.

Our only other player ever in a World Series is Jim Perry, who was with the 1965 Minnesota Twins, who lost to the Dodgers that year. But I think Jim is through. I brought him in to relieve Don Hood with two on, to face Jerry Remy, the Angels' little second baseman. Jerry Remy pulled Jim Perry for a three-run homer. Jerry Remy couldn't pull *me*. Jerry is 5-9 and 160 pounds. He had never hit a home run in the major leagues before. That pitch Jim Perry threw couldn't have had a thing on it. That pitch was the last straw. Jim Perry has got to be moved. Maybe tomorrow.

Cleveland, Tuesday, May 20

Off-day, but a big day. We traded Jim Perry and Dick Bosman to the A's for John (Blue Moon) Odom and about $25,000 in cash. I hated to give up Bosman, a really fine person. Bos was willing to do anything for the good of the ball club, but Phil told me that Charley Finley wouldn't make the deal without Bos in it. Charley's pretty smart. As much as I didn't want to move Bosman, the offer sounded good because it let me put Dennis Eckersley into the rotation and bring up Eric Raich from Oklahoma City as another starter. When we were discussing it in Phil's office, Ted Bonda turned to me.

"Would you make it?" he asked.

"I sure would," I told him.

"And if you make it, what?"

"Use a five-man rotation with Gaylord, Fritz, Kern, Eckersley, and Raich, and put Odom and Hood in the bullpen for long relief."

"Make the deal," Ted said.

Phil tried to call Finley back but the line was busy. He tried again. Still busy. Ted was so eager to complete the deal, he went over to Phil's desk and dialed Finley's number himself. Still busy. We decided to go upstairs to the Stadium Club for lunch. Phil usually has soup or chili for lunch. When he ordered chili, Ted and I did too. But just as it was served, Trudy came up to tell Phil that she had Finley on the phone. We thought Phil would be back in two minutes, but after maybe fifteen minutes he finally returned.

"What was the big delay?" Ted asked.

"I tried to get another $2,500 out of Charley," said Phil, "but he wouldn't go for it."

"You almost blew it over $2,500?" I said.

"I wanted a little more money," Phil said.

"You know Charley doesn't want to give up a dime, much less $2,500," I said. "But the deal's made?"

"The deal's made," Phil said.

"What else can we do?" Ted said.

Over our chili, Ted and I had talked about bringing up not only Eric Raich but also Rick Manning, the kid outfielder, and Larry Andersen, another righthanded pitcher. To make room for them, we would release Ken Berry and Leron Lee.

"You like Manning better than Tommy Smith?" Ted asked me.

"Manning can do more things," I said. "He runs better, he throws better."

"But if he comes up," Phil said, "he's got to play."

"Don't worry about that," I assured him. "He'll play."

"Let's do it all today and announce it today," Ted said. "It'll be a big story for the papers."

"We can't do it all today," Phil said. "The Cardinals are interested in Leron Lee for cash."

"Sell him then," Ted said.

"I've got to wait until Thursday," Phil explained. "Today we'll just announce the deal and Raich."

"That's enough to keep the writers happy," I said.

I know the writers will second-guess us for this trade. But we felt that if we went along with the older pitchers, within a year or two they wouldn't be back anyway. This was the time to trade them. To open up spots for some of our outstanding young people, to get us moving. I know the fans might think we're giving up on the season by making this trade. But to me, we would be giving up on the season if we didn't make this trade. Ted Bonda also showed me that he's not afraid to make a big move. After the 1973 season Phil wanted to trade Gaylord to the Red Sox for three of four pitchers who were being discussed—Lynn McGlothen, Marty Pattin, John Curtis, and Mike Garman—but I'm told Ted turned it down because of Gaylord's popularity here. Since then, Ted apparently has learned that popularity isn't everything.

But trading Jim Perry probably cost us a TV set for the clubhouse. I've been trying to get a TV set in there since spring training started. But every time I mention it to Phil, he puffs on his pipe and changes the subject. The other day Jim Perry told me he had a friend who would be glad to provide a TV set for the clubhouse.

"Anytime he's ready," I said.

I imagine now that Jim Perry will tell his friend not to bother. But as hard as this trade will be on Gaylord, he's a professional. He won't let it affect his performance.

Cleveland, Wednesday, May 21

The dh hit two homers tonight, his first since opening day, and we beat the Angels, 3–2, for Jim Kern's first major-league victory. Some of the Angels' writers wondered if Frank Tanana was tipping his pitches, as if that had to be the reason why I was able to hit two homers. But he hadn't tipped his pitches. I simply had put my thoughts together with his pattern of pitching. I knew him from when he came up with the Angels two years ago. He's got a decent fastball but he's not Nolan Ryan, he's not a real fastball pitcher. If he doesn't get his fastball exactly where he wants it, he's going to get hit. But when Dick Williams took over last year, he had him throwing even more fastballs, trying to do what we call "hump up," meaning get more on it. He also had him throwing a very lazy curveball. Plus, when I was up there hitting tonight, I knew the way the Angels think.

On the first homer, Frank started me with a curve for a ball because the Angels know I like to swing at a first-pitch fastball. Then he missed with another curveball. Two balls, no strikes. I was thinking he had to come with the fastball and he did. Inside, but not inside enough. I hit it over the left-centerfield fence.

Next time up, I flied out to center field on a curveball up and away. His curveball is lazily thrown, without a good motion. Then, for my third at bat, I figured they would change their pattern, thinking I would be looking for a curveball. Frank threw a fastball up and away and I hit it over the right-centerfield fence.

That's what I mean about putting my thoughts together with a pattern of pitching.

I wasn't reading Tanana's pitches, but I can read about 25 percent of the American League pitchers. One tip-off is the position of a pitcher's hands above his head in the windup. Some stop over their head on the fastball. Some go farther back on the curveball. Some go halfway back on the slider. Others keep their hands out in front on the fastball. Others go up high with their hands on the fastball, lower on the curveball. Another tip-off is where their fingers are on the ball, how much white is showing between their first two fingers. On a fastball those two fingers are slightly apart. On a curveball the fingers are together.

There's one pitcher who tips everything he does. If his hands come up above his head, it's a fastball. If they're in front of his face, it's a curveball. If they're off to the side, it's a change-up. And if they're not quite up to his face on the stretch motion, he's going to throw to first base.

This is why I keep telling our hitters that there is more to do in the dugout than laugh or joke or hang their heads. If they watch the other pitchers, they might learn something that they'll be able to use when they're batting, something that will help them be better hitters and help us be a better ball club. But there are some pitchers you shouldn't try to read. Nolan Ryan, for example. I've told hitters not to even try to read Nolan Ryan because I don't want them to make a mistake and get nailed by his fastball. Just look for his fastball every time. If it's a curve, be thankful.

Before the game, Phil told me that Lee MacPhail will be here Saturday morning for my hearing on the Neudecker incident.

John Odom and Eric Raich reported. I saw John quoted as saying, "I always wanted to pitch for a black manager." But when I told him I planned to use him in long relief instead of as a starter, he didn't seem thrilled with his black manager.

Cleveland, Thursday, May 22

Off-day. We called up Rick Manning, released Leron Lee, and discovered that John Odom wants to renegotiate his contract. He was making about $45,000 with the A's and he had an 0–2 record there with a 12.27 earned-run average. But he told Phil that he wants an $8,000 raise. Phil gave him a flat no.

Cleveland, Friday, May 23

We lost to the A's, 3–0, with Gaylord giving up two more homers—to Joe Rudi, which is understandable, and to Bert Campaneris, which is not. That's 12 homers off Gaylord, who hasn't been consistent. He hasn't been the leader of the staff like we thought he would be and like he has to be now with three rookie starters. He's got to give the kids an example to shoot at. But maybe he'll be stronger in a five-day rotation.

I put Rick Manning in right field. He got one of our three hits and almost made a diving catch. The kid wants to play.

Before the game I called John Odom into my office to talk over his contract situation. He was annoyed that Phil wouldn't give him the $8,000 raise.

"Why should he give it to you?" I said.

"Because I'm coming from a championship ball club," he said. "I won't be getting any World Series money this year."

"Did you talk to him about next year?"

"I didn't talk about nothin' but $8,000."

"Don't push people into a corner," I said. "Don't force him. Don't go up there upset and angry. Ask him, 'What if I do this or that, what'll that mean next season to me?' See if that helps."

"I'll see," he said.

Cleveland, Saturday, May 24

At my hearing today with Lee MacPhail in Phil's office, Ted Bonda made a good point. "The umpires," he told Lee, "are overreacting to Frank being the first black manager." Lee naturally didn't agree. The league office stands behind its umpires. In the hearing I had the feeling that I was being heard, but from Lee's expressions and comments, I wasn't surprised when he upheld the suspension.

"Let me talk to Jerry Neudecker again," Lee said, "and I'll announce it tomorrow, to begin Monday night in Anaheim."

Since it was a three-day suspension, I was tempted to request that it start the Monday of the All-Star break, but I didn't think Lee would appreciate my sense of humor. His umpires don't. But at least I've had the satisfaction of appealing and having a hearing. Maybe someday a manager or a player will win an appeal. Maybe.

Against the A's we had a 5–0 lead in the third after Rico and I hit back-to-back homers that knocked out Vida Blue, but Billy Williams hit a three-run homer off Eric Raich in the fourth. The A's went on to win, 10–5.

I got Raich out of there quickly in the fourth because I didn't want him to be the losing pitcher in his first major-league start. He seemed to get flustered when Joe Rudi hit a good sinker back through the box for a single before Billy Williams's homer. Down in Oklahoma City not many hitters could handle his good sinker. They can hit it up here. His presence on the ball club creates an unusual situation that might be unprecedented. His father-in-law is Russ Schneider; he met Russ's daughter Eileen at spring training three years ago. Russ was the official scorer today and he gave Bert Campaneris a hit on a bunt that Eric might have thrown him out on but Eric slipped. Not long after that, Russ's phone in the press box rang. It was his wife, Kay.

"How could you call that a hit?" Kay said. "That was an error."

Eric's mother-in-law already is defending his earned-run average.

I brought in John Odom in the sixth with us still ahead,

5–4, and two on. He gave up a single for the tying run, a walk that loaded the bases and, after a force-out at the plate, he walked in two more runs. I don't think it had anything to do with his contract problems. He probably was trying too hard against his old teammates. But that's not the way to convince the general manager that he deserves an $8,000 raise. Or the manager.

To complete my day, I met with some Stouffer's executives at the Top of the Town to discuss my visits to their frozen-food plant in Solon, Ohio, later in the season. They want me to talk about how a plant needs leadership and team unity the same way a ball club does. I'm not too sure they picked the right guy to talk about that.

Cleveland, Sunday, May 25

John Odom is threatening to jump the ball club. I don't like to get involved in a ballplayer's contract hassle, but I told John that if he does jump, he would be creating a situation that I would have to act on. He would be suspended without pay and fined.

"If you want a raise," I said, "it doesn't make much sense to lose money in fines. If you stay and perform well, maybe you'll get a big raise for next season. But as long as you're here, I expect you to do what you're supposed to do like everybody else."

He's going to Anaheim with us, but when he gets to Oakland on Thursday he's talking about leaving the ball club to drive home with his wife. He lives in Macon, Georgia, not far from Atlanta, and he would prefer to pitch for the Braves if Phil can arrange a deal. I hope he can. I want pitchers who want to pitch, not bitch. Dennis Eckersley wants to pitch. He shut out the A's on three hits, 6–0, in his first start before we lost to Dick Bosman, 6–3, in the second game. The kid now has pitched 20-plus innings without giving up an earned run. After six innings today he told me, "I'm pooped but I don't want to come out, I want to give you a little bit more." He pitched the last three innings on heart. And he never talked about demanding an $8,000 raise.

During the second game, Phil phoned me in the dugout to say that Lee MacPhail had announced that my suspension would begin tomorrow. I later saw a copy of MacPhail's statement. One part annoyed me. "Neudecker admits," MacPhail acknowledged, "that it is possible that he may have bumped Robinson in the course of the argument but that if he did, it was accidental and unintentional." For an umpire, it's always accidental. For a manager or a player, it's never accidental.

Anaheim, Monday, May 26

Since becoming a manager, I've wondered at times if my players were behind me. I've thought they were but I didn't know. I know now. On the plane coming out, Dave LaRoche told me that the players wanted to sit out my three-day suspension in a sympathy strike, protesting Lee MacPhail's decision as too harsh. Dave showed me a petition that all the players had signed.

"We the undersigned, in unanimous accord," it read, "hereby announce our disapproval of Mr. MacPhail's decision concerning the suspension of Manager Frank Robinson. We believe it was an unjust and unfair decision and, to show our disapproval, have agreed to sit out the suspension with him."

I was flattered that they were behind me that strongly but I suggested to Dave that the players reconsider.

"If you want people to know how you feel, tell the writers," I said. "If you want to support me, win the three games."

I also mentioned that a players' strike would force Mac-Phail to come down hard on the ball club itself as well as each player. The last time a major-league team had threatened to strike was in 1947 when the St. Louis Cardinals didn't want to play *against* Jackie Robinson; this time the Cleveland Indians didn't want to play *without* Frank Robinson—now that's progress. In the Cardinals' situation, Ford Frick, the National League president, warned of immediate suspension. I knew Lee MacPhail would react the same way.

"It wouldn't be worth it," I said. "And another thing— don't give the Angels three games. Win them instead."

And we won the first, 9–3, as Fritz Peterson went nine

innings and Charlie Spikes hit his first home run. As a player, I was allowed to work out before the game, but then I had to take off my uniform. Dave Garcia was the acting manager. I couldn't stay in the dugout or even in the clubhouse. I watched the game with Joe Tait and Herb Score in their WWWE radio booth. But even in a winning game, it was very frustrating. I couldn't talk to any players. I couldn't give any signs. About all I could do was bite my nails. And even though we won, Barbara had a headache. Driving back to our Bel Air home, about an hour up the freeway from Anaheim, she looked all worn out.

"I just used to have to worry about you," she said, "but now I've got to worry about the whole team."

How well I know. I've slept pretty well as a manager, but tonight I tossed and turned until about 5 o'clock. I kept thinking about our injuries. Rico Carty is out now with a pulled hamstring. Johnny Ellis is out with a pulled hamstring. Boog Powell is out with a bad back. Jack Brohamer is out with a bad hip. I'm out too. I just don't know what our lineup will look like.

Anaheim, Tuesday, May 27

Boog played despite his bad back and we won again, 6–3, with three runs in the eighth on four walks and Johnny Ellis's two-run single as a pinch hitter despite his pulled hamstring. Gaylord struggled with his control all the way in an eight-hitter.

Before the game, Phil told me that the Angels had complained to the league office that I had placed four calls to the bench from the radio booth during last night's game. Harry Dalton, the Angels' general manager, who's an old friend of mine from when he was the Orioles' general manager, claimed that the Angels' switchboard operator had handled the calls. I don't know where Harry got his information, maybe Dick Williams put him up to it, but I didn't place any calls to the dugout.

I did receive two calls. Our trainer, Jim Warfield, phoned to tell me that Rico had suffered a pulled hamstring. Jim called back to tell me it appeared to be a bad pull. That's all.

It would be foolish for me to risk extending my suspension or to risk forfeiting a victory by defying Lee MacPhail's orders, especially with Harry Dalton in the next booth, separated only by a glass panel. He could see anything I did. It also would be an insult to Dave Garcia's judgment as acting manager. But when Phil told me that Lee MacPhail had asked me to sit in another booth without a phone tonight, I agreed, though I thought it was silly. When we won, I wondered what excuse the Angels would come up with now.

Anaheim, Wednesday, May 28

We swept the three-game series from the Angels, 9–2—beautiful, beautiful. Eric Raich got his first victory by outpitching Nolan Ryan for all his relatives and friends. I'm told he had 68 names on the pass list. He grew up out here in Compton and he went to USC where he was on two College World Series championship teams. We're now 18–23, only 1½ games out of third place. Maybe my suspension was a blessing in disguise. Maybe it got this ball club together. If we can keep winning, we can move up quickly. I think this ball club has turned the corner.

"All we needed," I was kidded, "was a good manager like Dave Garcia."

But instead of taking even a little credit for the three-game winning streak, Dave seemed embarrassed. Even though he was the acting manager, he didn't use the office in the visitors' clubhouse. He dressed at his regular locker with the other coaches. That's the way he is. And when I got home in Bel Air after tonight's game, Barbara and the kids gave me my Father's Day presents two weeks ahead of time—two leisure suits, one white and one blue, and two colorful sports shirts. I'll fall asleep quickly tonight.

Oakland, Thursday, May 29

Off-day, but I celebrated the end of my suspension by taking Charlie Spikes, Oscar Gamble, Johnny Ellis, Rick Manning, and Alan Ashby out to the Oakland Coliseum for extra hitting. I even threw some bp. Manning is really something special. He's only hitting .211 now but he's a natural hitter. I've told the coaches to let him hit, not to fill his head with too much advice. I don't want him listening to different theories and getting confused. I just want him to go out and play. And hit.

Oakland, Friday, May 30

It looked like we might make it four in a row, but the A's won, 6–2, as Dick Bosman beat us for the second time since the trade. We had a 1–0 lead in the sixth with Jim Kern going strong even though he had been flirting with disaster. But he walked Billy Williams for the second time, then he walked Gene Tenace for the third time, to set up a four-run inning. He twice threw Tenace a curveball on 3 and 2 with nobody on. That's when a mature pitcher with confidence in his stuff will reach back and challenge a hitter with his fastball, especially if he's got a fastball like Jim Kern's.

John Odom has decided to stay with us. I used him in the eighth, just in time for him to throw Claudell Washington a home-run ball.

Oakland, Saturday, May 31

Dennis Eckersley again did all you could ask for. He stopped the A's, 4–1, on six hits. But his earned-run average is up to 0.28 because of the first earned run off him after 28⅔ innings. It might be a record for a rookie at the start of his career. But nobody knows for sure, because the record for earned runs isn't in the book. George Hendrick made it easy for the kid by hitting two homers. Tom McCraw also hit one. I put Frank Robinson in the lineup as the dh. Luckily he got three walks, because if Ken Holtzman had got the ball over the plate, he couldn't have swung too well. The manager's shoulder is bothering him again. He had another cortisone shot in Anaheim but apparently it didn't hit the spot.

Gaylord is acting up again. He wore white shoes in the

outfield during batting practice. White shoes like the A's wear.

I'm told that Charley Finley was with Phil in the Edgewater Hyatt House coffee shop after last night's game when Gaylord and Jim Perry sat down at another table. Charley sent Gaylord a pair of the white shoes that the A's wear. I was surprised that Gaylord would wear them, because they're Puma shoes, with the wing. Our ball club has a deal with Adidas, the one with three stripes. Adidas provides each player with three pairs, and extra pairs if anybody needs them. But then I'm not really surprised at whatever Gaylord does.

After today's game, I went over to visit my mother at her house on 73rd Avenue, only a few minutes from the ball park. My brothers Ellyon, Sylvester, Jesse, and Johnny and my sister Roberta were there, along with their wives and husband and kids. I had sixteen names on the pass list today.

Oakland, Sunday, June 1

We lost to the A's, 6–3, one of our worst games. Gaylord was wild. If he wanted to impress Charley Finley, he didn't succeed. Buddy Bell and Ed Crosby each made two errors. On one, Buddy outsmarted himself. Bert Campaneris was on first when Sal Bando popped up near the mound. Buddy tried to "exchange the runner," which was good thinking. The idea was to let the ball drop and force Campaneris at second while Bando, a slow runner, took first. But the ball hit the side of the mound, squirted away from Buddy, and both runners were safe. When you're going bad, you're going bad. And on our way off the field after the game, Tom Buskey had beer poured over him by a fan. I filed a complaint with the Oakland police and they got the guy. But the thing that annoyed me most was umpire Bill Haller's reaction to me disputing a call at the plate. Rick Manning slid headfirst and his hands were across the plate before Gene Tenace tagged him on the lower back.

"How could he possibly be out?" I argued.

Haller kept saying, "No, no, no," then he turned away to ask for some new balls.

"You want me to get in your face?" I said.

"Look," he said, turning back, "I respect you as much as any manager, as much as I respect Alvin Dark."

"What does that have to do with what I'm arguing about?"

Instead of answering, he turned away again. I'm becoming more convinced that the umpires are uptight about me and my situation as the first black manager.

Cleveland, Monday, June 2

Back home with an off-day and everybody talking about Nolan Ryan's fourth no-hitter. I was on the Angels with Nolan the previous two seasons, but before that we were always in opposite leagues. He was with the Mets while I was with the Orioles, then he went to the Angels in 1972 when I went to the Dodgers. As strange as it seems, I've only hit against him once—in an exhibition game when he was with the Mets before he found his control. I've never been afraid of hitting against any pitcher, it's just that Noland threw so hard and he was so wild then, I was as far back in the batter's box as I've ever been. He still knocked me down. By accident.

"Hey, just throw the ball over the plate," I yelled. "Over there."

I took three strikes that day and I was very happy, thank you. Nolan is always compared to Sandy Koufax now, but he's different. Any time that Koufax got in trouble, you knew the fastball was coming, not that you could always hit it. But when Nolan's in trouble, he sometimes tries to trick the hitter. For the last out in his no-hitter yesterday, he threw Bobby Grich a change-up for a called third strike. It worked because in that situation there's no way you should be looking for a curveball or a change. But it doesn't always work. A fastball pitcher gets himself in trouble sometimes by trying to trick a hitter instead of firing that fastball.

Cleveland, Tuesday, June 3

Another bad loss, 5–2, to the Royals, who have now won ten of their last eleven games. That's the kind of streak we need.

Instead, we've lost four of our last five. Fritz was sailing along with a 2–1 lead until his downfall in the sixth. And we couldn't do much with Dennis Leonard, a young righthander we hadn't seen before. And afterward, Bob Sudyk asked me a good question—if I'm experiencing the most difficult time of my career in baseball. I had to agree.

"I used to suffer through rough times as a player," I said, "but now it's twice as bad."

Or maybe 25 times as bad. To complicate my rotation, Eric Raich has the flu and can't start tomorrow, Don Hood isn't throwing well, and John Odom still wants to go somewhere else. Charley Finley is talking about taking him back with the A's, but I'm going to start him tomorrow. Maybe he'll give us four or five good innings.

Cleveland, Wednesday, June 4 .

Most of the players were outside for batting practice, but John Odom was sitting in front of his locker with a gloomy look on his face.

"What's wrong now?" I asked.

"What if I do well tonight?" he said. "Is that going to mess up my chances of getting away from here to another ball club?"

I couldn't believe what I was hearing.

"I've told you," I said, "your contract hassle with Phil is your business. But as long as you're a member of this ball club, I'll use you as I see fit and I expect you to go out there and give me 100 percent. If you go out there and win tonight, it's not going to hurt your chances of getting away from here."

"All right then," he said.

Maybe he knew something. He went out and put on the Blue Moon Odom Show with a two-hit shutout for a 4–0 win. He kept the ball down. He wasn't wild like he usually is. His velocity was good. It was a good win for us. It also was a good win for him in trying to go elsewhere because he showed he can still pitch. But when he came off the mound after the final out, he still had that gloomy look. The other ballplayers didn't know whether to congratulate him or not. Neither did I.

Cleveland, Thursday, June 5

Barbara finally arrived with the kids to spend the summer here, and when she looked at my batting average, she shook her head.

"I can't ever remember you hitting .220," she said.

"I've got more important things on my mind," I said.

Against the Royals tonight, we were down 7–3 after they jumped on Jim Kern, but we rallied to win, 8–7, on Buddy Bell's homer in the eleventh inning. Rick Manning singled to start our three-run eighth and tripled to drive in the tying run in the ninth. I got a single in the eighth. I'm up to .230.

Cleveland, Friday, June 6

Phil told me that Charley Finley doesn't want John Odom now but that the Braves had claimed him. Phil naturally wants more than the $20,000 waiver price. He asked me if I'd take Roric Harrison for him even up. Gladly. Back when I was with the Orioles, one of their best prospects was Roric Harrison, a big righthander with a live arm. He was traded to the Braves, where he was 11–8 two years ago, 6–11 last year before knee surgery. But then Phil suggested that I give Odom another start in Sunday's doubleheader with the Rangers, especially after his two-hit shutout.

"Maybe it will change his attitude," Phil said.

"I don't believe in telling him he's going to start just to make him happy," I said. "I was thinking about starting him. But only because he pitched well Wednesday night. Not to make him happy."

"Maybe if you called him in," Phil said, "we could both talk to him."

In my office downstairs, Phil told John that Finley had backed out of the deal. John glared at him.

"You're a liar," John snapped.

"Don't call me a liar," Phil snapped. "If you don't believe me, I'll get Charley on the phone. Ask him."

"I will," John said.

When the call went through, Finley apparently told John what he had told Phil, that the deal had fallen through. The way I understand it, Finley wanted John back but Alvin Dark didn't. When he got off the phone, John was more bitter than ever. Phil tried to tell him that if he pitched well, it would show up in his contract next year, but John didn't seem to be listening. He had his head down.

"Tell me something, John," I interrupted. "Will you pitch here and can you pitch here? Can you be happy here?"

"The only way I can be happy here is if I get my money and if I start," he said. "I'm a starting pitcher, like I showed you in that shutout."

"When was the last time you started?"

"Back in 1973 and 1972," he replied.

"I was in the other league in 1972, but I was in this league in 1973 and I never hit against you as a starting pitcher. Anytime we played the A's that year, the starters were Hunter, Blue, and Holtzman, sometimes Hamilton."

"I'm a starting pitcher. I have to start to be happy."

"You can't force any manager to start you if he thinks that's not the right thing to do. If you stay here, you'll be used as I see fit. Flat out—will you pitch here, can you pitch here?"

"No," he said.

"In that case," I said, "I want to tell you now in front of Phil so he'll know—if he can't make a deal to benefit this ball club, I recommend that you be suspended without pay. I don't want you here with that attitude. I've seen ballplayers with that attitude tear a ball club apart. But this ball club isn't in business to give you away. We're not going to release you because you don't like it here. We have to get something in return to help this ball club, somebody who wants to pitch here."

He stood up and started to leave.

"And another thing," I said. "As long as you're drawing a salary with this ball club, you'll continue to do what you're supposed to do."

"I'm not suspended?" he asked.

"I didn't say you were—yet."

After he left, I told Phil that I didn't want to use him at all now, either as a starter or in relief. Maybe that meeting steamed me up, because I hit two three-run homers off Ferguson Jenkins tonight and we beat the Rangers, 7–5. We have a new second baseman, Duane Kuiper, called up from Oklahoma City because Jack Brohamer had to go on the disabled list with his bad hip. Kuiper is the kid who didn't want to go to Oklahoma City and left his telephone number with the 312 area code on Trudy's desk. But he reported, like Phil predicted he would. And if Kuiper hits the way we think he can, he just might stay. I know that John Odom won't stay. His waivers expire Monday and by then, or before, he will be off this ball club, one way or another.

Gaylord Perry also might be off the ball club soon. Ted Bonda and Phil talked to me today about trading Gaylord before the June 15 trade deadline. We agreed that now is the time to trade him, if the right deal develops.

Cleveland, Saturday, June 7

We lost to the Rangers, 5–4, in twelve innings and Gaylord gave up 15 hits. Before the game, Harvey told me that John Odom had come to him.

"He says he's ready to pitch," Harvey said. "Ready to do anything to help this ball club."

"It's too late, the deal for Harrison has been made. And why go to you? Why not go to me?"

Phil had informed me that the deal with the Braves would be announced at 5 o'clock. I'm sure that Roric Harrison will fit into our organization better than John Odom did. But it was nice to know that John always wanted to play for a black manager.

Cleveland, Sunday, June 8

Another unhappy ballplayer. Before the doubleheader with the Rangers today, Johnny Ellis complained to me about having been fined $100 for missing a hit-and-run sign, fined $50 for not being on the field on time for batting practice, fined

$50 for signing up for early batting practice and not showing up for it. He also felt that the coaching staff has no confidence in him.

"I think I'd be better off," he said, "in another organization."

"If you feel that way," I said, "you have my permission to talk to Phil and see if he can trade you before the deadline. I don't want any players here who don't want to be here."

"I'll talk to Phil," he said.

John let his bat talk in the doubleheader. His two-run double was the big hit in the first game, which Eric Raich won, 3–2, and he hit a two-run homer in the ninth inning of the second game to put it in extra innings. We had some good relief pitching from Fred Beene (activated today when Ken Berry was released), Don Hood, and Tom Buskey, but we lost, 7–6, in the seventeenth on a single that caromed off Buskey's foot. We were only two hits away from sweeping the four-game series. Phil thinks I might have gotten those two hits if I had been in the lineup. But with my bad shoulder I feel I'm not able to swing the bat as well as I would like. I might be wrong, but I think Frank Robinson the manager is looking at Frank Robinson the dh objectively. But even without me, I believe this ball club is coming to life. If we can get some consistent pitching from Gaylord and Fritz, we can go someplace. With or without our unhappy players.

But the umpires continue to bug me, like Russ Goetz did in the first game.

Even though Jack Brohamer is on the disabled list, he's allowed to sit in our dugout with the other team's permission. When just about everybody got on Goetz for a call at first base that cost us a double play, Jack was among the loudest. Instead of saying something like, "You're in on a pass, Brohamer, quiet down," Goetz walked over to our dugout and chased him. I stepped up to continue the discussion, with my hands in the pocket of my red warm-up jacket. My suspension taught me to keep my hands in my pockets. But then Russ Goetz got to laughing, which didn't surprise me because he's always laughing. And that got me laughing.

"Kiss me," he said.

I puckered up and went "Mmmmm," but looking back on it now, I think we're all cracking up.

Cleveland, Monday, June 9

I made a mental mistake tonight, an inexcusable mistake, my most embarrassing moment as a manager.

We lost to the Twins, 11–10, in eleven innings after they scored four in the ninth to tie. But if I had been alert, I would have noticed that Danny Thompson and Dan Ford had been batting out of turn their first four times up. The way I understand it now, the Twins' manager, Frank Quilici, scribbled his batting order on a scrap of paper for field announcer Bob Keefer—with Thompson batting seventh and Ford eighth. That batting order was posted on the scoreboard. But when Quilici made out his official lineup card, he had Ford seventh and Thompson eighth. I never checked that official lineup card. But neither did Thompson or Ford, because they batted in the order on the scoreboard.

In a situation like this, it's not the plate umpire's responsibility to call it. The opposing manager has to charge the team with batting out of order. The thing to do is wait until the hitters involved do something, then protest. I imagine the plate umpire, Lou DiMuro, assumed I was waiting for that to happen. It did happen in the sixth when Ford tripled. But when I didn't protest before the first pitch to the next batter, I lost my opportunity to have Ford called out for hitting out of turn. The next batter, Steve Braun, grounded out, scoring Ford with what turned out to be an important run.

During the Twins' four-run rally in the ninth, Quilici realized the mix-up. He told them to hit in the proper order, Ford ahead of Thompson, and when Ford came up, Johnny Ellis complained to DiMuro, thinking they now were batting out of order. But it was too late for me to protest because now they were batting in the proper order. Thinking back, I must have had a mental blank during this game. I never looked at the Twins' official batting order when George Hendrick brought the card back from the pregame meeting with the umpires at home plate. I wasn't giving signs to Dave Garcia as quickly as I usually do. I even gave Dave the squeeze sign once when I didn't mean to. I just wasn't in the ball game, mostly because of a mysterious stranger who appeared in the Indians' office during the afternoon. Trudy Hargis phoned me immediately.

"This young guy was just in here, blond, greasy hair," she said. "He insisted he talk to you. I told him you weren't here, but he said it was very important that he talk to you, that if anybody else found out, it would be disastrous to you. Then he said he'd be waiting for you in the parking lot when you get here."

I didn't know what to think except the worst, because "disastrous" is a frightening word. Maybe this guy is a nut. And yet I couldn't tell Barbara to stay home with the kids tonight without making her suspicious. Kevin also had asked to drive down early with me, which was unusual because he's not a big baseball fan. I didn't want to disappoint him—or disappoint me for that matter, because I'm hoping he'll get more interested in baseball this year. When we arrived outside the ball park, I looked around for the blond guy but I didn't see anybody resembling Trudy's description. Two stadium policemen had been alerted. They escorted Kevin and me across the parking lot to the office entrance.

The blond guy never showed, but I kept wondering if he would. I was thinking more about him than about the Twins' batting order. As much as I was disappointed in us blowing a four-run lead in the ninth, I was more disappointed in myself.

Cleveland, Tuesday, June 10

We lost to the Twins again, 5–3, in twelve innings. Of our last five games, we've won one and lost four—all four losses in extra innings. If we had won those four, we'd be 1 game over .500 at 27–26 instead of 7 games under. As if that isn't frustrating enough, Jim Perry pitched a one-hitter for the A's against the Orioles tonight, not that I'm second-guessing myself on trading him. When you trade a ballplayer, you know he's not going to disappear, you know he'll do *something* for his new team. So he won a ball game. I still don't think he'll win many. And more and more, it looks like we'll make a deal for Gaylord before Sunday's trade deadline. Both the Royals and the Rangers are after him and we go to Kansas City tomorrow, then Texas for the weekend. While we're gone, Barbara has the silver Mercedes all to herself for the first time.

"Don't drive it," I told her.

"Try and stop me," she said.

"I'll check the mileage."

"By the time you get back," she said, "the mileage will be doubled."

Kansas City, Wednesday, June 11

Even before the Royals beat Gaylord tonight, 7–1, they weren't offering enough for him. They're talking about Paul Splitorff, Bruce Dal Canton, Al Cowens, and Vada Pinson and we want better than that. Once upon a time Vada Pinson would've been enough. Not many people realize that he's got more than 2,700 hits. But he's thirty-seven now. We were roommates on the Reds for seven years. We're still good friends. After the game he drove me back to the Sheraton Royal and tomorrow he's going to take me shopping for clothes.

As friendly as we are, I didn't tell Vada the Royals are offering him to us. That wouldn't be right.

I had another scene with an umpire. I got run by Ron Luciano, my second ejection. It started when George Hendrick got called out on a checked swing on an appeal from plate umpire Richard Garcia to Luciano, the first-base umpire. I didn't think George swung, but I'm not allowed to protest a ball or strike, so I was willing to forget it. But then I noticed Luciano jawing with Tom McCraw and I ran out. Luciano was telling Tom that a coach can't argue, that the next time McCraw said anything, he'd be gone. That made me hot.

"You mean to tell me," I said, "that a coach can't argue with an umpire?"

"That's right, I'll listen to you as the manager but a coach can't argue."

"My coach better argue with you," I said, "or he won't be coaching for me."

"We can't be fair with you," Luciano said. "You won't let us be fair with you."

"What are you talking about?" I said. "What do you mean, you can't be fair?"

He wouldn't explain what he meant. Instead, he started talking about how I'd been out there long enough. I reminded him that if he hadn't been arguing with my coach, I wouldn't have been out there at all.

"You're just wrong," I yelled.

For that, he threw me out. Walking back to the dugout, I turned to Bill Haller, the third-base umpire.

"Can coaches argue?" I asked.

"Yeah, coaches can argue," he agreed.

"Tell him that," I said.

Kansas City, Thursday, June 12

In the meeting at home plate, Ron Luciano said, "You knew what I meant last night. I meant that a coach can't argue on a checked swing, not that he can't argue, period." I told him he expected me to read his mind but that umpires never try to read the mind of a manager or a ballplayer to give him the benefit of the doubt, they just run him. Then we lost our fifth straight, 2–1, in ten, another extra-inning failure. It was a real heartbreaker for Eric Raich because the winning run scored on Johnny Ellis's passed ball. In the clubhouse later I told the players, "The way we're going, go get drunk tonight if you want to." And then I realized that Raich was still out in the dugout by himself. I went out to get him.

"Come on in," I told him. "You did everything you could. You can't ask more of yourself than that."

We're going to be depending on that big kid more than ever now. Phil phoned and asked my approval to trade Gaylord to the Rangers for three pitchers—righthanders Jim Bibby and Jackie Brown, and minor-league lefthander Rick Waits, who our scouts rate as having major-league ability now. We also got $150,000 in cash. I approved. The trade will be announced in Texas tomorrow after we arrive there.

Arlington, Friday, June 13

I never got to tell Gaylord good-bye. Phil asked me to have Gaylord call him and I told Phil's son, Mike, our traveling secretary, to give Gaylord the message. By the time we got to Arlington Stadium, the Rangers had held their press conference and Gaylord had changed clubhouses.

I'm sure most people will think Gaylord was traded because of a personality conflict with me, going back to that scene in the clubhouse late last season. But to me, there was no personality conflict. I think Gaylord feels the same way. The trade was made because Gaylord was not doing the job anymore, he isn't the pitcher he once was. In recent weeks, even before we traded his brother, Jim, I had the feeling that Gaylord wasn't really going all out, that he was just doing enough to be respectable but doing poorly enough to make us think about trading him. And all year long I haven't seen the tiger I used to hit against, the competitor. He wasn't throwing the ball with the same intensity. Or the same velocity. His record was 6–9 with a 3.55 earned-run average. He had given up 16 homers in 15 starts. Over his last 9 starts, he had a 2–7 record with a 4.22 earned-run average and 11 homers. He'll be thirty-seven in September, and at that age I don't think he's going to come around. He'll win some games for the Rangers but I don't think he'll ever be the Great Gaylord Perry again, the pitcher who was the Indians' franchise for three years.

Gaylord also was a bad influence on the young pitchers. Any pitcher of Gaylord's stature should be a big help to the young pitchers. But he wasn't. That was a pity because he could have taught them a lot. And it wasn't because I was the manager. I'm told he didn't help the young pitchers in previous years. Gaylord just took care of himself.

I was disappointed that Gaylord never tried to make my job easier. I'll always appreciate his gesture of tossing me the first ball on opening day. But he never asked if there was any-thing he could do to help me as a rookie manager. I never went to him either. But with a first-year manager, veteran players often will offer to help. Boog Powell and Dick Bosman did. Instead of helping, Gaylord seemed to go out of his way to make little comments, always negative comments. The first day of spring training, I had Gaylord, Jim, and Fritz in my office with the catchers to go over the signs they used last season. Afterward Gaylord told people, "That wasn't right, all the pitchers should've been in there." After some of my meet-ings, he said, "That's not going to help." And after his brother was traded, he kept saying, "I'm next." Not that I heard him, but his comments always got back to me, usually after the other players told the coaches.

The other players saw through Gaylord, especially the vet-erans. They didn't listen to him. They knew the way he is.

The only pitcher Gaylord had any effect on, other than his brother, was Jim Kern, the rookie righthander we sent back to Oklahoma City on ten-day recall to make room for our two new pitchers. I think Kern idolized him. It's too bad, because I think it's affected Kern's development. But for better or for worse, Gaylord's gone. Not that it made any difference tonight. We lost our sixth straight, 2–1, wasting another tremendous pitching performance, by Fritz Peterson this time. But at least we lost in nine innings.

Arlington, Saturday, June 14

With only 3 runs in 30 innings, I tried a gimmick to break the slump. I let the players pick the batting order out of a hat. I wrote the numbers 1 through 9 on scraps of paper and each of the starters picked one. Frank Duffy had only 2 hits in his last 35 at-bats, and when I held the hat out to him, I winced.

"Please don't draw number 4," I said.

He grinned, reached in, took out his slip, peeked at it, put it back, and drew another.

"Seven," he said.

"What was the first one?" I whispered.

"I'm not telling."

The batting order worked out pretty well except for Boog leading off. George Hendrick was next, followed by Rick Manning, Duane Kuiper, myself, Buddy Bell, Duffy, Charlie Spikes, and Johnny Ellis.

"I never batted cleanup before," Kuiper said. "Not even in Little League, and I was a star there."

Other managers have done similar things when their teams were in a slump. My second season on the Reds, we weren't hitting in midseason and Birdie Tebbetts threw the lineup card on the big table in the clubhouse.

"Fill it in yourselves," Birdie said.

I put myself down as the leadoff hitter that time. I had always wanted to be the leadoff man. But tonight nothing helped. We lost to the Rangers, 2–1, our third straight by that score, our seventh straight overall. Over our last 39 innings, we have scored only 4 runs.

I installed my first curfew tonight. The players had to be in their rooms two hours after the bus got back to the Sheraton Dallas, a long ride from the ball park. The bus didn't get back until about midnight, so it's more of a gimmick than a curfew. But maybe it will help.

Arlington, Sunday, June 15

We broke our losing streak, with Dennis Eckersley outpitching Gaylord Perry, 5–1, our future outpitching our past. Gaylord was throwing like he had for us. Not much velocity. He made a mistake on an 0-and-2 pitch in the first and Boog hit a two-run double. On our bench, there wasn't as much yelling at Gaylord as you might think. Brohamer got on him the most about his greaseball. Gaylord doesn't throw a spitball as such anymore. But he touches up the ball with K-Y jelly that he hides in various places—behind his neck, on his wrist, inside his glove, inside his belt, down the seam of his pants. It's a clear jelly and it sort of disappears. There's not much sense in me complaining to the umpires about it, because they either don't see it or don't want to see it. And we were winning anyway. Winning not only broke the losing streak. It also spared us the embarrassment of going home to read headlines like "Gaylord Beats Old Teammates."

The trading deadline passed. The Yankees, with three outfielders hurt, wanted Oscar Gamble or John Lowenstein for cash. No way. We also turned down the Angels' offer of catcher Ellie Rodriguez and lefthander Andy Hassler for John Ellis and John Lowenstein. But I would like to get Rodriguez to handle our young pitchers. John Ellis just can't seem to handle pitchers.

Cleveland, Monday, June 16

We're home all week against the Orioles and the Brewers and I was hoping we would get a winning streak going. But not tonight. In his first start for us, Jim Bibby didn't have good stuff and we lost, 8–3, to Jim Palmer, even though Palmer had to come out in the seventh because his arm was bothering him. But with his fastball, Bibby showed me that all he needs is control and consistency. The only pitcher who throws harder is Nolan Ryan.

Cleveland, Tuesday, June 17

I had another meeting to remind the players of their responsibilities. Not that it helped. We lost again, 5–3, our ninth loss in ten games, despite two homers by Boog and one by the manager. Mike Cuellar seemed to confuse our young hitters. Eric Raich wasn't able to keep his pitches down. With young pitchers, I know I've got to be tolerant of their inconsistencies. But talentwise, it's all there. When our new rotation gets rolling, we'll be rolling. But until then—patience.

Cleveland, Wednesday, June 18

Another loss, 13–6. Another disaster for Fritz Peterson, who was knocked out in the second. He's now 4–6. He's outstanding one game and horrible the next. I don't know what to do with him. I can't continually start him, figuring he's in for it after he pitches a good game, but I don't think he's the type who would be effective out of the bullpen. It was our tenth loss in eleven games and I guess I'm not as patient as I'd like to be. I lost my cool. What set me off was Ross Grimsley, leading 13–1, throwing me a 3-and-2 curveball with one on in the seventh. In that situation, a pitcher should be trying to make the batter hit the ball. I don't know Ross that well but I know him enough to kid him. The next inning, when Earl Weaver took him out after Boog's homer made it 13–6 in the eighth, I was the next hitter.

"No wonder you're 2 and 8," I yelled as Ross walked off, "throwing that garbage."

I was joking but Ross took it seriously. He yelled something back and then Dave Duncan got into it. Duncan's the catcher we traded to the Orioles for Boog and Don Hood just before spring training.

"At least," Duncan said, "he got your ass out."

"You got a lot of guts talking about somebody, the way you hit." I said it sharply because I dislike Dave Duncan totally. "For a nonhitter, you shouldn't be saying anything about hitting."

He was glaring through his mask.

"If you want a piece of me," I said, "let's go at it."

"Yeah," he said. "I guess I do."

He took his mask off and I tossed my bat away. But by that time, Rico Carty, who was out on deck, had moved between us and I was having second thoughts. I realized that if I punched Duncan, I might be suspended for having started the fight. I didn't want to be suspended again. But if I wasn't the manager, I'm sure I would've popped him. I just don't like Dave Duncan's attitude. Before the trade, I told the writers he would get the first shot at the catcher's job but that he would have to hit more than .200, which is exactly what he batted last season along with 16 homers and 46 runs batted in. He came back with the statement that I didn't realize his value as far as handling the pitchers was concerned, that he didn't think hitting was that important. He forgot that when he was with the A's, he wasn't known as a defensive catcher, he was known for his hitting. But when he came to the Indians and didn't hit, all of a sudden he's a handler of pitchers. But he's not that good to carry a .200 average. All he wants to do is hit his 15 home runs and drive in 40 runs. I remember when catchers used to be able to hit. Some still do—Johnny Bench, Thurman Munson, and Carlton Fisk, to name three. But most catchers cop out on their hitting now. They say they're too busy thinking, too busy handling pitchers.

I'll apologize to Ross Grimsley but I'm not apologizing to Dave Duncan—next time he says something to me, we'll probably go at it.

Cleveland, Thursday, June 19

Off-day, but when I dropped into Phil's office, he gave me his something-happened look.

"Have you heard?" he said.

"Heard what?" I wondered.

"Fritz cut the first two fingers of his pitching hand on the metal fender of his sit-down lawn mower. He needed three stitches in each finger. He'll have to be put on the 21-day disabled list."

For three weeks anyway, I don't have to think about how to use Fritz Peterson.

And tonight Pete Franklin, who has a sports talk show on WWWE, conducted a solemn burial of the Indians, complete with funeral music. We're in last place and we're 13 games under .500, but we're only 12 games out of first place. Pete Franklin just lost me as a listener.

Cleveland, Friday, June 20

On the editorial page of the *Plain Dealer* this morning, the lead editorial began, "The Indians have more than half a season left in which to prove they are a better team than the standings show today. Manager Frank Robinson has the same period of time in which to demonstrate improved judgment and maturity." It also mentioned that the manager

has not provided inspirational leadership. He has shown petulance. His run-ins with umpires and his recent hassle with some Baltimore Orioles may have been exciting but they did nothing to enhance his reputation as a model to be emulated. . . . Picking a lineup out of a hat, as Robinson did once, may be cute but it isn't practical. Neither is getting thrown out of ballgames. We hope the Tribe and its manager take a turn for the better.

But on the sports page, the headline over Chuck Heaton's column read, "Robby Satisfies Seghi" and down below Phil was quoted as saying, "From what I can see, he's doing everything he's supposed to. He's playing a sound game and has control of the ballclub. I'm well satisfied."

That's what is known as a vote of confidence, which makes me think I might be gone tomorrow. After a vote of confidence, a manager often is fired. Especially when his team has lost 11 out of 12, as mine has after a 6–0 shutout by Jim Slayton of the Brewers tonight.

But even in this slump, even getting knocked on the *Plain Dealer* editorial page, I feel secure. Not in my job, because I know I can be fired, but because I'm doing things the way I want to do them. If they don't turn out right, at least I managed the ball club my way. I'm not a worrier. I didn't worry as a ballplayer. I had more control over my destiny then. I only had to get *myself* out of a slump, not twenty-four other guys. But even as a manager, I'm not tearing my hair out. I'm not developing an ulcer. I'm not lying awake all night. The only ball games that bother me are when we play poorly. And walks, they bother me. And missed signs, they bother me.

Johnny Ellis missed the take sign twice tonight. In the fifth with one out and nobody on, we had him taking on Slayton's first pitch. He swung and topped a grounder to third. In the eighth, he was leading off and we had him taking on the first pitch again. He topped a grounder to second this time. Johnny Ellis, he bothers me too.

Cleveland, Saturday, June 21

We started Dennis Eckersley and we scored 9 runs and we won, right? Wrong. The Brewers scored 11 runs and now we've lost 12 out of 13, and we've dropped 15 games under the .500 mark and I've given up on finishing in first place, right? Wrong. Nobody has pulled away in our division. The Red Sox are only 2 games ahead of the Yankees, only 4½ ahead of the Brewers, only 7½ ahead of the Orioles, only 13 ahead of the last-place Indians, but we haven't had a hot streak yet. I'm serious. We're not this bad a ball club. We're due for a hot streak. I keep saying that but nobody seems to believe it except Barbara, and she better believe it.

Cleveland, Sunday, June 22

We won, 3–2, and not too proudly but we'll take it. With the bases loaded in the tenth, the Brewers' reliever, Ed Rodriguez, hit Rico Carty in the back, forcing in the winning run. We got good pitching from Jim Bibby and Tom Buskey and we're only 2 games behind the Tigers for fifth place. The way the Tigers are rebuilding, I never thought we'd be behind them at any time this season. But we are, mostly because each of our last three wins has occurred on Sunday, spaced a week apart. And now we're going to Boston and Milwaukee for a week, but I finally came up with a gimmick that worked. I switched my coaches—Tom McCraw went to third base, Dave Garcia to first. They'll stay there until we lose.

Boston, Monday, June 23

Shortly after we checked into the Sheraton Boston, my phone rang. Buddy Bell wanted to come up and talk to me. When he walked in, I knew from the look on his face that something was bothering him. He told me that he was unhappy with the way I've been playing him and with the way I've been handling him, that he wanted my permission to talk to Phil about being traded, that if he wasn't traded he probably would quit baseball.

"I can't play for you," he said.

"You can't play for *me*?" I said.

"Not the way things are going."

"Can you be more specific?"

"You ignore me," he said. "You don't pat me on the back when I'm going good, you don't chew me out when I'm going bad. It's like I'm not even here. I'm usually the only guy who gets pinch-hit for and if I'm not playing, you don't use me as a pinch hitter. I'm unhappy and when I'm unhappy, my family is unhappy. It's a bad situation."

"If you feel that way," I said, "there's not much I can say except that it might be best for you to talk to Phil and try to work something out."

When he left, I was really disturbed. Not because another ballplayer was complaining but because *Buddy Bell* was complaining. Buddy Bell—a class young man, the all-American boy, doesn't make waves, an even temperament, always does the best he can, the organizer of our Fellowship of Christian Athletes services on Sunday, our player rep since Dick Bosman was traded. *Buddy Bell* was complaining. I knew he was the type I had to talk to, that if I rested him, I had to explain why. The first time I did it, Frank Duffy came to see me.

"You better tell Buddy why he's not playing," Frank suggested. "He wants to be reassured."

I reassured Buddy that he was my third baseman. Later on I reassured him when I took him out again. But he's a regular, and I don't think I should have to talk to him every time I rest him. Our last two games over the weekend, I used John Lowenstein at third base because I wanted another lefthanded hitter in the lineup. To me, the reason was the stat sheet. Buddy Bell was batting .226, with 5 homers and only 19 runs batted in. If he was honest with himself, he should know why I took him out, he shouldn't need me or anybody else to tell him. But many of today's ballplayers aren't honest with themselves. My rookie year, I was 2 for 22 when we came back to Cincinnati after a road trip, and Birdie Tebbetts sat me down and talked to me. But he didn't have to. I knew I was 2 for 22, I knew it better than anybody. But nowdays you can't take anybody out without hurting his feelings. I think the front offices have contributed to this problem by rewarding players for mediocre performances. If a player has a big year, he wants a big raise—fine. But if he has a bad year, he refuses to take a cut, he threatens to retire, and the front office gives in. But taking a cut can give him an edge in salary negotiations the following year. I was making $115,000 with the Orioles in 1968 but I had a bad year—.268, 15 homers, 52 runs batted in, mostly because I had double vision for a month after a collision with Al Weis in trying to break up a double play. I agreed to a cut of $15,000, my raise from the year before. But after the 1969 season, when I hit .308 with 32 homers and 100 runs batted in and we won the pennant again, I could look the general manager in the eye. Harry Dalton upped me to $135,000.

The front offices also let too many ballplayers stay in the big leagues with batting averages of .230, .220, .210 year in and year out. I hate to go back to when I came up, but if you hit .230 for a month then, you were back in the minors. Maybe a .230 hitter stayed up if he had a great glove, as a shortstop or a second baseman. But a ball club carried only one .230 hitter then, if one. Now there are three or four or five on every ball club.

Buddy Bell is not usually among those .230 hitters. His lifetime average going into this season was .263, but I can't go by that. I have to go by what he's hitting now. Over the weekend when I took him out, he was hitting .226, which means he's not hitting the way he's supposed to. But apparently he can't accept that. He went to Phil, but Phil wasn't as disturbed by Buddy's complaint as I was. After their meeting, Phil sloughed it off. "He's young, he's a little confused now," Phil told me. "But he'll get over it." Probably before I do, because now I've got another problem. John Ellis came into my office at Fenway Park before tonight's game to complain about being fined a total of $300 for missing the take sign twice Friday night.

"You're just trying to stick it to me," John said. "To make an example of me."

Another case of a ballplayer not being honest with himself. Dave Garcia twice flashed him the take sign Friday night, but John never looked down to see if Dave was giving him a sign. When he came back to the dugout, I told him quietly, "You missed the take sign." He just looked at me. His next time up, he missed it again. The first time the fine was $100, the second time $200—that's not unreasonable for something that's unforgivable. I don't think I ever missed a sign. Most good ballplayers never miss a sign. It's just concentration. Certain signs fit certain situations. With a man on first or with men on first and second, nobody out, look for the bunt sign or the hit-and-run sign, occasionally the take sign. If the count is 3 and 0, 3 and 1, or 2 and 0, look for the take sign. And the sign isn't that mysterious. Dave Garcia held up the forefinger of his left hand—that was the sign that Johnny Ellis missed.

"But you've got to look at it from my viewpoint," John told me. "I'm up there concentrating on the pitcher."

"That's a selfish attitude," I said. "You're not thinking about the team, you're thinking about yourself. If you were thinking about the team, you'd look down for a sign like everybody else. You're just a selfish ballplayer, John, the fines stand."

"You never wanted me here," he said.

"If that was the case, you wouldn't be here," I said. "When we made the deal for Boog and Hood, the Orioles were willing to take either you or Dave Duncan, it was my choice. I chose you to be our full-time catcher, so don't say I didn't want you here."

"But you're always knocking my catching," he said.

We were both pretty hot by now. I reminded him that he had lied to me a few times when I asked him where certain pitches had been, that it was more important to tell me the truth as to where the pitches were than to protect the pitchers, that he was too buddy-buddy with the pitchers.

"You ask me about the pitches with the pitcher sitting right there," he said. "I can't show them up."

"If you feel that way, you'll never be a good catcher," I said. "I'm not second-guessing you. I'm the manager. I've got a right to know where a pitch was. If you think I'm hard, you should play for Earl Weaver, he wants to know everything. If you can't answer me truthfully because you're afraid of embarrassing a pitcher, you can't catch for me."

"You don't want me to catch anyway."

He didn't catch tonight because he's got a bad elbow, but

Buddy Bell played third base because the Red Sox started Jim Burton, a rookie lefthander. We played one of our best games, winning, 11–3. Frank Duffy knocked in five runs with a homer, two doubles, and a single. The manager knocked in three with a homer and a single, which surprised me because the situations with Buddy Bell and John Ellis had intruded on my concentration on the Red Sox pitchers. Eric Raich went seven strong innings and Dave LaRoche finished up. But even with the victory, I've decided to get tough with this ball club. As soon as we returned to the clubhouse, I called my coaches into my office for a quick meeting. I told them I'm putting in a curfew for the rest of the season—1 o'clock after day games, 2½ hours after the bus gets back to the hotel after night games. If the players are going to act like kids, we'll treat them like kids. With a curfew, I know what time they're supposed to be in their rooms. And they know.

Not that I'm looking to fine people. But without a curfew, if somebody strolled in at 4 in the morning, I couldn't fine him.

Usually my suite is on a different floor than the players' rooms are. But one time I was next door to Fritz's room. I didn't bother to change my room because we were only in that hotel for two nights. But when I finally fell asleep at 4, they were still going strong—Fritz, Ellis, and Fred Beene, they always ask for adjacent rooms.

I haven't had much feedback on guys staying up or staying out. But the Indians have been a loser for so long, the players don't really believe they can win when things start going bad. So they forget about everything else.

I still think my no-curfew theory can work with the right ballplayers, and I think I'll have the right ballplayers eventually. Having the right ballplayers is a big thing with me. I'm a great believer in attitude. I believe it's better to have a little less talented ballplayer with a good attitude than a little more talented ballplayer with a bad attitude. But because some of my ballplayers don't have a good attitude, from now on, no more babying of this ball club.

"From now on," I told the coaches, "things will be tough, tough, tough."

When the meeting ended, the writers naturally wanted to know what I had discussed with the coaches.

"Were you disappointed," one asked, "by something?"

"Just say I'm disillusioned, not disappointed."

Disillusioned is the word. I'm beginning to wonder if these ballplayers don't want to play for me because I'm black. I'm beginning to wonder if managing is worth it. The way things are going, if I was a quitter, I'd walk away from this job tonight—but I'm not a quitter.

Judgment Calls

Buddy Bell is leading the All-Star voting for American League third basemen, which surprised him as much as me. He had two hits tonight in our third straight win, 8–6, but in the ninth I took him out for a pinch hitter when Darrell Johnson, the Red Sox manager, did me a favor. We were behind, 6–4, with two on and Buddy coming up, but Darrell took out Roger Moret, a lefthander, and brought in Dick Drago, a right-hander. I sent Boog up to hit for Buddy and he doubled to left for one run, then George Hendrick hit a three-run homer, his second of the night. Tom Buskey got the win that tied us with the Tigers for fifth place and knocked the Red Sox out of first place. Jim Kern, back from Oklahoma City with Fritz out, had pitched seven good innings. But after the game, the writers mostly asked me about George's two homers.

"Why don't you ask him?" I said.

"He won't talk to us," one said.

"Have you tried to talk to him?"

"Not tonight we haven't, but he hasn't been talking to us."

"I'll bet you a drink he talks."

They left, but they were back right away. I owe them each a drink. I think George thought he was done wrong last year by some of the Cleveland writers. Rather than even talk to the Boston writers tonight with the Cleveland writers listening, he wouldn't talk to any of them. It's too bad, because it's important for every player's popularity and sometimes for his salary to tell the public about his game. The public is interested. But sooner or later, George will talk.

Some of the Red Sox aren't talking much either. They're bitching about the fans and the writers here—and they were in first place until tonight. I wonder what they would be saying if they had to go through what we've been through lately.

Boston, Wednesday, June 25

We swept the Red Sox series, 8–5, as Tom Buskey saved Roric Harrison's first win. The Duke looks like he's going to help us. We're getting seven or eight good innings out of our starters now, which has eased the burden on the bullpen. I was proud of the "little guys" as I call them—Frank Duffy got three hits, Duane Kuiper knocked in two runs, and Alan Ashby, our backup catcher, hit a two-run homer into the bullpen behind right field against the wind after the Red Sox had taken a 2–1 lead. It's amazing Alan hit the ball that far. He's also playing with a bad head cold, not that a bad head cold should stop anybody from playing baseball. But it stops some people. With four in a row, we're only 11 games out of first place.

I'm feeling better about this ball club now but my left shoulder is feeling worse than ever. I couldn't even take bp today.

Milwaukee, Thursday, June 26

Five in a row—9–2 over the Brewers with Dennis Eckersley pitching a five-hit shutout through eight innings before I brought in Jackie Brown at the start of the ninth. The kid had thrown 122 pitches and I didn't want him to throw any more. He forgets that he's only twenty years old and that he's not a big strong guy. His arm hasn't really matured physically. If he puts too much strain on it, he could hurt it. He doesn't understand that yet. All he wants to do is keep pitching. But he later told the writers something that bothers me.

"What's going to happen next winter at contract time," he said, "when the general manager says, 'Well, you didn't pitch many complete games.' I don't want to get screwed on my contract."

I'll take him aside and tell him the worst thing he can do is start negotiating his salary now. General managers don't want to read about a player talking about next year's contract when this season isn't half over. I'll also tell him that I'm concerned about him and his future, not about complete games. I'm sure Phil will consider this a complete game, like I do. But if this kid has any problems with Phil over salary, I'll go to bat for him.

Milwaukee, Friday, June 27

We won again, 6–1, for six straight, the Indians' longest winning streak in five years. This is the hot streak I knew we were due for. Jim Bibby made it look easy tonight, his first win for us. He burned his rising fastball by the Brewers—6 strikeouts and 12 pop-ups. The deal looks good. Gaylord has lost all three of his starts with the Rangers, giving up 19 runs in 16 innings. I'm sure he's still throwing the same stuff he did for us. That stuff is going to get hit.

Milwaukee, Saturday, June 28

To kill time before tonight's game, I saw *The French Connection II*, only the third movie I've gone to all season. The others were *Breakout* with Charles Bronson and *The Eiger Sanction* with Clint Eastwood. As a player, I sometimes used to see three in one day here or in Minneapolis or in Chicago, the three best movie towns in baseball. As a manager, I don't seem to have the time. But once a movie critic, always a movie critic. *The French Connection II* wasn't as good as the original. The plot wasn't as good. Our plot tonight also wasn't as good as it has been. Eric Raich had super stuff when he was warming up, but when the game started he had nothing. We lost to the Brewers, 10–6, breaking our winning streak. Eric didn't look physically sound. He was hesitating in his delivery as if he had a sore arm or a sore back. He was just flipping the ball up to the plate with nothing on it.

"Anything wrong?" I asked him.

"No," he said, "I'm all right."

I hope he isn't hiding an injury. But even with the loss, things are cool. Tomorrow my coaches switch back. Dave Garcia returns to third base, Tom McCraw to first base. And now, win or lose, they'll stay there.

Milwaukee, Sunday, June 29

We lost to the Brewers again, 4–3, which takes a little away from the road trip. We could have swept all seven games. But we're on the move now. Jim Kern's arm was bothering him, so I started Don Hood and it was 3–3 in the ninth when George Scott led off with a double. They bunted him to third, then I brought in Tom Buskey to walk Darrell Porter intentionally to set up a double play. But on the first pitch, Bobby Mitchell hit a fly to right to score Scott with the winning run. The writers wondered why I hadn't walked Mitchell to load the bases, with Pedro Garcia up next, but I wanted to give Buskey the opportunity to pitch carefully to Mitchell and hopefully get him out. If the bases are loaded, a walk or a hit batsman ends it. That doesn't give a pitcher much margin for error. That's the strategy Hank Bauer taught me. And it's good strategy. It just didn't work today.

Alan Ashby bruised his knee in a slide, so Johnny Ellis got to play for the first time since he hurt his elbow. Johnny told me yesterday that he was ready, but the way Ashby was hitting I wasn't about to take him out. But now Alan is hurt. It's weird how some problems solve themselves.

Cleveland, Monday, June 30

We swept a twi-nighter from the Tigers, 4–1 and 3–2, for eight wins in our last ten games. We're now within 2 games of the Orioles and 9½ games of first place. We're also 4½ games ahead of the Tigers, which is more like it. This is when managing is fun. Especially when you see new players developing. Roric Harrison pitched a seven-hitter and Eric Raich pitched a five-hitter, each a complete game. Eric was throwing very freely. Apparently he just had control trouble Saturday night, aiming the ball instead of firing it. Duane Kuiper got five hits in the doubleheader, Rick Manning got three in the second game, including a two-run single to left field off John Hiller in the eighth. John Hiller is maybe the best relief pitcher in the American League, a big lefthander. Afterward the writers wondered why I hadn't pinch-hit for Manning myself. But my shoulder won't let me swing the bat properly. Against an over-the-top fastball pitcher like Hiller, I figured Manning would have a better chance than I would.

Manning and Kuiper play this game the way it should be played—with enthusiasm and determination. Since they've come up, the ball club has new life in it. I find myself watching them almost like a fan.

We've added Bill Sudakis as a third catcher. He had been released by the Angels, where I knew him. He gives me two bats in one, a switch-hitter I can use as a pinch hitter. He also plays first, third, and the outfield. But to put him on the roster, we had to drop Tom McCraw as a player. He's still a coach, of course, but he can't return as a player until next season. I was sorry to drop Tom as a player, because he's still a good hitter. But it had to be.

Cleveland, Tuesday, July 1

We lost to the Tigers, 6–2, and I filed my first formal protest of a game to the American League office. With the score 2–2 in the seventh, Gene Michael led off with a single for the Tigers and Aurelio Rodriguez bunted down the first-base line. Johnny Ellis hurried out after the ball, but Rodriguez bumped him from behind, knocking Ellis off stride. Rodriguez beat the play at first base, leading to the winning run. I complained to plate umpire Jim Evans that Rodriguez had interfered with my catcher, but Evans contended that the runner had as much right to run to first base as the catcher had to field the ball, that it was a natural collision.

"It's like when a first baseman taking a throw is bumped by the runner," Evans said. "It's a natural collision."

To me, it was a natural protest. In the Official Baseball Rules, the definition of offensive interference is "an act by the team at bat which interferes with, obstructs, impedes, hinders or confuses any fielder attempting to make a play." But the umpire's judgment is more important than the rule. I won't win my protest.

Cleveland, Wednesday, July 2

We had a big win tonight, 3–2, over the Yankees and moved within 9 games of the Red Sox, who are back in first place. Dennis Eckersley didn't have his good stuff but it was good enough for six innings. With the bases loaded and two out in the seventh, Dave LaRoche struck out Alex Johnson to end that threat. Ever since Dave forgot about his forkball, he's struck out 41 in 36 innings with a 1.75 earned-run average and a 3–1 record. The winning run developed with two out in the eighth off Dick Tidrow when Duane Kuiper singled, went to third on Ed Crosby's single, and scored when Bobby Bonds's throw to third caromed off Duane's helmet down the leftfield line, too far for Tidrow to get the ball in time. That's how speed wins games.

Kuiper is up to .336 now and he can run. He can do more things than Jack Brohamer, who is still not 100 percent but keeps talking about how he wants to come off the disabled list. I've suggested to Phil that we don't take Jack off until after the All-Star break.

Cleveland, Thursday, July 3

This was a happy, happy night that I needed badly. We swept the Yankee series, 3–2, and moved within 8 games of first place. Boog Powell and Don Hood made our deal with the Orioles look good. Boog got the big hit, a two-run homer off Doc Medich in the sixth. His 12 homers are as many as he got all last season. Hood pitched outstanding except for two pitches to Bobby Bonds—a homer in the fourth, a homer in the ninth. After the second homer, Hood had thrown only 89 pitches but I brought in Dave LaRoche and he saved our tenth win in our last thirteen games.

The reason I needed a happy game was that Dr. Earl Brightman had told me I need an operation to correct my left shoulder.

"The tendon is torn in there," he said. "It won't get any better just resting it. Only an operation will fix it."

He used an arthrogram to discover that the tendon is torn. X-rays were taken, then Novocaine was injected into the shoulder to deaden it. I can take needles as long as I don't watch them go in. Once one of the spike wounds on my arm was being patched up, and I happened to glance at the needle going in and I fainted just like that. I haven't looked since. After the Novocaine took effect, another needle was used to inject a bluish dye in the shoulder joint. Then they put me under a special X-ray machine that showed where the dye was. Instead of staying in the joint, the dye spread into the tissue. That meant the tendon was torn.

"I don't know how you keep playing with that injury," Dr. Brightman said. "The pain must be terrible."

But pain is different for everybody. Some people can play with it, some can't. I knew the shoulder was bad even before I went to spring training. It's been bothering me for a few years. I knew this would be my last season, but I didn't want to tell anybody that the shoulder was the reason. I didn't want the other teams to know. I also knew I didn't want to go on living with the pain and the needles, as well as not being able to swing the bat properly. But at least now I'm relieved to know why the cortisone shots I've had weren't doing that much good. If the pain gets too bad, I'll have to make the decision of putting myself on the disabled list. I won't consider having the operation until after the season because I'll need three to five months to recuperate.

I won't mind the operation as much as I have the needles.

Cleveland, Friday, July 4

Another sweet 3–2 win, our third in a row by that score, in the opener of a big series with the Red Sox, and now we're only 7 games out of first place. Eric Raich didn't have his real good stuff and during the early innings he was complaining in the dugout about not being able to get much velocity on his fastball.

"Stay with it," Harvey Haddix told him. "Sometimes your fastball will come around."

"Or you might find," I mentioned, "that another pitch will be your best pitch."

His fastball came around and he pitched a gutty game. He stranded two runners at third base with less than two out. But when he looked tired in the eighth I brought in Tom Buskey, and in the ninth I brought in Dave LaRoche for the last two outs. LaRoche has now saved each of our last three wins. The big blow was Oscar Gamble's two-run homer off Luis Tiant in the seventh, his second homer in as many nights. We only got four hits. We haven't been getting that many hits lately. But they've been timely hits. They have to be timely to win three consecutive 3–2 games. As sweet as the win was, some of the older players had a scare in the sixth when Don Zimmer, the Red Sox third-base coach, ended up on the bottom of a scuffle between Buddy Bell and Bernie Carbo after a hard tag. Not many of the younger players realize that Don has a steel plate in his head from a beanball accident more than twenty years ago when he was a shortstop in the Dodgers' farm system. At the time he was unconscious for several weeks. When the scuffle started tonight, Don instinctively jumped between Bell and Carbo, but suddenly he went down unconscious in the middle of the players who had rushed out from both dugouts. He must have been struck in the head by a wild swing. Seeing him on the ground, Boog pushed everybody aside and got Don out of danger. Don was out on his feet. But apparently he's all right now.

Boog is nice to have around when a little muscle is required. The world is lucky he's an easygoing guy. But he's always there when he's needed.

I remember once when we were with the Orioles, we were coming out of Anaheim Stadium and somebody in the crowd near our bus was on me pretty hard. The guy even walked over near me to continue yelling. I stopped to see just how tough the guy wanted to get, but before anything happened, Boog was alongside me.

"Any trouble here?" Boog wondered.

"No," the guy said. "No trouble."

The guy walked away very quietly. Boog has that effect on people, just like Buddy's fight with Carbo had an effect on the big crowd tonight. Buddy has been booed recently because the Cleveland fans don't think he should be leading the All-Star balloting for third baseman. But his next time up after the fight, he got a big ovation. We had 36,124 for the holiday night game. Give the people in this town a winner and they'll come out.

Cleveland, Saturday, July 5

We beat the Red Sox again, 12–2, our fourth straight. Roric Harrison pitched an eight-hitter and Buddy Bell drove in six runs with two homers, one a grand slam, and a double. No-body's booing him now. We're only 6 games out of first place, but a bad scene with Jack Brohamer took some of the fun out of the win. The way Duane Kuiper is playing second base, I wanted to keep Jack on the disabled list until after the All-Star break. That meant he wouldn't go on our trip to California that begins in Oakland on Monday night. I had told him I didn't know he would be out since May 25 and I didn't know Kuiper would perform so well. But with his hip healed, Jack felt he deserved to be put back on the active roster immediately.

"I've got to play," he told me the other day. "If you don't want to play me, trade me. I'm sure the Yankees would take me. I'm only twenty-five, the next five years is when I'm going to make my big money."

I don't blame Jack for wanting big money. Back in April he told me, "I've got to play more to avoid a salary cut." Back in April is too early to be worrying about next year's salary. And before today's game Jack cornered Phil and demanded to be put on the active roster immediately. If he wasn't, he planned to file a grievance with Marvin Miller, the executive director of the Major League Baseball Players Association—the quickest way to antagonize a general manager. After their conversation, Phil came into my office, then he called Jack in.

"All right," Phil said, "you're going on the trip."

"But am I on the active list," Jack asked, "or the disabled list?"

"The disabled list," Phil said.

"Then I'm not going," Jack said.

"You're drawing a salary, you'll go if we tell you to go, damn it," Phil said. "You'll go."

"The hell I will," Jack snapped.

"Get the hell out of here," Phil told him. "Get the hell out of this office."

By now Ted Bonda had joined us.

"If we put Jack on the active list," Ted asked me after Jack had left, "who's the most likely player to go on the disabled list?"

"I am," I said.

"Nobody else?"

"I wouldn't want anybody else to go off, because nobody else is hurt. My shoulder's not right. It has to be me."

"All right," Phil said, "we'll activate him Monday night."

They called Jack back into my office and Phil told him that he would be activated for Monday night's game in Oakland.

"No," said Jack, "if I'm not activated now, I don't want to be activated Monday night. You've stalled me long enough."

"Get the hell out of here," Phil stormed again.

Jack left again, then Phil told Ted about the threatened grievance.

"Put him on," Ted said. "Frank comes off."

It wasn't the right thing to do, because the Red Sox started Steve Barr, a lefthander, today and they've named Bill Lee, another lefthander, as one of their starters in tomorrow's doubleheader. Even with my bad shoulder, I thought I might be able to do more against those lefthanders than Jack could with his lefthanded bat. But he had forced us to put him on the active roster. I understand his thinking. I just wish he had understood mine.

Cleveland, Sunday, July 6

Another great day. We lost to Bill Lee, 5–3, in the opener but we came back to win the second game, 11–10, and I mean came back. We were down 5–0 in the second inning, but this team showed me it has heart. George Hendrick, Boog Powell, and Oscar Gamble hit homers, then Dave LaRoche saved Fred Beene's first victory. With 7 out of 9 on our home stand, we've now won 13 of our last 17 and we're still only 6 games out of first place. We're in the race now as much as anybody.

Pete Franklin, the radio guy who buried us on WWWE last month, is around the clubhouse again, but the players and I mostly ignore him.

If we can win 2 out of 3 in Oakland and sweep 3 in Anaheim this week, we can be only 3 or 4 games out at the All-Star break. This town would really be jumping. We had 58,781 in the ball park on Bat Day, the biggest crowd in the major leagues this season. It's great to see that many people out. I wish we could take all those people to Oakland and Anaheim with us. But not umpire Armando Rodriguez. On a close play at first base in the opener, he called George Hendrick safe, then he changed his mind and called him out. But not decisively. It looked to me like George had beaten the throw by a stride. Arguing with Armando is difficult. He was born in Cuba and lives in Mexico and he doesn't speak enough English to express himself properly. Even more frustrating, he doesn't understand enough English to really know what you're saying. I finally gave up and turned to go back to the dugout.

"Sorry about that," Armando said.

Whatever the hell he means by that.

Oakland, Monday, July 7

My problems with the umpires really got ridiculous tonight. We lost to the A's, 7–3, but I was gone in the third inning. From the start the plate umpire, Larry Barnett, wasn't giving Dennis Eckersley the low pitch. The kid is a sinkerball pitcher. He's got to get those pitches for strikes. I thought the kid had Billy Williams struck out on a sinker in the second, but Barnett called it a ball. The next pitch, Billy hit a two-run homer. I hollered about that, not screaming like Earl Weaver does, but yelling pretty good. Between innings, I went out very calmly after Jim Perry had thrown some greaseballs. All the years I hit against Jim Perry, he had nothing that sinks. He was always a fastball-slider pitcher. But tonight his ball was sinking. I had to suspect something, especially since he had one of the best teachers in the world in Gaylord—and also the way he's been pitching. He knows he needs an extra pitch to win.

"He's mixing a few in," I said.

"No," said Barnett, "you've got the wrong Perry."

"He needs it to win now," I said.

"All right, I'll try to watch him."

In the third, Eckersley threw a two-strike pitch to Reggie Jackson across the middle of the plate above Reggie's knees.

Johnny Ellis didn't even have to move his glove. I couldn't believe Barnett called it a ball.

"Hey," I yelled, "poke a hole in your mask."

He spun around and shouted, "You're out of the game." I couldn't believe that either. I ran out to find out why.

"You don't tell me that," he said.

"You got to be kidding," I said. "Everybody yells that."

"Nobody yells it at *me*," he said.

Maybe not, but I've heard managers and ballplayers yell it for years. All it means is, poke a hole in your mask so you can see the ball better. Until tonight, I've never seen an umpire run a manager or a ballplayer for saying it. I think he ran me because he was tired of listening to my hollering. But to me that's not a sufficient reason. Of my three ejections, this and the one with Ron Luciano in Kansas City were undeserving. The umpires are too uptight about me and my situation.

"Barnett," I told the writers later, "would not run any other manager for saying that."

It's harassment. I always get short answers from umpires. Anytime that I dispute something, they snap, "Because I said so," or "Because I wanted to," or "Because that's the way it's going to be." Even when I'm discussing something, they say, "All right, let's go, you've been out here long enough." They're keeping me from doing my job. And they're not doing their job. Tomorrow I'm going to call Dick Butler, the supervisor of umpires, and make a formal complaint.

Oakland, Tuesday, July 8

Dick Butler wasn't in the league office but Lee MacPhail was. He agreed that I shouldn't have been ejected for yelling, "Poke a hole in your mask." He also agreed that some umpires are quick on the trigger.

"I'll get back to you," he said, "after I see their game report."

I also phoned Phil to tell him that I was tired of keeping quiet, that it was time to give the umpires a blast. I didn't have to wait long for the opportunity. Before going to the ball park

I was in the coffee shop at the Edgewater Hyatt House when Russ Schneider sat down.

"When you said last night that Barnett would not run any other manager for saying what you did," Russ asked, "did you mean what it sounded like you meant?"

"What did it sound like I meant?"

"That it's because you're black."

I told him, "That's right," and then I explained all the resentment and frustration that had been building up inside me. And it's still there. Not long after tonight's game started, I strolled out calmly to tell Hank Morgenweck, the plate umpire, "If you guys have anything against me, don't take it out on my ballplayers, that's all I ask." He flared up, trying to convince me the umpires aren't against me. But when I turned to go back to the dugout, Marty Springstead had come halfway down the line from first base.

"Get back in the dugout," he yelled.

"I wasn't talking to you," I snapped.

"You're always crying and complaining," he said. "I don't want to talk to you."

"I hope I don't have to talk to you."

Springstead told the writers later that as the crew chief, he was trying to protect his umpires. But the umpires didn't cost us tonight's game. The A's clobbered us, 15–5. Don Hood started and he didn't pitch poorly, but he didn't pitch well either. He had a 2–0 lead in the first but then the A's came back with four runs, including three on Gene Tenace's homer, a fly ball that Charlie Spikes jumped for and accidentally slapped over the fence with his glove. Three days ago Charlie would have caught that ball.

Oakland, Wednesday, July 9

When we're in California, my phone always starts ringing early because of the three-hour time difference from the Eastern cities. But today it rang early and often. Several writers called to ask about my quotes in Russ Schneider's story in the *Plain Dealer* which the wire services picked up. Phil called to tell me he would back me up all the way. He also told me that the league office, as expected, had disallowed my protest of last week's game with the Tigers over the catcher's interference ruling. It seems like everything that's happening involves umpires. And at the Oakland Coliseum, it continued. I was in my office with the writers when Russ Schneider began wondering how many American League umpires I rated as creditable.

"I'd have to see a list of all of them," I said.

"Here they are," he said, handing me a scorecard.

I rated ten as creditable, meaning not bad—Nestor Chylak, Larry Barnett despite his ejection of me Monday night, Marty Springstead despite yesterday's scene, Bill Deegan, Don Denkinger, Jim Evans, Richard Garcia, Bill Kunkel, Jim McKean, and Dave Phillips.

That left thirteen others I don't consider creditable, plus Terry Cooney, who hasn't handled enough of our games for me to rate.

To me, Nestor Chylak is the league's best umpire. He works at his job. He's always watching what's going on. His calls are the most consistent, both behind the plate and on the bases. He's not involved in many arguments—that's usually the sign of a good umpire. And when he is in an argument, he keeps his cool.

Barnett could be very good if he concentrated more on his job. Denkinger could be excellent.

Springstead has a strange strike zone. It's smaller both top and bottom, but at least he's consistent with it. His problem is that he's always got a chip on his shoulder. His temper gets the best of him.

Deegan could be very good if he stopped thinking that he knows it all just because he's been around a few years.

Evans should get better when he realizes that his temper is too quick, that he should listen more, that maybe he's not always in the proper position to make a call. I wish Evans had Garcia's conscientious attitude. When we were in Boston two weeks ago, I was walking away from the pregame meeting at home plate when Garcia told me, "I had a bad night on low pitches last night." His honesty was refreshing.

"Admitting that," I told him, "will make you a better umpire." Not many of them admit it.

Kunkel is another who could be even better, but he has to show his authority every once in awhile.

McKean should be better once he gets his feet on the ground. He seems a little scared now. He's also in with a bad crew, meaning Jerry Neudecker and Art Frantz.

Phillips will be better when he learns to take the initiative more instead of deferring to the older umpires.

As for the others, Ron Luciano is the biggest disappointment to me. He once was one of the better umpires, but he got carried away with his clowning, his acting, and all his publicity. But even before that, he sometimes got personal, which an umpire shouldn't do. In my years with the Orioles he once told me, "You're overpaid, you're not a real superstar."

I told him, "If you were black and you did what you do, they'd call you a clown instead of colorful." In recent years, he's not bearing down, he's not concentrating. He should be a good umpire, but he's not.

Bill Haller would be all right if he didn't let his temper get the best of him. Jerry Neudecker is just bad, so is Joe Brinkman, Lou DiMuro, Russ Goetz, George Maloney, Hank Morgenweck, Merl Anthony, Art Frantz, Nick Bremigan, and Larry McCoy.

The last umpire I want to see at home plate is Larry McCoy, because his strike zone changes from pitch to pitch. He's in and out, up and down. In the minor leagues he wore his chest protector inside his coat. Now he's wearing it outside like most American League umpires do, which means he's working over the top of the catcher. Not quite 6 feet, he's too short to work from there. But the thing I can't understand is that the league office permits three umpires to wear their chest protectors inside their jackets and all the rest to wear them outside. The league office's explanation is that Denkinger, Evans, and Phillips are more comfortable wearing them inside, that they are better umpires that way. What the league office apparently doesn't realize is that the strike zone with those three umpires is lower because they're judging pitches from inside the catcher's left shoulder instead of above his right shoulder. Because of the American League custom of permitting its umpires to wear their chest protectors outside, the American League strike zone has always been higher than the National League strike zone. But now, with three umpires using the National League style, the American League is asking approximately 180 batters and 120 pitchers to adjust to three umpires. It should be the other way around. Make the three umpires conform to wearing their chest protectors outside like the other twenty-one umpires do. I've asked umpires if they didn't agree that the strike zones of those three umpires had to be lower. They naturally insisted that the strike zone is the same. No way it can be the same. If an umpire is working at a lower angle, his strike zone has to be lower.

But the umpire problem involves much more than the strike zone. Just as expansion lowered the standard of ballplayers, it also lowered the standard of umpires.

Before expansion there were fewer major-league umpires. There also were more minor-league umpires who were qualified to be in the major leagues. As a result the major-league umpires had more pressure on them. If they didn't do a good job, they were in trouble. But now that job pressure doesn't exist. They know they're here as long as they don't do anything embarrassing off the field to jeopardize their job. In their security, they're more short-tempered in arguments. They hear everything and react to it. Umpires used to let you have your say and then walk away, and you knew that was it. But now they come at you. Their security also has made them lazy. The next time you're at a major-league game, watch the umpires between pitches. When the pitcher gets the ball back from the catcher, most of the time none of the base umpires are watching him. The umpire at first base will be looking in the stands, the umpire at second will be smoothing the dirt, the umpire at third will be talking to the coach. The pitcher could be doing something to the ball that maybe only one of the base umpires could see, but they're seldom watching. Two weeks ago Jim McKean was on first base. For three straight pitches, he was fooling with something on his finger. He looked up just as the pitch was thrown, then he looked down at his finger again. And sunflower seeds—most of the umpires are always popping sunflower seeds.

By the nature of their job, umpires are dictators. If nobody is allowed to challenge their decisions, they soon begin to think that everything they call has to be correct, just because they have called it. Especially when they are not subject to any pressure from the league office.

Until this season, I never had many serious problems with umpires. But now I'm arguing for twenty-four other players. Popping off like I did isn't going to make me too popular with the league office or with the umpires. It will probably get me fined again. Even so, I felt I had to do it to protect my ball club. But sometimes I wonder if the other ballplayers appreciate me putting myself on the spot for them. I thought they would be fired up today. They were completely flat. Our dugout was the quietest I've ever seen in twenty years in the major leagues. No chatter at all. They just sat there, too tired even to talk to each other. I don't know why. Maybe it was the delayed reaction of the time change from the flight out here or having to play a day game after a night game or just that they don't give a damn. But when your dugout is that quiet, you're going to lose. And we did, 3–1, to Dick Bosman on four plays that should have been made but weren't.

With one out in the first, Eric Raich walked Billy North, who likes to run. And with Claudell Washington up, Bill Sudakis called for a pitchout on the first pitch, but North didn't go. Sudakis looked over to me and I nodded, meaning call for another pitchout. He did, North went, but Sudakis dropped the ball. Washington then beat out a roller to deep short, then Reggie Jackson knocked in North with a single up the middle. Joe Rudi lifted a high foul near the A's dugout but Buddy Bell lost it in the sun. Rudi then hit a short fly ball behind second base that either Frank Duffy, Duane Kuiper, or George Hendrick should have caught. But none of them really went after it. Duffy told me later that he had it lined up but lost it in the sun, then neither Kuiper nor Hendrick moved in quick enough. It fell for a double as Washington scored.

In the fifth, with Phil Garner on second, Oscar Gamble tried to make a shoestring catch on North, and when he didn't make the catch he threw to second instead of to home. Garner had stopped at third, but when he saw Oscar's throw going to second he scored. It was George Hendrick's responsibility to tell Oscar to throw home.

Four plays that should have been made and weren't. We've reverted back to the way we were playing before our hot streak. What makes it worse is that the Red Sox have won 3 games while we lost 3 here. We're only 9 games out of first place but we're only ½ game ahead of the last-place Tigers—that's how tight the AL East is. But with 3 weekend games in Anaheim, maybe we can get it down to 7 games by the All-Star break.

The ball club went down to Anaheim tonight but I stayed in Oakland for my mother's eightieth birthday party. She admits to eighty anyway.

Her birthday isn't really until July 21, but they had the party tonight so I could attend. My brothers Ellyon, Jesse, Johnny, and Sylvester were there along with Sylvester's wife, Verdis, and their three boys. After the roast beef, fried chicken, macaroni and cheese, and jelly roll, Verdis was talking to Johnny.

"Isn't your birthday soon?" she asked.

"Yeah," he said, "my birthday's the ninth."

"What do you think today is?" she said.

"Hey, yeah," he said. "Today's the ninth."

I need a few laughs like that to help me forget about the umpires and about three straight losses.

Anaheim, Thursday, July 10

Off-day in the Grand Hotel across the street from Disneyland and an unprecedented day in All-Star Game history. Buddy Bell announced his withdrawal from the American League team because he didn't think he deserved to be on it.

Through the years I've known players who withdrew from the All-Star Game for selfish reasons. They wanted to go fishing or play golf during the three-day break. But this is the first time I can remember a player having an unselfish reason. Buddy finished third in the fans' vote at third base behind

Graig Nettles of the Yankees and Sal Bando of the A's, but Alvin Dark of the A's, the All-Star manager, wanted to select Buddy over Bando as the backup third baseman. Alvin and Lee MacPhail, the American League president, phoned Buddy to try to change his mind. But he kept telling them he didn't deserve to be on the team. He told me the same thing when he asked my thoughts before the final voting was announced.

"I've talked to my dad a few times," he said, referring to Gus Bell, my old teammate, "and he thinks I should accept."

"I feel the same way your father does," I said. "It's an honor to represent the league, something that comes once a year."

"But the way I'm playing, I don't deserve to be an All-Star," he said. "Nettles deserves it ahead of me, so does Dave Chalk."

I couldn't argue with him there. He's hitting .235 with 8 homers and 31 runs batted in, not exactly All-Star statistics. And he has been erratic defensively.

"But sometime in your career," I said, "you may be having a year when you feel you deserve it but won't get it."

"That's not the point," he said. "Other third basemen deserve it more than I do this year. It's not right for me to go."

"I have to respect you for that," I said. "I think that's great. Too many people don't think about other people, they just think about themselves, but I still wish that you'd accept."

"I can't," he said. "I just can't."

And he didn't. Alvin Dark chose Dave Chalk of the Angels as his backup third baseman and George Hendrick as a reserve outfielder. George will be the Indians' only player on the American League squad. I'm glad George made it. He's been our best player. He deserves to go. And deserving it was Buddy's argument. I just hope that the next time I take Buddy out for a pinch hitter, he will realize that he didn't deserve to be up there.

But my biggest surprise today was that Lee MacPhail phoned Buddy Bell instead of me.

Anaheim, Friday, July 11

We bounced back tonight, rallying to win, 5–3, after another communications gap helped the Angels take a 3–2 lead in the sixth. We were leading, 2–0, when Jerry Remy bunted himself on, stole second, and went to third on Johnny Ellis's bad throw. Dave Collins chopped a grounder on one hop between the mound and first base. Roric Harrison fielded the ball, turned, and looked toward home plate. He had no play on Remy, who can really run, but he had a play at first— except that nobody was covering. Boog got caught in no-man's-land coming in for the chopper and Duane Kuiper hadn't gotten over in time. Collins then stole second and went to third when Ellis threw wild again. Collins scored on Joe Lahoud's double and Lahoud later scored. If Johnny Ellis had yelled to Harrison to throw to first base immediately, either Boog or Duane would have had time to get there.

"Nobody said a word," I told the players in the clubhouse. "We're just not communicating. Like the ball in Oakland that dropped behind second base. Nobody yelled until it was too late. And tonight nobody yelled on that chopper. Yell so that the other guy knows what's going on. Communicate."

But tonight at least it evened out. In the seventh Duffy doubled and Lowenstein doubled to tie the score. Rick Manning then hit a long line drive to left-center that Mickey Rivers, the centerfielder, and Collins collided on. No communication. When they leveled each other, Rick got an inside-the-park-homer, his first major-league homer.

"I hit a slider," the kid told the writers with a laugh. "I knew it was gone the moment I saw the ball lying at the base of the fence."

Anaheim, Saturday, July 12

We beat the Angels tonight, 9–1, with Oscar hitting a three-run homer off Nolan Ryan in Dennis Eckersley's sixth win. The kid was terrific again. I would have preferred to start him tomorrow because he had a tough game Monday night in Oakland, but the league office wouldn't let me. I had been notified about ten days ago that the kid was under consideration for the All-Star team and to plan my rotation so he wouldn't start the Sunday before the All-Star game. But when the kid wasn't selected, Phil phoned the league office to see if I could pitch him tomorrow.

"They said no," Phil told me. "They said it wouldn't be fair to the Angels because they had to schedule Ryan the same way."

To me, that was the Angels' problem, not mine. Ryan was selected for the All-Star team, Eckersley wasn't. I think Eckersley then should have been excused from the league's policy not to start an All-Star pitcher the Sunday before the game. I think it's wrong for the league office to dictate that policy. The league office is putting the All-Star game ahead of the pennant race, an exhibition game ahead of a regular-season game. To me, the All-Star game is strictly a showcase of the best players. Even though the American League has lost ten of the last eleven games, that doesn't prove the American League is weaker. I believe the National League is stronger because their teams are stronger, not because they win the All-Star game almost every year. I've played in the All-Star game for both leagues and it never bothered me if I was on a losing team, just like I didn't take it too seriously if I was on a winning team. With either league, I wanted to win. But if my team lost, no big deal.

As a manager, I resent the league office telling me when or when not to use a pitcher.

With the All-Star break, if I had a workhorse pitcher, I could start him tomorrow, give him three days' rest, then start him Thursday in our next game. That way I'd be getting maximum use out of him, getting an extra start out of him that might make the difference in winning the division title. But the league office wouldn't let me. That's wrong.

Anaheim, Sunday, July 13

We swept the Angel series, 8–7, on Dave LaRoche's seventh save, but Rick Manning really deserved the save. He made two diving catches in left field that prevented at least two runs in the sixth, at least one run in the seventh. Going into the All-Star break, we're still 9½ games behind the Red Sox, who look like they're going to be tough to catch. But we're only a game out of second place. After losing 3 straight in Oakland, the sweep was sweet. The Indians have now won 13 straight games in Anaheim Stadium, tying the American League record for consecutive victories in another team's ball park. But since the first 7 were against the Angels when I was with them the last two years, the record doesn't mean much to me.

But the big kick for me was winning all 6 games here this season. I don't have anything against Anaheim or the people or the players, but I enjoy beating Dick Williams's team. He thinks he's the great tactician. He thinks he can do no wrong. He thinks he's it. And in his heart, he knows he still owes me $500.

Cleveland, Monday, July 14

No game, no workout, no office, no nothing. After our charter got us home about 5 in the morning, I slept most of the day, then I read the columns by Hal Lebovitz in the *Plain Dealer* and Bob August in the *Press* that concerned my pop-off on the umpires. The columns appeared last week but Barbara had saved them for me.

"I wish it were possible," Hal wrote, "for all managers who gripe as much as Robby to be ordered by the league president to put on an umpire's suit for two weeks. . . . I have been on both sides, in the umpire's uniform and on the coach's bench. I have discovered that when a manager or coach begins to officiate, he can't concentrate on his own job."

But he's talking about when he was an umpire and a coach on the sandlots, a big difference from the major leagues.

"This business about racial discrimination is ridiculous," Hal also wrote. "My black friends laugh at this charge."

My black friends don't laugh at it. They know it exists. And they know that if it's not changed, it will continue.

"I wish," Bob August wrote, "he would shut up and give a rest to his grievances against the umpires, but I am not going to issue a plea that he change roles and emerge as a serene, more accommodating human."

But if I did shut up when bad calls went against my ball

club, Hal Lebovitz and Bob August would be the first to criticize that.

Niagara Falls, Tuesday, July 15

I drove Barbara and the kids up here to see Niagara Falls and do something with them for a change. Being a ballplayer is tough on your family, but being a manager is worse. And up here maybe the nicest part is the anonymity. It's nice to be recognized. I'm not knocking it. But it's also nice not to be recognized. Walking toward the Falls today, only two people recognized me, a middle-aged man and his wife. I noticed them peeking at me. Then they approached me.

"Aren't you Frank Robinson?" the man said.

I nodded and we chatted. Other than that, I was just another guy relaxing with his wife and kids. Relaxing and meditating, mostly on my problems with the umpires. Even while watching the All-Star game on TV tonight, I was thinking about the umpires. And the more I thought about it, the more I came to the conclusion that it's not doing me that much good to get on them. They're not going to change a call. Even when I'm convinced I'm correct, the more I get on them, the more they think I'm crying and complaining. In the long run, that hurts me and my team.

Niagara Falls, Wednesday, July 16

The ball club had a workout today, but being on the disabled list I was excused by the manager, who knew that I wanted to stay in Niagara Falls with my family. Except that it didn't turn out that way. Barbara and the kids were up early but I kept sleeping.

"Let's go," Barbara was saying, "let's go down for breakfast."

I turned over and she stalked out with the kids. They had breakfast, then they took a ride on "The Maid of the Mist" that goes under Niagara Falls, and when they returned Barbara was really stalking around.

"Let's go home," she said.

"But we're not leaving until tomorrow," I said.

"We're leaving now," she said.

We left. I drove three hours back to Cleveland in silence. Nobody was talking to the manager. I don't blame them. The manager hadn't managed his family too well on this road trip.

Cleveland, Thursday, July 17

Not long after I got to my office, John Stevens phoned, asking to see me. He's the American League's umpire consultant now but he once was a good umpire, an umpire you could talk to. He started in by saying, "What can we do to help you get along with the umpires, what can we do to make things better?" Right away I was encouraged. He was trying to come up with something constructive. I told him I didn't want any special treatment, I just wanted to be treated like the other managers. No quick ejections. No quick put-down answers.

"Some of the young umpires are impatient," John agreed.

"But it's not the young umpires I'm having trouble with."

Then he mentioned something that really disturbed me— that several umpires had complained that every time I walked away after an argument, I pointed to the skin on my arm and asked if that was the reason the call had gone against my team.

"I did that once, John, that's all," I said.

It happened in Kansas City after the argument with Ron Luciano over the checked swing. Luciano had said, "We're trying to be fair with you but you won't let us." Walking off after I had been ejected, I asked Bill Haller if coaches could argue, as Tom McCraw had done. And that, I told John Stevens, was when I pointed to my skin.

"That's the only time," I said, "and I was wrong for doing it even once."

I didn't ask him the names of the umpires who had accused me of that. It's better that I don't know. But overall, I had a good meeting with John Stevens, a meeting that I hope will cool things between the umpires and me. I'm ready to cool things. I hope they are.

Then we lost to the A's, 6–3, our 9th loss in 11 games with them. We seem to save our worst for them.

We got two early runs but Eric Raich gave up homers to Reggie Jackson and Sal Bando that got the A's going. I didn't mind Bando's homer. It was on a good pitch, a fastball low and away. Bando still hit it out. Not much you can do about that. But the homer by Reggie was off a fastball on an 0-and-2 count. No pitcher should give up hits on an 0-and-2 count, especially to a hitter of Jackson's caliber, a good hitter and a power hitter. In that situation, I know how I think. Any hitter of Reggie Jackson's caliber is an even better hitter with two strikes on him.

Cleveland, Friday, July 18

We lost to the A's again, 7–6, and at least we're finished with them for the season. I'm also finished with Johnny Ellis as my regular catcher. The problem with Ellis has been building, building, building, and tonight it finally exploded. He was batting .217 when I sent up Bill Sudakis to pinch-hit for him in the eighth. He stormed back to the dugout and started throwing his catcher's equipment around. His mask almost hit me.

"John, are you mad at me?"

"Yeah," he snarled, "I guess I am."

"Well, are you?"

"Yes," he said.

"You're lucky you're even here with the average you've got."

"Yeah," he snapped, "and you're lucky you're here yourself."

"I'll be here a lot longer than you will."

I ordered him into the clubhouse, then I sent our batboy, Mike Moulder, in to tell him not to leave. After the game I closed the clubhouse and told the players, "If there's anybody here who thinks he can't play for me, if there's anybody here who thinks he's bigger than the team, just stand up or come into my office and we'll arrange to get you out of here." Nobody stood up. Nobody came into my office. After a few minutes, I sent for Johnny Ellis and when he arrived, he was all apologies.

"I know I was wrong," he said. "It won't happen again."

That's the way Johnny Ellis is, that's his sob story. He comes on like a little kid.

"I'll apologize," he said. "To the whole team."

"That won't be necessary," I assured him.

"You should've known I was upset," he said. "You shouldn't have said anything to me."

"*I* shouldn't have said anything to you?"

"Yeah, you knew I was upset," he said.

"John, evidently the way you are, the way you react, the way you think people are second-guessing you, maybe you can't play for me."

"I guess that's right."

"Well, since you feel you can't play for me," I said, "I don't want you to play for me. From here on out, as long as you're here, you will not be my catcher. You'll still be on the team. But you will not be my regular catcher."

That stunned him. He left without a word.

He probably thinks I won't stick by what I said. He doesn't know me. I'm tired of his selfishness. I want my players to know they're here to play for the team, not for themselves. No individual is bigger than the team. If Johnny Ellis comes to me now and tells me he'll do anything to help the ball club, I'll use him as I see fit—as a catcher, a first baseman, a pinch hitter, whatever. But if he doesn't tell me that, he won't play for me at all. That's what I'm going to tell Phil tomorrow. I'm also going to tell Phil to try to move Johnny Ellis to another ball club, as quickly as possible. But that won't be easy. We're not going to give him away.

We've already moved Jim Kern back to Oklahoma City on option to make room for Fritz Peterson, who is off the disabled list. His fingers have healed. Jim Kern has a 1–2 record for us but he objected to returning to the minors.

"I don't want to go back there," he told me. "I'd rather go home and work out."

He lives in Midland, Michigan, which is about a two-hour drive up from Detroit.

"I can take my family home and come back here in September like I would anyway," Kern said. "I think I've proven I can pitch up here. I don't have to go back to the minors."

"How can you say you've proven yourself?" I said. "You've

won only one game in almost two years. If you'd proven yourself, you wouldn't be going back to Oklahoma City again."

But then he got down to the real reason why he didn't want to return to the minors again.

"My wife's never liked me playing baseball anyway," he said. "She doesn't want to go back."

I sympathized with that. The first year Barbara and I were married, she didn't like me traveling. She later got accustomed to it but she never got to like it. I didn't blame her. Marrying a ballplayer requires a big adjustment, especially when he's on the road.

"Maybe the best thing," I told him, "is to take your wife home to Michigan, leave her there, and go to Oklahoma City to pitch. It's only for a few weeks. Maybe she'll realize she needs you, that baseball isn't so bad after all. It might help your marriage."

Then he mentioned how he had to forfeit a deposit on his apartment in Cleveland, about $350.

"Talk to Phil about it," I said. "If he agrees to give you the deposit, will you go to Oklahoma City?"

He agreed that he would go. I found out later that he went upstairs, talked to Phil, got the money, came back down to the clubhouse, packed his gear, and left. I was disappointed that he didn't stop by to tell me that everything had been straightened out. The manager likes to know. More and more, I'm realizing that managing doesn't involve just baseball. Tonight I was a combination marriage counselor and real estate adjuster for Jim Kern. And a cop on the beat for Johnny Ellis.

The Warden
Blows His Stack

Cleveland, Saturday, July 19

I told Phil about the Johnny Ellis situation. He had seen the temper tantrum from upstairs and he promised to back me all the way. He also promised to make a few phone calls. Then we proceeded to lose a twi-night doubleheader to the Angels, 8–0 to Frank Tanana, who seems to be coming into his own, and 3–2 to Bill Singer, who was lucky. Losing to the Angels really annoys me because we're a better ball club. Between games, the Great Wallenda did his high-wire act. He had the wire set up across the infield from one side of the stadium roof to the other. Our public relations director, Randy Adamack, told me that the Great Wallenda wanted to drop a baseball when he got halfway across.

"You want one of the players to catch it?" Randy said.

"No way," I replied. "Not one of my players. Somebody might break a finger. Not one of my players."

Not even Johnny Ellis.

Cleveland, Sunday, July 20

At breakfast, Barbara suddenly said, "When did *this* happen?" and showed me the *Plain Dealer* sports section. Across the top was a big headline, " 'Won't play Ellis again'—Robby." I had already read Russ Schneider's story.

"Oh, that's nothing," I said.

"But why didn't you tell me?"

"You don't want to hear that."

I'm not the type to bring my work home. Especially the trouble. And by the time I got to the ball park, I had more trouble. Trudy told me that Susie Tedrick, the switchboard operator, had received a threatening phone call from a lady.

"The lady said," Trudy told me, "to tell Frank Robinson that he's going to be shot when he comes back from the road trip if Johnny Ellis isn't playing by then."

I knew I wasn't going to tell Barbara about that either, but I didn't take it seriously. I just can't believe that anybody would get so upset about a manager benching a player that he or she would shoot the manager. I worried more about my ball club winning, and it did, 10–4, knocking out Dick Lange in the third. Don Hood pitched well, then Tom Buskey saved him. Oscar hit a triple, double, and single. Buddy hit a three-run homer, Rico hit a two-run homer. Rick Manning hit his first over-the-fence homer. He's my centerfielder now, with George in right. Some centerfielders don't like to move to right or left, but George seemed to prefer it.

"That's my natural position," he told me.

When he came up with the A's, he played center because Reggie Jackson was in right. When he came here, he played center because Charlie Spikes was in right. Now he's in right, probably to stay.

We're still in last place but we're only 6 games in the loss column out of second place, only 4 games in the loss column out of third. And we're only 9 games under .500. We're not dead.

Cleveland, Monday, July 21

We won, 2–1, in eleven innings, the type of game that some people consider boring but to me it's baseball at its best. Especially when you win. Fritz Peterson started his first game since coming off the disabled list last Friday, and I was hoping for five good innings, maybe six. He gave me seven. Maybe he was helped by the 10 pounds he put on while he was on the disabled list.

"I'm 205," he told me, "but I feel good. I feel stronger than before."

"Let's see how you pitch at that weight," I said. "Then we'll decide."

I got on Boog, Johnny Ellis, and Charlie Spikes for being overweight last month. They didn't think I had noticed because I didn't say anything right away, but I noticed, just like I had noticed that Fritz was heavier. But off his performance tonight, Fritz looked faster than before he cut his fingers. He can stay at 205 until he shows it hurts him. Dave LaRoche got the win when Oscar Gamble homered in the eleventh off Ed Figueroa, the Angels' starter. Oscar even called his shot as he went up to hit.

"You won't need that bat," he yelled back to Buddy Bell, who was on deck. "I'm takin' this dude deep."

But then Oscar says something like that just about every time he goes up there to hit. His trouble is he's always trying to hit the ball as far as he can. He could hit for a good average if he worked at his skills. But when he's not in the lineup, he doesn't sit on the bench and sulk. He's always talking things up. And he's doing a good job as the Kangaroo Kourt judge.

Before the game Johnny Ellis told me he was willing to do anything to help the ball club. At least now I'll use him as I see fit, unless we make a deal. Phil put him on waivers to see what teams are interested.

We pulled into a tie with the Tigers for fifth place, but beginning tomorrow in Texas, we've got a long road trip that also takes us to Detroit, Baltimore, and New York for a total of 14 games. I'm hoping to be only 6 or 7 games out of first place when we return.

Arlington, Tuesday, July 22

On the plane down here to open our road trip, I read where Billy Martin is out as the Rangers' manager and Frank Lucchesi is in. It reminded me that in Anaheim last year, Billy called me over during batting practice for a private talk.

"I'm going to manage this ball club for another year," he said, meaning through the 1975 season, "then I'm going to move upstairs as the general manager and I'll hire you as manager."

He sounded sincere and I appreciated his confidence in me, but I didn't get all excited about it. Too many things can happen to plan that far ahead, as I discovered last year and as Billy has discovered now. With him gone, the Rangers won't be as tough to manage against. Billy was unpredictable. He might hit-and-run with men on first and second, he might try to steal third. I found myself yelling to my players to watch out for moves like those when Billy was the Rangers' manager, moves other managers seldom make. That's what made Billy a good manager in the dugout. But he's always had trouble getting along with the owners and other front-office people. That's why the Rangers fired him. It also was why the Tigers and the Twins fired him. No wonder Billy was talking about moving upstairs as general manager himself. But if he had, he probably would have had trouble dealing with his manager. That's the way Billy is. That's probably the way he always will be.

The *Plain Dealer* also had a column by Chuck Heaton suggesting sarcastically that if Forrest Gregg, the new coach of the Cleveland Browns, were to handle his team the way I've handled the Indians, he would be "seeking other employment" by midseason. I thought it was a cheap shot, especially since Chuck will be covering only the Browns from now on. Until now he had occasionally done columns and features on us.

We opened our road trip with Gaylord Perry stopping us cold, 4–0, a 2-hitter with 13 strikeouts. Give him credit. When he gets it together, Gaylord can still make a batting order look helpless. He mixed a few greaseballs but it didn't really matter. That's not what he was getting us out with. He just had good stuff. He's now pitched three shutouts in his last four starts. But we're not sorry we made the trade. Jim Bibby came out of the bullpen tonight to pitch three shutout innings. Jim looks like he's coming around.

Arlington, Wednesday, July 23

Duane Kuiper has a torn ligament in his left knee. He got it last night when Roy Howell, the Rangers' third baseman, slid hard into second base. Duane went down in pain, but when he got up he seemed all right. He wanted to run it off and stay in the game. I insisted he go to the clubhouse and have ice put on his knee.

"Knees are funny," I told him. "It might feel all right now but it might not be all right."

Sure enough, he woke up in the middle of the night in tremendous pain. He'll be out for at least two weeks, out for the season if he needs surgery. We'll miss him. He's hitting .294, playing a solid second base, and giving us speed on the base paths. To replace him, I'm coming off the disabled list. But not to play second base. Jack Brohamer played there in tonight's 9–8 loss. Jack walked and scored our first run after the Rangers had taken a 5–0 lead against Roric Harrison, who didn't help himself with two of our six errors. We were trailing, 7–2, going into the ninth but we scored five runs. We went ahead in the thirteenth on Rick Manning's baserunning. He had singled and when Rico Carty singled, Rick raced to third, hurrying Lenny Randle into a throw. When the throw was wild, Rick scored. The kid has great baseball instinct. Dave Garcia hadn't waved him to third, the kid just went. But in the bottom of the thirteenth the Rangers scored twice. What hurt was Charlie Spikes misplaying Tom Grieves's line drive. That let in the tying run and put the winning run at third. Grieves then scored on Mike Cubbage's sacrifice fly.

This ball club has me baffled. We're just not improving the way we should.

Arlington, Thursday, July 24

I had another rap session tonight. I told the players, "We played last night like we hadn't seen a baseball field in six months. We have to be more alert and more aggressive day in and day out, not just when we feel like it." Not that I'm blaming them for everything. I asked if I was putting too much pressure on them but they said no. I asked if my hassles with the umpires had put too much pressure on them but they said no. I also reminded them that despite my hassles with the umpires, I wasn't blaming the umpires for the way we were playing and I didn't want them blaming the umpires. The umpires didn't put us in last place. We put ourselves there.

"But the big thing is, we're not thinking," I said. "We're just not thinking."

They agreed. They always agree. But the same things keep happening. When tonight's game started, John Lowenstein led off with a homer off Steve Hargan, then singles by Rick Manning, Boog Powell, and George Hendrick produced a 2–0 lead. But then a thunder-and-lightning storm hit, and the game was washed out. Dennis Eckersley had warmed up, so I won't even be able to open with him in Detroit tomorrow night in the crucial series for last place. To look at the Tigers rebuilding with all their kids, then to look at our ball club with the ball-players we've got, to think that we're battling the Tigers for last place—it's very discouraging.

Detroit, Friday, July 25

We lost to the Tigers, 4–3, which dropped us into last place by 1 game. Don Hood had good stuff and he was leading, 1–0, in the sixth. My pitchers have been told not to give Willie Horton anything good to hit. If they walk him, fine. But don't give him a pitch he can pull. Hood did. Willie lined a single to left to drive in the tying run. Before the inning was over, the Tigers had all their runs. I probably would have used Tom Buskey in relief that inning, but he has a bad back, what Dr. Earl Brightman diagnosed as a growth on a vertebra. Buskey is the type who'll pitch in pain, but he hasn't been able to pitch in four days. His back must really be bothering him. To give him time to get well, we'll put him on the disabled list and call up Rick Waits, the minor-league lefthander we got from the Rangers in the Gaylord Perry trade.

We got some good news too. Duane Kuiper won't need surgery for his knee. But his left leg is in a hip-to-ankle cast. I'm beginning to think that Dr. Brightman manages this ball club as much as I do.

Detroit, Saturday, July 26

I didn't know how far Dennis Eckersley could go. He had to leave the ball park in the fifth inning last night with a virus. And before today's game, he told me, "I feel lousy but I'll give it a try." I wish all my pitchers gave it a try like this kid. He shut out the Tigers, 6–0, on 7 hits with 10 strikeouts and only 2 walks. He was challenging the hitters like he did earlier in the season. His record is 7–3 now with a 2.30 earned-run average. And this win was a big one. It ended a three-game losing streak. It also got us back into a virtual tie with the Tigers for fifth place. And it looks like the Tigers have lost

John Hiller for the next few weeks. He's got a bad back and a bad arm. Without him, their bullpen won't be the same.

I'm not thinking about first place anymore, not the way the Red Sox are playing. But second or third is still within reach if we want it bad enough. I know I want it bad enough.

Detroit, Sunday, July 27

We split a doubleheader with the Tigers, winning 7–2 with Jim Bibby saving Fritz, after an 8–7 loss that Dave LaRoche let get away. Dave's human.

The split kept us in a virtual tie with the Tigers for fifth place. But we're only 7 games behind the second-place Orioles and we open a three-game series in Baltimore tomorrow night. I thought we got some bad calls from the umpires in the opener. The crew for this series was Marty Springstead, Larry Barnett, Don Denkinger, and Hank Morgenweck—the same crew that was in Oakland when I popped off nearly three weeks ago. With runners on second and third in the ninth and two out, Springstead called Rico Carty out on strikes after Bob Reynolds had gone to 3 and 0 on him. The next pitch was around Rico's ankles. Strike one. Rico swung at the next pitch. It looked like a ball from the dugout, but maybe he was afraid to take it. The next pitch looked both low and outside. Rico took it. Strike three. Game's over. I wanted to yell but I kept my cool. Kept my mouth shut too. Maybe it'll help, maybe it won't. I'll never know unless I try it.

That reminds me. Lee McPhail told Phil to have both of us drop by the American League office Friday when we're in New York for a weekend series. He wants to talk to me about my blast in Oakland at the umpires. I've always wondered what color the carpet is in the league president's office. I'll not only find out what it looks like, I'll find out what it's like to be on it.

Baltimore, Monday, July 28

We moved to within 6 games of the Orioles with a 7–5 win in ten innings on Charlie Spikes's two-run single. Rick Waits got his first major-league victory in his first appearance for us, even though the manager didn't quite plan it that way. The manager goofed. Judging by the outcome, maybe I should goof more often.

Going into the ninth we were leading, 5–2, but the Orioles rallied for three runs. We thought we had turned a game-ending double play, but on a bang-bang play at first, Nestor Chylak called Tommy Davis safe as the tying run scored. Rico Carty argued the call and I hurried out of the dugout. But not to argue. I wanted to calm Rico down and keep him from getting ejected. But as I approached, Rico had already cooled off. That's when I noticed Jackie Brown standing near the first-base line with his head hanging, like he was really disgusted. Without thinking, I walked toward him.

"Get your head up," I said. "C'mon, let's go, let's get that third out."

As soon as I spoke to him, I realized I had goofed. Harvey Haddix had been out to talk to Jackie earlier. I now had technically made the second trip to talk to the pitcher, meaning under the rules that Jackie Brown had to be relieved. I peeked at the bullpen. Harvey had told Rick Waits to loosen up and, God bless him, he was throwing. I knew the plate umpire, Terry Cooney, would invoke the second-trip rule but I figured I would play dumb. At least that would give Rick more time to warm up. I walked Jackie back to the mound.

"I made a mistake," I told him. "I shouldn't have said anything to you."

Jackie understood. After a while, Terry Cooney strolled out from behind the plate with his mask off. He was looking at the bullpen.

"You want the pitcher?" he asked me.

"What pitcher?" I said, straight-faced.

"The pitcher warming up. It's your second trip."

"No, it's my first trip," I said.

"No, no, Haddix was out here before to talk to him."

"Are you sure?"

"I'm positive."

He had me. He knew it. I knew it. He knew I knew it. I really had goofed. But my new lefthander, Rick Waits, saved me. I had him walk Lee May intentionally. Then Earl Weaver sent up my favorite catcher, Dave Duncan, to hit for Jim Northrup, a righthanded batter for a lefthanded batter. Of all people, I didn't want Dave Duncan to beat me with a base hit. He didn't. Rick Waits got him for the third out. The next inning, I had to bring in Fred Beene to get the last two outs, but Rick Waits had showed me something. Not that the manager planned it quite that way.

Baltimore, Tuesday, July 29

We lost to Mike Torrez of the Orioles, 7–1, tonight in the worst type of game for the manager. The losing manager anyway. We were tied, 1–1, when Don Hood walked Mark Belanger and Ken Singleton to open the third. They both came around to score on a sacrifice bunt and Lee May's double, then May scored on Bobby Grich's single. Fred Beene got us out of that inning but he opened the fourth with four straight walks. Rick Waits gave up a two-run single by Grich, but the walks had given the game away. Those giveaway losses really drive me up the wall.

Baltimore, Wednesday, July 30

We beat the Orioles tonight, 3–1, in the best type of game for the manager. The winning manager anyway. Dennis Eckersley outpitched Mike Cuellar—youth against age: the kid who comes right at you with a good fastball, a sidearm curveball, and a change-up, against the crafty oldtimer who keeps you off balance with his off-speed stuff. The kid pitched a four-hitter, struck out nine, and walked four. He's leading the league now with a 2.16 earned-run average and a .727 won-lost percentage on an 8–3 record. But he needed a two-run homer by Johnny Ellis in the eighth to win. The writers wondered if I'm not relenting in the Ellis situation by using him. He also hit a triple and a double in our win here Monday night.

"I told you," I reminded the writers, "that once he told me he would do anything to help the ball club, I'd use him as I see fit. But he's not our regular catcher and he won't be."

Rico Carty had doubled and Cuellar had a 3-and-0 count

when I signaled Dave Garcia to give John the hit sign, meaning he had the green light to swing if he liked the pitch. Thinking that John would be taking, Cuellar threw a fastball down the middle. Mike's fastball isn't that fast. John swung for his first homer in more than six weeks. John didn't miss that hit sign.

But even with the homer, Phil is trying to work out a deal for John with the Twins, who claimed him off the waiver list.

Since the Twins have the worst won-lost record in the American League, they have first shot at the waiver list. But when they claimed John, we recalled him from the list because we didn't want to lose him for the $20,000 waiver price. Then the Twins offered us catcher Phil Roof for him even up, but Phil asked for both Glenn Borgmann, a catcher, and Jim Hughes, their rookie righthander. The Twins turned that down quickly. For better or for worse, I imagine Johnny Ellis will be around for the rest of the season. Tonight at least, it was for the better.

New York, Thursday, July 31

Off-day, which gave me a chance to walk down Broadway to see *Jaws* tonight. I was startled a few times by the shark, but I never was scared. It's only a movie. I didn't think the movie was as good as Peter Benchley's book. The movie didn't follow the book. I think it would've been a better movie if it had.

New York, Friday, August 1

Lee MacPhail has a rust carpet in his office. I mostly listened as he and Phil discussed the umpire situation. But he told me that he couldn't let my blast in Oakland go by without calling me in. He showed me the column Hal Lebovitz had written in the *Plain Dealer* about being an umpire himself. Lee evidently liked that column more than I did. But he acknowledged that some of the young umpires are trigger-happy. I asked him again if yelling "Poke a hole in your mask" was a valid reason for being ejected.

"No," he agreed.

I told him that some umpires are so trigger-happy, and not

just the young umpires, that they can run you for anything at all. That's not right. We also got into the rule about fraternizing on the field. He mentioned that my ball club was one of the worst offenders. That rule is a sore spot with me.

"Just what is fraternizing?" I asked.

"Well," he said, "if you say hello to somebody on another team and move on, that's not fraternizing. But if you stand there talking to him, that's fraternizing. You've been reported for fraternizing."

"Can't a manager talk to other ballplayers?"

"Not on the field. Not more than a hello."

"I've seen other managers do it. I've seen ballplayers stand around talking to ballplayers on the other team all during bp."

"They're not supposed to," Lee said.

"But the way the schedule works, sometimes you don't see a friend of yours for several weeks. You can't just say hello to him and move on. That's not even polite. But if you talk to him, you might be reported."

"That's the rule," he said.

He also brought up an incident I hadn't been aware of. Before our doubleheader in Detroit last Sunday, the Tigers had a ceremony commemorating their seventy-fifth year in the American League and honoring several of their oldest living former players. I stayed in the clubhouse but some of my ballplayers were playing flip in front of the dugout. They get in a circle and, using only their gloves, flip a ball to each other. They were doing it while the ceremony was going on.

"The Tigers filed a complaint," Lee said.

"I don't blame them. It won't happen again."

Other than that, I mostly listened because I knew that whatever I said to Lee MacPhail, it wouldn't really change the way he feels about his umpires. I also think he realizes that I've changed my outlook on his umpires.

I've also changed my outlook on Eric Raich, who couldn't get anybody out in the third inning in a 5–4 loss to the Yankees tonight. He's got a 5–6 record now. I'm thinking about taking him out of the rotation. I'm not seeing the good sinker and the good slider that he had when he first came up. He's not getting the ball down like he was then. He's got to get the ball down to win up here. He proved he can win. But he'll have to prove it all over again.

After the game, the rumor was all over Shea Stadium that the Yankees have fired Bill Virdon and will hire Billy Martin tomorrow. I thought that Virdon might be in trouble, but I'm surprised at the Yankee owners hiring Billy after he's been canned by three ballclubs. I always figured Billy was too strong-willed for the Yankee owners to consider.

Back at the New York Sheraton, a letter from T. J. O'Hays was waiting for me. Apparently he lives in New York and had delivered the letter himself, because it didn't have a stamp on it. The letter read:

Frank, just a few lines to fill you in on my condition. I have resumed my very strenuous exercise routine after about three false starts (the shoulder could not hold together the first three times so I waited and waited, what a drag). Meantime though, I worked on what I could and got my legs in better shape than I ever did. I used heavy ankle weights (that karate men use). I've been walking a great deal with them on and then running carefully because I don't want to pull anything else. I can't tell you how strong they make your legs, because they build up the lifting muscles of the thigh in front. And they extend the legs forward for sprinting. Of course you have to work at it. I've had to drop about five pounds that I got because of the depressing impotent feeling I got from not being able to throw or workout. I ate too much but that's coming off now. I'm on a strict diet. I can make the throwing motion now without pain. But it's amazing how weak I got. I was down to two pushups from 200 but I'm 1.000 % better and getting stronger by the day. I don't want to rip it again so I'm going to take 15 more days before trying to hum the pelota. I'll call you or see you then if the arm holds up. I'd love to help you now but I don't ever want to rip a shoulder again. I have a feeling, always did, that it's knitting stronger than before. I had a slight tear last winter playing handball and it evidently didn't knit. I perfected the shoe for the slide in the meantime.

Incidentally, that Ellis broke my balls in the locker room over the new slide and I thought he was the rottenest bastard I ever met. My arm was hanging off at the time and this prick was making fun of my slide. I had a mind to catch him on the toilet bowl and push his face in but I didn't want to cause a problem.

Frank, some people only understand force. They misunderstand kindness for weakness. It's their fault they were brought up that way. For instance I had to take care of a friend of mine who refuses to stop drinking (I haven't had a drink in 10 years). He bullys people and I had to use karate on him because of my shoulder. Also a prostitute grabbed me when I went to the Port Authority to pick up my luggage. She knocked off my baseball hat (asking me if I wanted to buy some you know what). When I went to pick it up after I told her I didn't want her favors, she started to kick me. I belted her with a backhand left and another prostitute came at me. This was three months ago. I threw a fake right at her and had to run like hell from the pimp. What a town. Lost my favorite hat but it was about to fall apart anyway.

What I'm really worried about is you changing your mind about me and deciding to forget about the slide. Although you've been the one guy who has never gone back on your word, God knows baseball is full of the other kind. So please, I'll try to never let you down if you don't let me down. Say hello to Jackson for me. If you remember, he's a good man in my book.

Your friend,
T. J. O'Hays

P.S. Hang in there and don't kill anyone. See you around the 15th of August, God willing. P.P.S. I've been thinking about the roll on close plays at first base when the pitcher takes the throw and has to sprint to first.

Now that's a full day in baseball—from being on the carpet in Lee MacPhail's office to getting a letter from T. J. O'Hays.

New York, Saturday, August 2

In the exchange of lineup cards at home plate, I looked at Billy Martin and laughed.

"What's the secret?" I said.

He laughed because he knew what I meant. When we began this road trip, he had just been fired by the Texas Rangers and now, before we even get back to Cleveland, he's got another job. I wonder if I'll get another job that fast when I get fired, as all managers eventually do. I wonder if I'll want another job, the way things are going. We lost to the Yankees again, 5–3, when Jim Bibby failed in relief. I brought Jim in to replace Fritz Peterson in the sixth with a 3–1 lead and a runner on second. He gave up a run-scoring single to Ed Herrmann that inning, then gave up three consecutive singles to open the eighth. I brought in Dave LaRoche then but he wasn't sharp and the Yankees had three runs. Bibby doesn't seem to be able to get the big out or to get the big play behind him. Something always happens. Every staff seems to have one of those pitchers. But the thing I like about him is that he's a hard worker. He doesn't moan and groan and he doesn't make excuses. With his stuff, maybe we can get him straightened out and take that hard-luck tag off him.

But the whole team has to be straightened out. Instead of gaining ground, we're losing ground.

We've lost 7 out of 11 on this road trip that ends with a doubleheader tomorrow. We're 8 games behind the Orioles now. We're still in fifth place by 2 games but only because the Tigers have lost 6 in a row. I had planned to go to a good Mexican restaurant for dinner but I ordered room service instead. I'm concerned that the way we're playing, the fans might get on us pretty hard when we get home. I don't want Barbara and the kids to have to listen to any ugly things.

"If we don't snap out of this slump," I told her on the phone tonight, "maybe you better go home next week instead of waiting until school starts."

She tried to cheer me up, but it's not easy. I even made my first curfew check tonight. I talked myself in and out of it about four times before I decided to do it. The way we're playing and with a doubleheader tomorrow, I wanted to see if the players are thinking, *Hey, let's get in tonight, let's be ready.* It's not in my nature to be a warden. It's not in the nature of most managers. But sometimes it's got to be this way. All my years in the majors, I remember only two bed checks. Back around 1960 with the Reds, we lost to the Dodgers in Los Angeles and we had been playing so poorly that Fred Hutchinson had batting practice *after* the game.

"He might check tonight," the older guys were saying. "Better stay in tonight."

Sure enough, Hutch checked. And last year, not long before the Angels traded me, Dick Williams checked. It was my turn to check tonight. Shortly after 1 o'clock, I took my room list and started checking. If the little button in the doorknob had been pushed in from the inside, I didn't check the room itself. If it wasn't, I knocked. I only had to knock at maybe a dozen rooms. When the players answered, they stared at me in surprise. I just told each one to lock his door.

"Is that all?" Dave LaRoche said, laughing. "I thought you'd come to tell me I was starting tomorrow."

But there was no answer in the rooms of four players—Dennis Eckersley, Rick Manning, Charlie Spikes and Bill Sudakis. I'll call them into the warden's office tomorrow before the doubleheader.

New York, Sunday, August 3

One by one, the curfew breakers entered the warden's office. Dennis Eckersley had his right hand on his stomach like a little kid who's hungry.

"I went out for something to eat," he said. "I got hungry."

"You got hungry?" I said. "You got hungry at 1 in the morning after a day game?"

"I'm always hungry," he said.

My other twenty-year-old rookie, Rick Manning, told me he had been out with friends.

"I decided to stay over," he said.

"That's not the way it's done," I told him. "Even if it's with relatives, you have to get permission."

Charlie Spikes had a better reason.

"I was in my room," he said, "but I had changed rooms. You must've checked my original list."

My room list didn't show the change.

"You're off the hook," I told him.

I let the two kids off the hook too. As rookies, I gave them the benefit of the doubt. This time. But the warden fined Bill Sudakis $200.

"You got me," he said. "I was out."

I think the warden felt worse about the fine than he did. It doesn't bother me to fine a player for missing a sign, but fining a player for missing curfew is like spanking your own children. It can hurt you more than it does them. But sometimes you have to do it. Then we lost the first game to the Yankees, 12–1, which hurt even more. But we came back to win the second, 3–2, on Rico Carty's fourth hit, a two-run homer off Dick Tidrow in the eighth. After that, Rick Waits, Jackie Brown, and Dave LaRoche each helped to preserve the win. The more I see of Waits, the more I like him. He lets me hold LaRoche until I really need him. But as strange as it might seem, Fred Beene helped us win the second game by taking a beating in the first game. Beenie relieved Roric Harrison in the fifth with the Yankees leading, 4–0, with runners on second and third. By the time the inning had ended, the Yankees had an 11–0 lead.

"I'm not punishing you or anything," I explained to Beenie in the dugout, "but I'm leaving you in there to finish. No sense using anybody else."

Beenie understood. At least he said he did, and I hope he did. I admire a pitcher who understands that. It's not easy to accept. But when we needed Waits, Brown, and LaRoche in the second game, their arms were fresh. Beenie had kept their arms fresh.

After the split, I called George Hendrick into my office. He hasn't been swinging the bat good. He hasn't had a homer since July 6, almost a month. He's knocked in only seven runs since then. His average has dropped to .264.

"Anything wrong?" I asked.

"No," he said. "Nothing wrong."

"Anything bothering you?"

"I'm a little tired, that's all," he said. "Maybe two or three days' rest would help me."

"I'll give you two days off," I said. "If you feel you're ready Wednesday, let me know."

I hope the rest helps. We need George's bat.

Cleveland, Monday, August 4

We beat the Tigers, 6–4, even though Dennis Eckersley didn't have his best stuff. My yardstick for him is, when he doesn't get strikeouts early in the game, he doesn't have his best stuff. He had two strikes on several hitters in the early innings but he couldn't get the third strike. Even so, he got his ninth victory. Jim Bibby did a good job in relief, then Jackie Brown got the final out. We're still fifth, 8 games behind the second-place Orioles, but we've opened up a 3½-game lead on the Tigers who have now lost 8 in a row. Winning tonight kept the fans off our backs, even though they booed me when I took Eckersley out.

I've changed my mind about sending Barbara and the kids home. I need them around.

Cleveland, Tuesday, August 5

We beat the Tigers again tonight, 8–4, in almost a replay of last night's game. Eric Raich didn't have his best stuff but Jackie Brown and Rick Waits preserved his sixth win. Rico Carty drove in four runs with two singles and a sacrifice fly. Rico is really swinging the bat. In a letter to me last Winter he wrote, "Let the players do the job for you." If they all did their job like Rico does, I could. He's our best pure hitter, a thinking hitter. He's thirty-five now and he's a real professional. When he wasn't playing much early in the season, he didn't like it but he didn't bitch about it.

"Don't worry about the Big Mon," he told me in his Dominican Republic accent. "The Big Mon is all right."

Since then the Big Mon has been the dh almost every day

and the Big Mon has been more than all right. He's the club leader at .307, only one point below his lifetime average. Of all the veteran major leaguers entering this season, he had the fifth-highest lifetime average, behind Ralph Garr at .327, Rod Carew at .323, Hank Aaron at .310, and Pete Rose at .309. And if he had been healthy, his lifetime average probably would be even higher. He missed the 1968 season because of tuberculosis and the 1971 because of a knee injury. He has also had three shoulder separations. But he's still producing and still smiling.

Cleveland, Wednesday, August 6

We beat the Yankees, 5–3, for four in a row. Rico hit his 11th homer, a three-run shot in the sixth, then Dave LaRoche saved Fritz Peterson's 6th win. It was Fritz's fourth strong performance since he put on 10 pounds after slicing two fingers on his lawn mower. That weight must agree with him. LaRoche arrived in the eighth with none out, the score 5–2, and Bobby Bonds on second after a double. Bonds stole third, then Lou Piniella singled for a run. Roy White doubled, then I had Thurman Munson walked intentionally to load the bases even though he represented the potential winning run. With the game on the line, Dave struck out Graig Nettles, Chris Chambliss, and Sandy Alomar for his 9th save. Around the American League, there are several outstanding relief pitchers —Rollie Fingers of the A's, Rich Gossage of the White Sox, John Hiller of the Tigers until he got hurt. But to me, Dave LaRoche has been as valuable to us as any of those relief pitchers is to his team.

I didn't even ask George Hendrick if he wanted another day's rest. I kept him out. The way we're going, I'll keep him out against the Yankees tomorrow night too. Then he should be ready to go in our weekend series with the Royals.

Cleveland, Thursday, August 7

I got a nice letter from President Ford, thanking me for speaking at a Shriners' banquet in Norwalk, Connecticut, last Sunday night. Barbara put it among our souvenirs. But our souvenirs won't include the 6–3 loss to the Yankees tonight. Thurman Munson and Graig Nettles hit homers off Don Hood, but our baserunning hurt us even more.

Rick Manning led off the first with a single, but when he tried to take second on a short passed ball, Munson threw him out. That probably cost us a run because Buddy Bell followed with a walk, Oscar Gamble doubled for one run, and Boog Powell walked. Charlie Spikes singled for another run but he took a wide turn at first base and didn't get back in time. That may have cost us another run, maybe several runs. And in the seventh Oscar was asleep leading off first when Munson picked him off. I didn't get on the players about it. Manning made a mistake in judgment but at least it was an aggressive mistake. Our first-base coach, Tom McCraw, was as much to blame for Spikes and Gamble as they were. It's the coach's job to make base runners aware.

I wish I could show videotapes of Maury Wills's lectures in Tucson, but they don't fit the old videotape machine we have here. I'm told it would cost about $2,600 for a new machine. We're not drawing that well in fifth place. We're not even drawing well enough for Phil to put a TV set in the clubhouse. But at least we got Cy Buynak a washing machine. He had a dryer but no washing machine.

Cleveland, Friday, August 8

I had urged all the players to participate in the Rally Round Cleveland Day parade downtown at noontime, but it wasn't a command performance.

"Any major-league team is part of the community," I told them last night. "There are certain things a player owes the city that he plays in."

Eleven players didn't show, which disappointed me. But so did the way the parade was conducted. We rode in cars in silence for maybe half an hour with no signs identifying who was in each car. And there was no sound car until the parade was almost over. Half the spectators didn't know what was going on or who they were watching. It was too bad. It could've been a good parade, for both the city and the ball club. At the parade I met Doug Metcalf, the national free-fall parachute champion who floated down into the stadium from a small plane before tonight's game with the Kansas City Royals.

"I'll come down at home plate," he told me, "and deliver the game ball."

He landed behind the pitcher's mound. Close enough. Then we beat the Royals, 4–3, with Oscar Gamble hitting a two-run homer in the eighth and Dave LaRoche doing his number in the ninth. With the tying run on second and one out, I let him pitch to two righthanded batters, Harmon Killebrew and Al Cowens, and he got them both—Killebrew on a pop-up, Cowens on a groundout. The way LaRoche is pitching, he can get anybody out. That's why I left him in, against the book. And against Jeff Torborg's thesis. My bullpen coach has a degree from Rutgers in education and a master's degree from Montclair (N.J.) State in athletic administration. Once he was counting the balls as he put them into our big brown-leather ball bag.

"I think," he said, smiling, "that I'm overeducated for this job."

Jeff's thesis for his master's degree was titled "The Analytical Study of the Effects of Platooning in Baseball," a compilation of more than 250,000 at-bats over the last five years. He discovered that righthanded batters have hit .264 against lefthanded pitchers and .254 against righthanded pitchers, that lefthanded batters have hit .270 against righthanded pitchers and .255 against lefthanded pitchers.

"But you have to read my full thesis," Jeff said. "Those statistics represent the average batter against the average pitcher."

The way Dave LaRoche is pitching, he's not the average pitcher. The way Dave LaRoche is pitching, he can get anybody out anytime.

Cleveland, Saturday, August 9

Old-Timers Night—the Indians honored their 1948 World Series champions, the last time the Indians won it all. I've known a few of them, like Lou Boudreau, Joe Gordon, Al Rosen, and Larry Doby, but Doby didn't show. I understand he's annoyed that I got the manager's job instead of him.

I finally met Johnny Berardino, an infielder in 1948 but now an actor who portrays Dr. Steve Hardy in "General Hospital," the TV show. Back when I was in the minors, I remember reading that Johnny Berardino had taken out a $100,000 insurance policy on his face. I've never forgotten that. I enjoyed meeting him, but I'm not big on Old-Timers games. Maybe someday I'll go back to Baltimore for one, but that would be the only place. If there. I just don't believe in them. I appreciate that the fans enjoy them, but I can't understand how some of the real Old-Timers haven't gotten hurt or had a heart attack in the games. Being introduced is enough.

I didn't even watch the Old-Timers game tonight. I stayed in the clubhouse. I wish I hadn't watched our game either. We lost to the Royals, 6–4, with Buddy Bell making two errors that were responsible for the runs that beat us. Buddy's in one of his fielding slumps again and the fans got on him pretty hard. I'll use Ed Crosby at third tomorrow, then we go to Chicago and Minnesota and by the time we come home, maybe the fans will have forgotten Buddy's two errors tonight.

All the Old-Timers had a party at the Cleveland Sheraton after the game. I was invited but I didn't go. I didn't belong there. I wasn't on the 1948 World Series team.

Cleveland, Sunday, August 10

I'm learning that if I want somebody walked, I can't let my pitcher work carefully on the hitter, hoping that the hitter might go for a bad ball. Anytime that I want somebody walked from now on, I'll order him walked intentionally. I learned that lesson again today in our 5–1 loss to the Royals when John Mayberry hit a three-run homer off Eric Raich in the third. With runners on second and third and two out, Raich went to 2 and 1 on Mayberry and Johnny Ellis looked over to see if I wanted to put Mayberry on. I motioned to keep pitching to him but carefully. I was hoping that Mayberry, a big swinger, might jump at a bad ball and pop it up. Eric threw a curveball outside. Ball three. Eric would throw another bad ball and if John didn't go for it, then he could work on Hal McRae.

Instead, the next pitch to Mayberry was a curve inside that hung—just where he likes the ball. Home run.

Even so, we might have won with a couple of timely hits. But we didn't get them. We seldom do. Al Fitzmorris started for the Royals and had nothing, but he got away with it until we got him out of there in the sixth on Frank Duffy's walk, steal of second, and Boog's double. Nelson Briles relieved and we still couldn't do anything. After the game, I surprised my ballplayers by ordering a workout tomorrow except for Boog, Rico, Manning, and the pitchers. It's our first off-day after 25 consecutive game days. I'm sure they had assumed I wouldn't call a workout. But an off-day without a workout at this stage of the season is a luxury that a winning ball club deserves. The way we're going, this ball club doesn't deserve it.

Cleveland, Monday, August 11

We had a good workout. As each hitter finished his turn in bp, he came down to first base where I talked to him about taking a longer lead. Just about everybody got a longer lead today than I've seen for two months.

"You sure your lead hasn't been shorter?" I asked them.

"Oh, no," most of them said. "I always lead off here."

But in a ball game their leads had to be shorter because they were getting back too easy on the pickoff throws. I don't mind them conning me today as long as they get a longer lead from now on. We also released Bill Sudakis in order to get Duane Kuiper back on the active list. The way things are, Sudakis was the most expendable player. Releasing him bothered me personally because after the Angels had let him go, he had offers to go to Albuquerque in the Dodgers' farm system, to Hawaii in the Pacific Coast League, and to Japan, but he wanted to play for me because of our friendship on the Angels and the Dodgers where I worked with him on his hitting.

"We've got to put Kuiper back on," I explained. "We've got to let somebody go."

"I understand," he said. "My mistake was not taking the Dodger offer instead."

Hindsight makes it seem that way. Shortly after he signed with us, the Dodgers lost two catchers, Joe Ferguson and Steve Yeager, and if he had been at Albuquerque, he probably would have been called up. But at the time it wasn't a mistake. I was just sorry it didn't work out. The way our roster is now, I've got two infielders on the bench, Kuiper and Ed Crosby, that let me pinch-hit for Bell, Duffy, or Brohamer if I want to. Being able to maneuver is important. With the White Sox starting three lefthanders against us in Chicago beginning tomorrow, I'll keep Brohamer at second base, but Kuiper is available now if I need him.

After the workout, Buddy, Buskey, and I talked to Phil about the American League crackdown on complimentary tickets for the ballplayers—four for family, two for friends.

The way it was, if a ballplayer needed five tickets for his family, he had to pay for the fifth, which I think is ridiculous. Phil agreed. From now on, the ballplayers will be able to swap their family tickets among themselves but the limit stays at two tickets for friends. I'm in favor of that. I couldn't believe it when Eric Raich asked for 68 tickets in Anaheim when he pitched there. Inviting your family is fine, but not the neighborhood. The most comps I ever remember a player getting was 104 for Curt Blefary once when the Orioles were at Yankee Stadium several years ago. The most I've ever had was about 16 for my family in Oakland, where Charley Finley is very strict on comps. Most ball clubs figure that the visiting team is entitled to 180 tickets. As long as the list is within the limit, fine. But not Charley O.—not even with all the empty seats in his ball park.

Chicago, Tuesday, August 12

It looks so easy when you win sometimes that you wonder why you can't do it all the time. Or at least half the time.

Fritz Peterson again was outstanding for seven innings tonight, then Dave LaRoche was Dave LaRoche in a 6–3 victory over the White Sox for his 11th save, his season high in the majors. George Hendrick hit a two-run homer and Johnny Ellis knocked in two runs with a double and a single. It was George's first homer since July 6, and he had only driven in six runs in the five weeks since then. Maybe the homer will get him going again. I've suggested that he take his stance 6 inches close to the plate in order to cover the outside corners.

"Your stance is so closed and you're so far away from the plate," I told him recently, "you can't reach outside pitches."

But he is very aware of the inside pitch. When he has to swing at pitches on the outside part of the plate, he usually hits ground balls or easy fly balls. He's reaching too much to hit a line drive. I didn't order him to change his stance, because I don't believe in that. Ordering a hitter to change his stance, especially during the season, will create more problems than it will solve. Sometimes you just have to wait for a hitter to get so down he'll be glad to accept a suggestion. But not George, not yet anyway.

We moved to within ½ game of the fourth-place Brewers and we're not worrying about the Tigers anymore. They've lost 17 in a row.

Chicago, Wednesday, August 13

We lost to the White Sox in twelve innings, 4–3, with Rick Waits walking in the winning run on four pitches to Tom Varney, who is not a good hitter. Waits threw four pitches down low. He never made an adjustment to get his pitches up. In that situation, with the bases loaded, the 3-and-0 pitch to a hitter like Varney shouldn't be questionable. But he was low again.

Don Hood had pitched six good innings. Dave LaRoche got us through the ninth, but I didn't want to overwork him. I brought in Jim Bibby, who was all right until he opened the twelfth by walking Carlos May, which was asking for trouble. May went to second on Johnny Ellis's passed ball. I had Bibby walk Ken Henderson intentionally, then I brought in Waits and Jorge Orta hit a line drive that took a bad hop and bounced off Frank Duffy's shoulder. Duffy looked everywhere except where the ball was—between his feet. Now the bases were loaded. Waits got a force-out at the plate but then he walked in the winning run. Of all the ways there is to lose a baseball game, walking in the winning run is the worst.

But this was Waits's first appearance in White Sox Park, where the mound is maybe the highest in the league. In contrast, the mounds in the visiting bullpen are almost flat.

I can understand the bullpen mounds not being too high here because they're in foul territory. You don't want to risk a player tripping over a high mound and breaking an ankle running after a foul ball. But the mounds in the White Sox bullpen are higher than the mounds in the visiting bullpen. That's not fair. Especially when the regular mound is so high. The high mound helps Jim Kaat and Rich Gossage, who come over the top with their pitches. Through the years, the White Sox have been known to tamper with their field. When they had good bunters and fast runners, they used to tilt the dirt near the third-base line to keep bunts fair. They also watered the grass heavily in front of the plate to keep the bunts from rolling too far. Now that the Angels are bunting and running, they do that too. The height of the infield grass is also important. With their slow infielders, the Twins let the grass grow thick. But in our ball park, I've ordered the grass to be cut low. Defensively, we've got infielders who can cover the ground. Offensively, we hit a lot of sharp grounders that low grass will help skip through for base hits.

But the mound situation in White Sox Park is something the league should investigate. And something the umpires should check.

Chicago, Thursday, August 14

We don't seem to want fourth place. We wasted an opportunity to tie the Brewers tonight by losing to the White Sox again, 6–4. We also lost Johnny Ellis with a pulled hamstring.

He'll go on the disabled list and we'll call up Rick Cerone from Oklahoma City, the kid catcher from Seton Hall who was our No. 1 draft choice. The shame of Ellis's injury is that he was starting to swing the bat well. He hit his seventh homer and a single, lifting his average to .233, then he pulled up lame scoring from second to give us a 4–3 lead against Jim Kaat in the seventh. But the White Sox came back with two off Roric Harrison, including the tying run on Pat Kelly's homer that I disputed because of fan interference.

It was similar to the play here that led to my argument with Jerry Neudecker and my three-game suspension. But this time I kept my cool.

To me, it was very clear that a fan in the right-centerfield bleachers had reached below the level of the fence and interfered with the ball as George Hendrick jumped for it. The second-base umpire, Ron Luciano, had hustled out there and had a good view but I still think he blew it. I argued that Kelly should have been called out on fan interference.

"The fan touched it," Luciano said, "but he was up in the stands. It would've been a homer even if he hadn't touched it."

I didn't agree and neither did George, who was sure that he would have got his glove on the ball, at least keeping it in play. But the real issue is that the American League should order the White Sox not to sell tickets in the first row of the bleachers, maybe the first two rows. In old Yankee Stadium, they never sold tickets in the first row where a fan could affect the outcome of the game.

In the eighth Jackie Brown gave up a homer to Bill Stein, their third baseman who was batting eighth. We've been hurt by those guys at the bottom of the lineup all year long.

Harrison didn't have his control. One of the few pitches the Duke got where he wanted was a fastball behind Carlos May's head in the first inning. May had slid high into Frank Duffy last night. I like my pitchers to protect their teammates. Knockdown pitches are part of the game. Sometimes a batter has to be moved away from the plate. But throwing at somebody's head is not part of the game. If a pitcher feels he has to throw at a batter's head to get him out, I don't think that pitcher belongs in the big leagues. Next time, I hope the Duke aims below the batter's waist or at least below his shoulders.

Minnesota, Friday, August 15

Speaking of knockdowns, I ordered a batter hit tonight. We played poorly again, losing to the Twins, 8–4, and dropping 2 games behind the Brewers for fourth place. Dennis Eckersley didn't have much. I had to bring in Fred Beene in the third when the Twins took a 5–1 lead. But the reason for the knockdown developed in the second when the Twins had runners on first and second with two out and their catcher, Phil Roof, bunted for a base hit. To me, Phil Roof was trying to show us up. It was uncalled-for to bunt for a base hit in that situation, especially with their ninth-place hitter, shortstop Luis Gomez, up next. Gomez can't hit his way out of a paper bag. Neither can Phil Roof.

"The next time Roof comes up," I told Beenie in the dugout later, "I want him hit on the knee. I don't care if it takes four shots. I want him *hit*."

That's my way of saying hit a batter anywhere from the waist down. In the fifth the Twins were leading, 8–3, when Roof came up with nobody on. Beene took one shot and missed, then he hit him on the second pitch, a good shot on the thigh near the knee. As he went to first base, Phil assumed correctly that I had ordered him hit and he was hollering at me.

"If you want me," I told him, "come on."

He never moved. He's lucky I don't believe in ordering a pitcher to throw at a batter's head, to "stick it in their ear," like some managers do. If the batter were to be seriously injured, the first thing a pitcher would say is that he was only obeying orders. I don't want that on my conscience. That's not part of the game. I know. I've been thrown at. By the best.

Don Drysdale was the toughest knockdown pitcher I ever faced. He was mean enough to do it and he did it continuously. You could count on him doing it. And when he did it, he just stood there on the mound and glared at you to let you know he meant it. With my stance, leaning over the plate, I had to contend with inside pitches. My first year in the minors, I got hit in the forehead. But the pitcher wasn't aiming at me, he was just wild. With the Reds, getting hit was part of the game, but Birdie Tebbetts kept complaining that the pitchers were throwing at me. After a while, I began to believe him.

My worst knockdown scene occurred in 1961 when the Reds were in Los Angeles for a big weekend series with the Dodgers before the All-Star break. That was before the divisions. We were leading the league, with the Dodgers second.

We won a twi-night doubleheader Friday but the Dodgers won Saturday to cut our lead to 4 games. Roger Craig started against us Sunday and I hit a two-run homer in the first and singled in the fifth. To show how much the Dodgers wanted the game, Walt Alston used both Sandy Koufax and Drysdale in relief. In the sixth, when Joey Jay, a pitcher with an .065 batting average, doubled for two runs, Drysdale was really steaming. He threw a pitch behind Don Blasingame's head, he threw two close pitches at Vada Pinson, then he knocked me down twice.

"That's enough," the plate umpire, Dusty Boggess, yelled. "Another one and you're gone."

Drysdale threw another one inside. I looked at Dusty and Fred Hutchinson came out to argue that Drysdale should be ejected.

"No, no," Dusty said. "It wasn't that far off the plate."

But then Drysdale made sure Dusty wouldn't have any excuses. His next pitch drilled me. Dusty threw him out. Drysdale later was fined $100 and suspended five days. My next time up, I hit a two-run homer off Turk Farrell to put us ahead, 10–3, then I hit a three-run double to give me 4 hits and 7 runs batted in. We won, 14–3, we led by 5 games, and we went on to win the pennant. Games like that earned me a reputation I always enjoyed.

"Don't throw at Robinson," some managers used to say. "It makes him a better hitter."

But it works the other way with some hitters. That's why pitchers throw at them.

After our loss tonight, I met with my coaches in my suite at the Leamington Hotel until 3 o'clock. We talked about everything, but mostly about why this ball club accepts defeat when it gets behind. We also talked about a lack of execution of fundamentals, especially bunting, baserunning, and preventing the opposition from taking the extra base. We talked about how some of our pitchers aren't mean enough to keep batters from digging in at the plate. I don't mean throwing at them. I mean throwing inside to keep them thinking. But mostly, it came down to that attitude of accepting defeat. This ball club just surrenders. I've never been on a ball club that acted this way. And if I'm going to be the manager, it won't continue.

Minnesota, Saturday, August 16

I finally blew my stack today. We lost to the Twins, 9–1, we accepted another defeat. Nobody swung the bat aggressively, Buddy Bell and Duane Kuiper threw the ball away, Eric Raich and Jackie Brown gave up 20 hits. When it was over, I closed the clubhouse and kept the players sitting at their lockers for maybe two minutes while I got myself together. I didn't want to yell. I didn't want to put on an act. I knew I had to be myself. Otherwise the players would see right through me. Now that I think about it, my tone of voice was different than it has been in any other clubhouse meeting. Above my normal tone, but not yelling, not acting. I told them that they were accepting defeat too easily, that they were making too many excuses for themselves, that the pitchers were letting the hitters at the bottom of the batting order kill us. I told them that they're playing to get the game over as quickly as possible, that whether we win or lose it doesn't matter, that all they're thinking about is getting dressed and getting out on the streets to have a good time. I told them that we still have six weeks to go, that we're going to play good baseball the rest of the season, that we're going to finish strong.

"You're pussies," I told them. "You talk tough in the dugout and in the clubhouse, but once you're out there between the white lines, you're pussies. You lay down and accept defeat."

I talked for about ten minutes and after I had my say, that was it. I didn't storm around anymore, because that wouldn't be me. I remember Birdie Tebbetts once knocking all the hair tonic bottles off the shelf in the locker room john, but all the players shrugged and looked at each other because that wasn't him. Fred Hutchinson was different. You expected Hutch to stalk around with the veins in his neck popping out. After we lost a doubleheader to the Mets at the old Polo Grounds in 1962, their first year, Hutch stayed in the dugout when the players went to the clubhouse, which was out in centerfield. When he didn't show, we looked out the window and he was still sitting in the dugout. In the dark. All the lights had been turned off. Finally the clubhouse phone rang.

"Hutch," the clubhouse man told us, "will be here in 15 minutes. He wants everybody gone when he gets here."

I never saw ballplayers move so fast. Some guys hadn't even bothered to get undressed, much less showered. But they did now. They were all out of that clubhouse by the time Hutch arrived. Another time in old Crosley Field, he threw his desk chair through the clubhouse window. In the tunnel to the clubhouse in Milwaukee, he reached up and ripped the small protective screens off the lightbulbs on the ceiling, one by one. But the scene I remember best was in old Forbes Field in Pittsburgh after we had led the Pirates, 6–1, with two out and nobody on in the ninth. When the smoke cleared, we had lost, 7–6. From right field I could see Hutch stomping toward the Pirates' dugout that led to both clubhouses.

I hurried through the bullpen exit because I wanted to get to the clubhouse before Hutch did. I wasn't thrilled by the loss, but now that it was over I wanted to see what Hutch would do.

I beat him into the clubhouse and sat at my locker, peeking up as he came in. Instead of unbuttoning his shirt, he just popped it with his hands. The buttons flew all over. Then he picked up the wooden folding chair in front of his locker and slammed it to the floor. It bounced but it didn't break. Not a splinter off it. He picked it up again, whoom, like he was really going to show that chair this time. Again, not a splinter. And a third time, not a splinter. Now he just glared at the chair, reached down, opened it up and calmly placed it in front of his locker as if to say, all right, chair, you win.

I didn't try to break any chairs today.

Minnesota, Sunday, August 17

Maybe my blowup did some good. We routed the Twins, 14–5, on 20 hits. We got 8 runs in the second after George Hendrick's three-run homer in the first. By the third, Fritz had a 13–0 lead, but that inning Rick Manning had been hit in the thigh by Mark Wiley, intentionally I thought. In the dugout I called Fritz aside.

"I want you to hit Carew on the knee," I told him, but then I realized Rod Carew would be the third hitter that inning. "No, the situation might not be right. Hit the first batter instead."

Fritz threw a couple of pitches inside to Jerry Terrell, the Twins' shortstop. But they weren't that close. From the dugout I hollered, "Get the hitter now," meaning for him to work on Terrell, then take a shot at Dan Ford or Carew, or both. But he didn't take a shot at anyone. When he came into the dugout, he said, "Sorry about that, I couldn't get him." I just looked at him. He hadn't let *me* down. He had let his teammates down. They're the ones who might be thrown at.

With the Reds once, I got knocked down, and when I went to the outfield, Bob Purkey knew I expected him to protect me. His first pitch wasn't as close as it should have been. He turned around and waved at me, as if to say that he would get him on the next pitch. He did.

I don't think Fritz has the stomach to throw at hitters. Eckersley and Harrison do, so does Bibby, but this ball club never had a reputation for pitchers who threw at anybody. Some people thought Gaylord was a tough pitcher but I never did. Once when he was with the Giants and I was with the Reds, he yelled, "I'll stick one in your ear tomorrow" but I hit a home run instead. I became convinced that Gaylord wasn't tough early this season after Rod Carew stole home on him. When Carew let his bat fly toward him after a close pitch, Gaylord never said a word, never moved off the mound. The next pitch, Gaylord threw it right over the plate. To me, after Carew let the bat fly, Gaylord should have taken Carew's cap off with the next pitch and hollered, "Now that's a knock-down pitch." But old Gaylord wasn't as tough as he likes people to think.

Other than Fritz letting his teammates down, George baffled me by trying to bunt in the first with runners on first and second and nobody out.

On the first pitch, I thought he was faking. After he squared around the second time and took another ball, I signaled Dave Garcia to give him the hit sign. The next pitch he swung lazylike. That disturbed me because I figured he must be angry. But on a fastball, he popped his three-run homer. I didn't say anything to him then, but the next inning I called him aside.

"What was your thinking on the bunt?" I asked.

"I wanted to move two men into scoring position."

"Why?"

"So they could both score on a base hit," he said.

"Your thinking is fine, but the situation is wrong."

"Why's that?"

"Boog is the next hitter with a lefthander pitching," I said, meaning Bill Butler. "Boog's chances of hitting are less than yours are. In that situation, I want you swinging away. If there's a tough righthander out there, that's different. Or late in the game, bunting might be the right move. But the first inning is too early for you not to be swinging away."

"I understand," he said.

His homer helped us really put a ball club away for the first time all season. We're only a game behind the Brewers for fourth place. We've opened up a 7-game lead on the Tigers, who finally won last night after losing 19 in a row. We go home now for 3 games with the Rangers before going to Kansas City next weekend. If we keep winning, I'll know my blowup did some good.

Cleveland, Monday, August 18

We moved into fourth place by sweeping the Rangers, 4–3 and 4–2, in a twi-nighter. Gaylord didn't pitch and he won't unless we get rained out tomorrow, but he let the writers know he's winning again. Before the doubleheader Russ Schneider stopped by my office with a message from Gaylord, who has won six of his last seven starts, including four shut-outs. His record is up to 13–15 now.

"Gaylord said," Russ told me, " 'Tell 'em that's how much they know about pitching. Tell them I was only in a slump, like I tried to tell them when I was over there. Tell them pitchers have slumps like hitters do.' "

Gaylord didn't say anything about his brother, Jim, who was released by the A's last week and apparently is through. But when we traded Gaylord, we knew he wasn't through. We knew he still had some good games in him. But not enough good games to justify keeping him. Rick Waits will mean more to the Indians' future than Gaylord would have meant. Waits was the minor-leaguer in the deal. At least he was a minor-leaguer then. He's a major-leaguer now. He was outstanding again in the first game tonight, relieving Don Hood with none out in the third and allowing only two hits the rest of the way for his second victory. To me, his future is as a starter, not a reliever. We've got to get him into the rotation soon. In the second game Roric Harrison and Dave LaRoche com-bined for a five-hitter. I brought in Dave after the Duke had walked Toby Harrah in the seventh.

"Don't take me out," the Duke said. "I was just pitching around that guy."

He stepped to the edge of the grass behind the mound, with his back to me. I knew he was steaming but I didn't mind that.

"Were you pitching around Cardenas too?" I asked.

In the fifth he had walked Lee Cardenas, then a triple by Bill Fahey and a single by Dave Moates had cut our lead to 3–2.

"When you walked him," I said, "they got two runs."

Harrison doesn't like to come out, but I don't mind that. Like when he started in Baltimore for the first time since the

Orioles traded him to Atlanta before we got him, he was leading, 4–2, but there were runners on second and third with nobody out.

"Don't take me out," he said.

"I can't leave you out here."

"I want to beat these guys," he said. "I want to show them I can pitch up here."

"Fine, but not tonight."

"Just one more hitter."

"I can't leave you out here," I said. "I don't want to lose a ball game because *you* want to stay in."

"All right, all right," he said.

The Duke is angry inside but he doesn't make a scene. I like that. He's a competitor. So is John Lowenstein, who hit a homer and two singles to help win the second game while I gave George Hendrick a rest. The more I see John, the more I like him. He's always ready to play, and when he's not playing, he doesn't bitch about it. Between games tonight, he didn't expect to play so he stuffed himself with two chicken-loaf-and-cheese sandwiches and two cream sodas. Then he saw his name in the lineup.

"It was necessary," he told Bob Sudyk later, "that I belch quickly."

He's the funniest guy on the ball club. He claims he's got the biggest fan club in baseball, the John Lowenstein Apathy Fan Club—millions belong to it. He's been on this ball club since 1970, longer than any of our other players, longer than the manager, longer than the general manager, longer than the executive vice-president.

"Only major talents," he told Sudyk last week, "stay with one club through a career. My longevity therefore is even more significant. I don't want to be a star but I'd like to twinkle a little."

John Lowenstein can twinkle for me anytime. Because he's so versatile and because he's got a good attitude, I consider him one of the few players we can't afford to trade. But after John and most of the players had dressed and gone, Frank Duffy and Dave LaRoche stopped by my office.

"Do you have time to talk?" Frank asked.

I had planned to meet Ed Keating in the Theatrical for a drink, but I knew Ed would understand if I kept him waiting a few minutes.

"I've always got time to talk," I said.

I thought they just wanted to check something out with me. I didn't realize they wanted to check out the whole ball club. They told me that Buddy Bell is very down now, that they feel I should pat Buddy on the back more, especially now because the fans were still on him tonight. While we were on the road, I thought the fans might forget about booing him, but they haven't. Buddy went 0 for 3 in each game tonight, and after he grounded out his last time up, the fans got on him hard. Back in the dugout he growled, "I want to get out of here, I want to be traded." I didn't take him that seriously. I've heard ballplayers say that for twenty years, but most of them don't really mean it. As soon as the cheers return, they forget all about the boos. Buddy just has to learn to cope with the boos, like other ballplayers have. I told that to Frank and Dave but they thought Buddy was a special case.

"Pat him on the back more," Dave said. "Talk to him more."

Frank then brought up the Jack Brohamer case. I put Duane Kuiper back at second base in Minnesota without telling Jack why I was taking him out.

"Did you have a reason," Frank asked, "for not telling him?"

I told him I didn't. I also told him I consider my office to be on a two-way street but it seems to be a one-way street for players. When a player feels I'm wrong, he seldom walks down the street leading to my office, he usually waits for me to walk down the street to his locker, and I don't think I should have to do that.

"But that," Frank said, "is like telling the player that you're not going to lower yourself to go to him."

I disagreed. I reminded him that when Jack Brohamer wanted to come off the disabled list, he walked in my door and we got it straightened out. And now that Jack is out of the lineup, if he wants to know why, he can come to me as well as I can go to him.

"But maybe you're right," I conceded. "I'll call Jack in and tell him why he's out of the lineup."

Then we got into the George Hendrick situation. George started out great but in July he just stopped hitting. When he was hitting, nobody complained about his casual style. But when he's not hitting, he looks like he doesn't care. To me, George is the type of individual who just doesn't push himself. I don't think he realizes how good he can be if he were to push himself. Or maybe he just doesn't care how good he can be.

"I'll be honest with you," I said. "I still don't know how to get the best out of George, but I'm going to keep trying to find out."

We also talked about the lack of a leader. We agreed that we don't have one player who will walk up to a teammate, look him straight in the eye, and tell him, "You were horseshit tonight." Other teams have those players, especially the A's, but we don't.

"As co-captain, I guess I should do that," Frank said, "but that's not my personality. I couldn't say that to a player. I'd be an outcast."

"But a leader can't worry about that," I said. "He's got to be able to tell a teammate that he should've made that play or that he was loafing."

As we kept talking, we agreed that we're tired of hearing that this ball club has the potential to be a winner. Potential, my ass. Produce, that's the name of the game. We also agreed that one reason why this ball club has accepted defeat easily is that it's been a losing ball club. It *expects* to lose. That losing attitude is difficult to change. But as long as I'm the manager, I told them, I won't give up trying to change it.

"Have you been asked to come back?" Frank asked.

"No," I said. "Nobody's said anything to me yet."

"If you're asked," Dave said, "will you come back?"

I told them I really hadn't made up my mind yet.

"I hope you do come back," Frank said. "The ball club is

just starting to grasp a lot of things you told us in spring training and all season. It's just starting to sink in. Pretty soon it's all going to come together."

"I haven't given up on a .500 season," I told them. "I'm not going to let the ball club give up either."

I looked at my watch. It was nearly 2 o'clock. We had been talking for almost three hours. I thought about Ed Keating still waiting for me in the Theatrical and I assumed he had the sense to go home. I knew I wasn't going to stop in for a drink now. I knew I would have enough trouble making Barbara believe that I was in my office talking to two of my ball-players until 2 o'clock in the morning. But at least she had to give me credit for coming up with a new one.

Cleveland, Tuesday, August 19

All that talking didn't help us tonight. We lost to the Rangers, 2–1, with Dennis Eckersley wasting a tremendous five-hitter. His only real mistake occurred in the seventh when he challenged Jim Spencer with a fastball after getting him out earlier with breaking balls. Spencer hit the fastball down the right-field line for a homer that decided the game. The kid is still our best pitcher, but I'm thinking about a new rotation— Jim Bibby and Rick Waits promoted from the bullpen to join Fritz, Harrison, and the kid. Don Hood and Eric Raich will go to the bullpen. Hood has great stuff but he's high-strung. Maybe the bullpen will relax him. Raich also needs to relax. He's in a unique pressure situation with his father-in-law covering the ball club. He's very determined to make it. Maybe too determined. Maybe the bullpen will ease his pressure.

Cleveland, Wednesday, August 20

Off-day with no workout. I stopped by the ball park to see Phil, but he was upstairs having lunch so I went home. Ed Keating came over for dinner. His wife, Carol, and their kids are in Atlantic City, where Barbara and the kids visited them last weekend. Barbara wanted to have Ed over tonight just as a thank-you for him and his family being so nice to her and the kids this summer, especially when I was on the road. Carol had them over sometimes, took them places other times. Knowing they were enjoying themselves made it easier for me to concentrate on my job.

Kansas City, Thursday, August 21

In his subtle way, Phil was puffing on his pipe the other day when he mentioned Jackie Brown had a 4–0 record as a starter against the Royals for the Rangers last year.

"When we go to Kansas City," he suggested, "Jackie might be worth a start there."

I took the suggestion and I'm glad I did. Jackie pitched a nine-hitter and we won, 7–3, with George Hendrick and Oscar Gamble hitting home runs. We've won 4 of our last 5 and I'm starting to talk up catching the Yankees for third place. We're only 5 games behind them. We can finish third, we can finish above the .500 mark. Last year when we still had a chance to win the division, nobody mentioned it, like there was no way we could do it. That won't happen this time.

Even though we're 10 games under the .500 mark, I'm not going to let this ball club die.

Kansas City, Friday, August 22

Another win, 9–5, for 5 in our last 6 since I blew my stack. Fritz got his 5th straight but Jim Bibby saved it by retiring the last 12 batters in a row. Bibby's ready to go back into the rotation now. Rico got three hits, including his 15th homer. His average is up to .310 now with 51 runs batted in. Rick Cerone also got his first major-league hit, a bouncing single to left. The kid has a future as a catcher. He's got a great arm and he handles the pitchers well. Right now he's a mechanical hitter, too stiff. But with minor-league experience, maybe he'll loosen up.

Kansas City, Saturday, August 23

We won again, 7–1, with Rick Waits pitching a five-hitter in his first start. He's sneaky-fast. That type is always tough to hit because you're not ready for his fastball. We've now won 6 of our last 7. The loss dropped the Royals 8½ games behind the A's in the AL West after they had been only 5½ behind when we arrived.

Whitey Herzog doesn't know it but he taught me something. When he took over as the Royals' manager from Jack McKeon a few weeks ago, he talked about how the Royals still had a chance to overtake the A's for first place. When we got here Thursday, he was quoted about still hoping to finish first and how "we've been playing the tough ball clubs and now we've got Cleveland coming in," like we were patsies. I don't think he meant it like it sounded but I didn't care. I told our players about it, hoping it would fire them up. Maybe it helped.

"But on other teams I've been on," I told Tom McCraw, "the manager wouldn't have to do that. Half a dozen players would beat him to it."

As a manager you really have to be careful what you say about other ball clubs and how you say it. You also have to be careful not to gloat. After each win here, I didn't mention the Herzog quote to the writers. I didn't want to give the Royals something that would fire *them* up.

Kansas City, Sunday, August 24

We missed sweeping the four-game series when Al Fitzmorris stopped us, 5–2, but more frustrating, we missed an opportunity to close in on the Yankees, who lost a doubleheader to the Angels.

We're 4½ games out of third place, with 37 to play. Roric Harrison didn't keep the ball down. Don Hood pitched four scoreless innings in relief, but he was called for a balk again on his pickoff move to first base. That's his fourth balk, and after the inning I went out to talk to Nestor Chylak, the umpire who had called it.

"What did he do this time he didn't do last inning?"

"Everything," Nestor said. "The whole move stunk."

"But what was there that made you call it?" I asked.

"He hung the runner up with his leg, he can't do that."

"That's part of a move for a lefthander as long as he doesn't pause for five seconds."

"But then," Nestor said, "he stepped directly toward the plate."

"That's ridiculous. No lefthanded pitcher is going to step directly toward home plate."

"He did," Nestor said.

I'm beginning to think that Don Hood's pickoff move fools the umpire as well as the base runner. It's almost as good as Danny McDevitt's move, the best I ever saw. He was a little lefthander with the Dodgers whose move wasn't predictable. When most lefthanders look at the base runner, they're going to pitch to the plate. When they're looking away with their head, they're usually going to come over to first base. But with Danny's move, you never knew.

And with Don Hood's move, you never know. The base runners don't know. The umpires don't know.

Being Rehired
Is More
Important

We're home this week against the White Sox and the Twins and I planned to sleep late, but Trudy's phone call got me up.

"Mr. Bonda wants to see you in his office at the Investment Plaza building," she said. "Mr. Seghi will be there too."

I was wide awake now. I was sure they wanted to talk to me about next year. I also was sure that they would ask me to return. I had thought every so often about not wanting to come back, but now I wanted to. As bad as things were sometimes, I never thought I would be fired. But driving downtown, it was comforting that we had won six of our last eight. In the meeting Ted and Phil made it clear right away that they were happy with the way I've managed the ball club. They asked me back as the manager and also as the dh. But being the dh depends on my shoulder.

"When we talk contract," I said, "I'd like to negotiate two separate contracts—one as a manager, one as a player-manager."

I'd like to play again next year, because my shoulder wouldn't let me play as much this year as I wanted to. It's not the 3,000 hits and the 600 home runs. I'd like to reach those milestones, but if I had been able to play pain-free this season and didn't reach them, that would have been it. But because of my shoulder, I wasn't able to give the Cleveland fans what I had hoped to give them. If surgery corrects my shoulder, then I'll give it another shot as the dh next season. But there's no way I'll know until I test the shoulder in spring training.

"That's why I want two different contracts," I said. "I don't want to sign a player-manager contract and feel like I have to play if my shoulder isn't right."

They agreed to that. They didn't even discuss money. I made $180,000 this year as a player-manager. I imagine they'll offer me that much as a player-manager again, but I don't know what they'll offer me as a manager—probably $50,000, maybe $65,000 tops. If my shoulder doesn't let me play, a manager's salary would be a big comedown.

"You've got to play," Barbara said when I told her about the meeting. "We can't afford for you *not* to play."

She's always kidding me about that. But she knows and I know we'll learn to live on less. We've also got $40,000 a year for five years coming from the Orioles as deferred income when I stop playing. We won't exactly be destitute.

Against the White Sox tonight, I celebrated with my ninth homer and Dennis Eckersley pitched a three-hitter. We won, 5–1, for 7 out of our last 9. We're only 4 games behind the Yankees.

Eckersley is 10–5, and after his first few pitches I turned to Harvey Haddix in the dugout and said, "The kid really has his stuff, we're not going to need but one or two runs to win this ball game." He had a no-hitter through six innings, but when Bill Melton singled in the seventh I wasn't as disappointed as the kid was. Anytime a young pitcher throws a no-hitter, he has a tremendous amount of pressure on him to live up to it. The kid doesn't need that kind of pressure yet. My homer gave him some breathing room. We were leading, 2–1, in the eighth when George Hendrick singled. Jim Kaat had gotten me out twice, a strikeout and a fly ball. I figured he would try to keep the ball away from me, but he threw a slider down and in that didn't do much. I was fortunate to get all of it and I hit it over the leftfield wall. Charlie Spikes followed with another homer, his eighth, a line shot off a change-up curveball.

The big play for us was a leaping catch above the centerfield fence by Rick Manning in the third that robbed Jorge Orta of a three-run homer. Rick had run across the worst-looking outfield I've ever seen in a major-league ball park.

They had a rock concert in the stadium Saturday night that drew more than 60,000 people. Some of the crowd roamed all over the outfield, wearing away some of the grass. When it rained hard Sunday, deep muddy areas developed. Our groundskeepers, Harold and Marshall Bossard, did a great job smoothing it out as much as possible. But it still wasn't a major-league outfield. Other parts of the field also were slick. Duane Kuiper fell running from third to home, but he got up in time to score. In the Kangaroo Kourt later, Duane had some fun with Art Modell, the Cleveland Browns' owner who also operates the Stadium Corporation that put on the rock concert.

"I want Mr. Modell fined $1 for embarrassing the ball club when I fell," Duane said, "$1 for stinking up my uniform, and $1 for the overall lousy conditions of the playing field."

To me, baseball is a grass game. Artificial turf adds an artificial element that baseball is better off without. But if Cleveland Stadium is going to jeopardize the grass by putting on rock concerts and football games during the baseball season, then I vote for artificial turf. It's better than the swamp the outfielders were in tonight. And the Indians would be a good artificial-turf team. We hit a lot of sharp ground balls. Those grounders shoot through an artificial-turf infield for base hits.

Cleveland, Tuesday, August 26

More rain washed out tonight's game with the White Sox and deepened the mud in the outfield. We'll play a twi-night doubleheader tomorrow. We purchased Bob Reynolds, a right-handed reliever, from the Tigers for the $20,000 waiver price. Phil had mentioned that Reynolds was on waivers and I said, "Get him." When nobody below us in the standings claimed him, he was ours. He didn't do much with the Tigers since they got him from the Orioles three months ago, but he didn't have a chance to do much. He might just need work. He had a good arm with the Orioles when I was there. I had hoped to get the Orioles to include him with Boog and Don Hood in the Dave Duncan deal. All he needs to be sharp is work. He's a two-pitch pitcher who works the outside corner. He rarely comes inside. He needs his control. If he has it, he'll help us.

Cleveland, Wednesday, August 27

We split with the White Sox tonight. Jim Bibby lost a three-hitter, 2–0, then Fritz won a five-hitter, 5–0, for his sixth straight. But the manager's shoulder went again. Claude Osteen threw me a fastball away and as I swung, I could feel the tendon tear a little bit more. The pain prevented me from taking a full come-around swing and I popped up to first base. My left arm went limp. It really hurt. I went up again and got a good pitch. I even thought I had a good chance of pulling it out, but it sunk at the fence. The way my shoulder feels as I'm getting ready to go to bed, I don't know when I'll hit again. I need the laughs we had before the doubleheader.

Duane Kuiper got a letter from Art Modell, saying, "Attached is my check in the net amount of $2, of which $1 is deducted, and fining you $1 for running out of the base line from the spectators' standpoint." Art can take a joke.

In the Joe Garagiola/Bazooka Big League Bubble Gum Blowing contest, Eric Raich blew an 18¼-inch bubble for the major-league lead. It was the silliest thing I've ever seen in a clubhouse, all the players cheering louder and louder as the bubble got bigger and bigger. Boog nudged me.

"I haven't seen this much fuss in a clubhouse," Boog said, "since we won the World Series in Baltimore."

It also was somewhat historic. Two females were in our clubhouse for the bubble-gum contest—Jackie York, our promotion director, and Marie Vidmar, a TV camerawoman. I knew Jackie would be there but I didn't know about the camerawoman until the security guard at the clubhouse door told me.

"There's a girl here," he said. "Can she come in?"

"She's working, right," I said. "Then let her in."

That's how I feel about females in the clubhouse. If she is a member of the working media, she has a right to come in. But she should have the decency to do her job and leave so that the players don't have to sit around for an hour waiting to take a shower, just as the players should have the decency to cover themselves.

Cleveland, Thursday, August 28

Off-day, and Barbara and the kids flew back to Los Angeles to get ready for school. After seeing them off, I thought of the time they came out to the airport to pick me up from a road trip. I was antsy because they arrived a few minutes late. Barbara apologized but Nini just looked at me.

"Daddy," she said, "it didn't kill you to wait for us."

Another time, when I was leaving on a road trip, she looked at me and shook her head.

"Daddy," she said, "you just come home to get your clothes washed."

At times like that I think Nini is raising me, instead of the other way around. But as much as I was away, Barbara and the kids seemed to have a good time because the Keatings were so nice. And their three kids—Kelly, Eddie, and Karen —are close to our kids' ages. Around our apartment, there weren't many other kids for them to play with, but Nini took swimming lessons and Kevin joined a motorcycle club. More important to me, Kevin took a big interest in baseball for the first time. He usually went to the ball park with me. Even when I had to go downtown early, I had my orders.

"Don't forget," he would say, "to come back and get me before you go to the ball park."

When the game started, he would join his mother and sister in my box behind home plate. Being the manager's wife made it tough on Barbara because she couldn't socialize with the other players' wives as she had in Cincinnati, Baltimore, Los Angeles, and Anaheim ever since we were married. Soon after she arrived in June, she was at a game when Carol Hendrick stopped by to say hello. They talked for a few minutes, then Carol excused herself.

"I better not stay," Carol said. "The other wives might not like it."

Barbara didn't agree. She thought she could maintain a relationship with the other wives. But then the Johnny Ellis situation developed.

"I guess it's better," Barbara told me, "that I don't get to know the wives too well."

Instead, she got to be great friends with Carol Keating, which was perfect because Ed and Carol aren't part of the ball club. At least it was perfect except for the day when I was on the road and Barbara drove the kids over to Carol's house. When she parked the Mercedes, she left the sunroof and the windows open. When a thundershower struck, she remembered. Too late. She and Carol bailed out the Mercedes and dried it up inside. But she didn't tell me about it until a few weeks later when we were winning.

I was a little upset. But like Nini might say, getting my Mercedes all wet inside didn't kill me. Nini is raising me pretty well.

Cleveland, Friday, August 29

We beat the Twins tonight, 9–6, on Rick Manning's grand slam after the manager conned an intentional walk. With a 5–4 lead, Alan Ashby led off the eighth with a single and Frank Duffy doubled. With first base open and lefthander Vic Albury pitching, I pinch-hit for Duane Kuiper, assuming that the Twins would order me walked intentionally. I also assumed that the Twins didn't know that my shoulder wouldn't let me swing the bat. But the Twins didn't order me walked. On the first pitch, Albury fired his fastball. I thought I'd outsmarted myself. But when the fastball missed for ball one, Frank Quilici decided to put me on. Rick followed with his grand slam, his first in the major leagues. But in the Kangaroo Kourt later, he was fined $1 for hotdogging it around the bases. I was running ahead of him, so I didn't watch him but the other players were laughing about the way he was timing his trot to step on each base in stride.

It takes practice to develop a home-run trot. Most of all, it takes home runs. I might run around the bases faster than anybody who hit a lot of homers. My thinking was to get around the bases and get off the field.

Hank Aaron always was smooth, trotting with his elbows up. Of course he's had more opportunity to work on his trot than anybody else has ever had. Willie Mays would look at his homers as he ran down the first-base line. Or sometimes he would run hard to first, round the bag, and then go into his trot. Mickey Mantle liked to watch his homers. Harmon Killebrew sometimes would stay in the batter's box, drop his bat, and watch it go out. Stan Musial acted like he was embarrassed. He trotted with his head down. Some hitters trot too slowly, especially those who don't hit many homers. Curt Blefary was the slowest I ever saw. With the Orioles once, he must have taken 25 seconds. He really overdid it. But young players sometimes don't know how to trot. I remember Vada Pinson running around the bases as a rookie almost as fast as if it had been an inside-the-park homer.

"Learn how to act those things out," I kidded him later. "Or else don't hit them."

Vada learned, just as Rick Manning will. All hitters want to learn a home-run trot. I don't think Rick will ever be a big home-run hitter. But as he fills out and gets stronger, he should hit maybe 15 to 20 a year. More important, he's going to be a dependable .300 hitter. He's a delight to watch. He's a throwback to the old-timers. He enjoys playing baseball. He doesn't ask for a rest like some young players do. I can't understand how a young player can get tired playing baseball. They don't really need a rest. They just think they do because they surrender to a slump instead of fighting their way out of it. And some young players don't get the proper sleep. Just because they're on the road, they think they have to go out on the town.

Rick Manning doesn't ask for a rest. He wants to play. You can see that in his exuberance on the field. But in the clubhouse he's a quiet, friendly kid. Except that tonight he was a little excited after his first grand slam. Even if he hasn't developed a home-run trot.

Cleveland, Saturday, August 30

Our twi-nighter with the Twins was rained out. We've got a doubleheader tomorrow but they don't come back here and we don't go to Minnesota again. If it rains again tomorrow, as forecast, we'll be wiped out of all three games, which means we can't play any more than 159 games, three short of the full schedule. Watching the rain outside Phil's office, I talked with him about Steve Kline, the righthanded pitcher who needed surgery for a torn Achilles tendon last winter and hasn't been able to pitch all season. Phil calls him the Phantom because he shows up whenever he wants to, then disappears whenever he wants to. Now he wants to play winter ball in the Caribbean but he feels betrayed because Phil can't get him a job.

"I'd love him to pitch winter ball," Phil said, "but I don't know if he can."

"That's what I told him," I said. "And he told me he'd go down there for nothing. I told him, 'Now you're really making a mistake, you know how expensive things are.' But then I told him if he shows you he can pitch, I know you'll try."

"I will try," Phil said. "Nobody wants him to pitch more than I do."

But if he can pitch and a job opens up, I hope the Phantom can be found.

Cleveland, Sunday, August 31

In my office, Cy Buynak hung a uniform with number 40 on the back. Very funny.

I turned forty today and Barbara and the kids phoned to make sure the big birthday cake arrived in the clubhouse. She had ordered it before she left. She and the kids wished me a happy birthday. My big present was a gift-wrapped box of Geritol, a denture cleaner, Preparation H, a tube of Ben Gay, some Ex-Lax, and an arthritis painkiller. I'll probably never know for sure, but it's something Trudy Hargis would do. And some of the players enjoyed kidding me about my old age.

"Now we know why you got Reynolds," somebody said. "To issue him number 40 so you don't have to wear it."

My number is 20 but when I joined the Indians last season, George Hendrick was wearing it. That was all right with me. As far as I was concerned, he had it first. But he offered it to me.

"If you want 20, you can have it," George said. "You deserve it more than I do."

"I really appreciate that," I said. "But it's your number. I'll take it only if you want me to have it."

"I want you to have it," he said.

He kidded me about it ever since. Every so often I'll hear his voice behind me.

"That number would look better on my back," he'll say.

"With a body like that?" I'll say. "You got to be kidding."

"People are always comparing me to you," he'll say. "I should be wearing that number."

"You couldn't carry my glove."

And then we'll both laugh. I like to needle players. People who don't know me think I'm very insulting sometimes. But that's just my sense of humor. Early in the season I think some of my players didn't realize that. All they knew was that I was the boss and they took me seriously. But now they know when I'm joking. I also know which guys to joke with. Ed Crosby has a sense of humor on the same wavelength as mine. So do Boog, LaRoche, Eckersley, Manning, and Kuiper. I've been on Kuiper lately because he has his knee taped up like a mummy.

"I thought you were tough," I told him the other day. "I didn't know you were a candy ass."

He wanted to cut the tape off right there. He wasn't too sure that time if I was kidding or not. I've learned to be careful who I kid with. John Lowenstein has a great sense of humor but it's dry, it's different than what Barbara calls "my biting humor." I tried to kid John a few times and he just stared at me. I know better than to needle Duffy or Buddy because they're too sincere. And as outgoing as Rico is, I never really know what he's thinking so I don't needle him. All this has been part of my education as a manager. If you're a manager, you can't ever be too old to learn. And for a manager, his fortieth birthday is almost a kindergarten age.

But the birthday present I really wanted today, a sweep of the Twins, never had a chance to materialize. We get rained out again. Now we've lost the opportunity to play three games with the Twins because we don't go to Minnesota again. The way we're playing, we might have won all three. That could prevent us from finishing third and finishing at or above the .500 mark.

And when we arrived in Baltimore tonight, it was still raining.

Baltimore, Monday, September 1

In the morning, we got the word that our big Labor Day doubleheader with the Orioles had been rained out. But I had my own doubleheader—two full-course dinners within about two hours. Boog probably could have handled them with a few hamburgers in between, but I'm not a big eater. I went over to Marci and Buzzy Kolodney's house in the afternoon and they celebrated my birthday by ordering Chinese food. Their children, Jill and Ricky (whose birthday also was yesterday), enjoyed the feast. And then I went over to see Linda and Gordon Schwartz and their children—Barbara, Craig, and Howard—without realizing that they planned to have dinner at an Italian restaurant. Just to be polite, I ordered veal parmigiana.

"Spaghetti comes with that," the waiter said.

"I think I'll skip the spaghetti," I said.

Baltimore, Tuesday, September 2

We finally got to play again. We lost the opener to the Orioles, 3–2, but Jim Bibby pitched an eight-hitter with no walks in winning the second game, 2–1. Bibby needed Dave LaRoche to get the final out. But ever since Jeff Torborg helped Bibby improve his slider, he's looked like an altogether different pitcher. In the opener, Dennis Eckersley had to leave after six innings because a blister had broken on his middle finger. I didn't want to take a chance on him tearing up his finger and missing the rest of the season. We lost when Bob Reynolds asked for trouble by walking Don Baylor to open the tenth inning. Bobby Grich singled for the winning run.

But the Oriole who beat us was Brooks Robinson with four big plays. Big for any other third baseman, but for Brooks three of them were somewhat routine. In the tenth he bare-handed John Lowenstein's topped grounder and threw him out —for Brooks, that's like brushing his teeth, he does it every day. The same inning he backhanded Boog's liner over the bag. In the ninth he dove into the hole for Buddy Bell's liner, another typical great play. But in the eighth Brooks did something I never saw him do before, and I played with him five years. He dove to his left to stop Rico's one-hop shot and sprawled on his knees with his body facing left-centerfield. Still on his knees, he somehow turned his torso toward first base and threw Rico out.

In the dugout I just stared. When he made the play on Buddy in the next inning, I applauded. Brooks is the best third baseman I've ever seen. Old-timers talk about Pie Traynor and I'm sure he was good, but Pie Traynor couldn't have played third base better than Brooks Robinson does. No way.

Milwaukee, Wednesday, September 3

Before the ball game tonight, I had a short meeting. Coming over from Baltimore, some ballplayers were boisterous on the plane, shouting at the stewardesses, playing their tape recorders too loud. Nothing serious, but I wanted to head it off before it got worse. It's easy to be boisterous when you're winning. And our magic charm did it again. Fritz Peterson beat the Brewers, 11–3, with help from Bob Reynolds the last three innings. Afterward I told Bob Sudyk that I have decided I wanted to come back as a manager. The reason I told him goes back several weeks when he asked me about returning next year.

"I don't know," I said, "if I want to come back."

"When you know," he asked me, "will you tell me?"

In recent days Russ Schneider had been asking me the same type question but in a different way. Russ wanted to know if I had been asked to come back. I felt that wasn't a question for me to answer. That was for Ted Bonda and Phil Seghi to answer. But the Sudyk question, in my mind, was different. It involved whether I *wanted* to come back.

I felt that I owed it to Sudyk to answer his question.

"I don't know how you want to handle this," I told him tonight, "but I told you I'd tell you when I came to a decision. I want to come back and manage next season if they'll have me."

"Have they met with you?" he asked.

"We meet all the time," I said. "I talk to Phil every day, you know that. He and Bonda have asked me if I want to come back."

"Can I speculate on it?" he asked.

"You can do anything you want," I said. "Just don't quote me on it."

Milwaukee, Thursday, September 4

Phil was on the phone from Cleveland early. Ted Bonda had called Phil after seeing Sudyk's story in the *Press*.

"Did you see the paper?" Phil asked me.

"How am I going to see the paper?" I said. "I'm in Milwaukee."

"He quotes you as saying you'll be back."

"He quotes me!" I said. "Read it to me."

"He quotes you as saying, 'I have met with Ted Bonda and Phil Seghi and they indicated they wanted me to continue. I have decided I would like to come back and continue managing. I only made up my mind about it recently. I've been mulling it over in my mind for weeks. For a while I wasn't certain I wanted to return.' These are the only quotes he uses."

"I asked him not to quote me," I said. "I told him I had decided I wanted to come back. I told him he could speculate. But specifically, I told him not to quote me."

Not long after that Russ Schneider of the *Plain Dealer* phoned me. I denied the quotes that Sudyk had attributed to me. But that's all I denied. I didn't deny Sudyk's story as such. I didn't deny that I was invited to return. I didn't deny that I was willing to return. I only denied the quotes. But that was enough for Schneider, because he enjoys putting it to Sudyk anytime he can. Sudyk didn't enjoy my denial. After we beat the Brewers, 10–5, for Roric Harrison's seventh win, I was walking into the Marc Plaza Hotel when Sudyk asked me to have a drink with him. He was upset that I had denied the quotes he attributed to me.

"It's the worst attack I've ever had on my integrity," he said.

"I didn't deny your story," I said. "I just denied the quotes. I told you that you could speculate, but I asked you not to quote me."

"Well, it's out of my hands now."

"What do you mean, it's out of your hands now?"

"My editors are dealing with this," he said.

"As far as I'm concerned," I said, "it's over."

I got up and went up to my room. To me, it is over. To me, the most important thing that happened today was not Bob Sudyk's story. The most important thing was winning our 12th game in the last 16, our 3rd in a row. And now we've got a 4-game series against the Tigers starting in Cleveland tomorrow.

Cleveland, Friday, September 5

Bob Sudyk apparently isn't talking to me now. But that's more of a problem for him than it is for me. He's got to cover the ball club and I don't see how he can cover it properly if he doesn't talk to the manager. But tonight there wasn't much to talk about. We lost to the Tigers, 11–2, the *Tigers*—one game I really want to forget. I was hoping for a sweep of this 4-game series and now we've got to win the next 3. But the Yankees lost a doubleheader to the Orioles, so we're only 3 games out of third place.

Cleveland, Saturday, September 6

Now we're only 2 games out of third place. The Yankees lost again after Dennis Eckersley stopped the Tigers, 4–2, for his 11th win. The kid had a three-run lead in the ninth, but with two on, one out, and Gates Brown announced as a pinch hitter, I brought in Dave LaRoche to lock it up. He did, but not without making things uncomfortable. To counteract LaRoche's lefthanded breaking stuff, Ralph Houk sent up Bill Freehan to hit for Brown and Freehan blooped a single, loading the bases. LaRoche walked John Veryzer, forcing in one run. But then he got the final two outs. The last out was a sinking liner by Billy Baldwin that Rick Manning caught on the run.

"You always make it hairy," I told LaRoche later.

Eckersley's earned-run average is down to 2.35, second to Jim Palmer in the league. Almost as important, the kid didn't develop a finger blister like he did in Baltimore on Tuesday night. Sometimes blisters can become a chronic problem for a pitcher.

Cleveland, Sunday, September 7

We swept the Tigers, 7–2 and 9–0, moving to within 1½ games of third place and 8 games of second place. Nobody seems to believe me when I talk about the possibility of finishing second. We can do it if we stay hot and if the Orioles go into a slump. Nobody believed me when I talked about finishing at .500 but we're only three games under now, with a 67–70 record, including 15–5 since I blew my stack in Minnesota three weeks ago. I wish I had taped that oration for future use.

In the opener Tom Buskey worked the last three innings to save Jim Bibby's second straight win. Buskey looked like he did before he hurt his back. George Hendrick and Oscar Gamble hit homers but the big play was Alan Ashby protecting the suicide squeeze in the sixth. Rico was running and when Alan squared around to bunt too soon, Joe Coleman pitched high and outside. I thought Rico would be an easy out, but Alan reached up and fouled off the pitch. Then he singled to give us a 4–2 lead. Alan is a good bunter because he works at it. He knows how to deaden the ball by snapping the bat back, creating backspin. Another good bunter is Ed Crosby, our utility infielder. John Lowenstein is a good drag bunter. But those three are about our only good bunters. The others don't work at it. In batting practice, each hitter is supposed to lay down one bunt before taking his eight swings. But most of them don't take that one bunt seriously. George once bunted so carelessly, I had to get after him.

"Each time you don't lay down a good bunt," I said, "I'll subtract it from your swings."

He wound up with only two swings. Then he went to the outfield and sulked instead of taking any more bp. George isn't the only one who thinks bunting isn't important. But that protective bunt by Alan Ashby, even though it was foul, showed how important it can be. In the second game, Oscar hit a homer for the third straight game and Fritz pitched a ho-hum shutout for his twelfth victory, his eighth in a row. He had a five-run lead after the first inning but when we didn't score in the second and third, he stomped around the dugout before we batted in the fourth.

"C'mon, guys," Fritz said, "I'm not used to working with only a five-run lead."

Sure enough, we got three more runs that inning. We've got to keep Fritz happy.

Cleveland, Monday, September 8

To inspire the hitters, one of Fritz's uniform tops was hung in the dugout. It worked. We beat the Red Sox, 4–1, with three runs off Rick Wise in the fourth after Alan Ashby apparently had flied out to end the inning. As he swung, Alan's bat was tipped by Carlton Fisk's glove. Rico was on third, Oscar on first. I had Oscar running and when Fisk saw Oscar take off, he reached for the pitch and scraped Alan's bat with his glove. Bill Deegan, the plate umpire, immediately called interference, awarding Alan first base. Frank Duffy then singled for two runs, and when the ball got past Fred Lynn on a bad bounce in our messy outfield, Alan also scored. But it all developed because Oscar was running.

"When a runner is going," I reminded the players in the dugout, "you never know what will happen."

Even a catcher as good as Fisk can get too anxious. But if Oscar hadn't been running, the inning would have been over. John Lowenstein added a homer in the fifth and Don Hood pitched a seven-hitter for his sixth win. I'm starting to believe that lefthanders can beat the Red Sox easier than righthanders can, especially lefthanders who don't depend on a fastball. Lefthanders have an edge against Yaz, Fred Lynn, Cecil Cooper, and Denny Doyle, assuming Doyle stays in the lineup.

Of their righthanded hitters, Jim Rice is dangerous but Dwight Evans and Rick Burleson aren't real hitters yet and Rico Petrocelli isn't the hitter he used to be. Maybe this is the secret against the Red Sox the way it was against the Yankees, but the lefthander has to get his breaking ball over or the Red Sox will sit on his fastball. On my way back after the meeting at home plate with the umpires, an old guy who sits behind our dugout almost every game was yelling at me.

"How can you start Hood?" he was yelling. "You better get somebody warmed up."

I don't know his name but I know his face. He's a great old guy. He's always yelling but I enjoy him because he's never vicious. He's just trying to help me manage my ball club.

"You better get somebody warmed up right now," he yelled.

"Right now," I said, "before he throws the first pitch? I can't do that. It would shatter his confidence."

"All right," he agreed. "Let him throw one pitch."

As it turned out, I let Don Hood throw nine innings. I don't think the old guy objected.

Cleveland, Tuesday, September 9

On my way back after the meeting with the umpires at home plate tonight, the old guy was in good voice again.

"How can you start Waits?" he was yelling.

"You told me that about Hood last night," I said. "And look what happened."

"You were lucky. You won't be lucky two nights in a row."

But we were. Actually, we weren't lucky as much as Rick Waits was good. He pitched a five-hitter and we beat the Red Sox again, 3–2, in ten innings. He retired 20 of the last 21 batters. He threw mostly breaking balls, which again points up my theory that a lefthander can beat the Red Sox with breaking stuff. Our win developed when George Hendrick doubled, Buddy Bell was intentionally walked, and Alan Ashby singled off Bill Lee past Rick Burleson into left field. In the on-deck circle, Alan was looking over his shoulder, expecting me to send up a pinch hitter, but there was no reason to. Alan was batting only .221 but he's been one of our hottest hitters lately and that's what I go by. He's a switch-hitter who swings better lefthanded. Against Lee, he was batting righthanded but he got the winning run in. We're the only team in the league to have an edge on the Red Sox this season. They've just about got our division wrapped up with a 5-game lead on the Orioles, but we've beaten them 9 out of 14, with 4 in Boston the final weekend.

"I hope we've got it clinched," Don Zimmer, the Red Sox's third-base coach, told me tonight, "before that final weekend."

That's about the nicest compliment my ball club and I have had all season. We're now only 1 game under .500, with the Orioles coming in for a 3-game series. If we can sweep them, we'll be only 5 games out of second place. We're still 1½ games behind the Yankees for third place, but we play them 3 in Shea Stadium this weekend.

Cleveland, Wednesday, September 10

On the way to the ball park, Ed Keating and I stopped in Ted Bonda's office to talk with him and Phil about my two contracts next season. Ed is no longer with Mark McCormack's firm. He resigned to go into business for himself. In an amiable letter last week, I notified Mark's firm that I was terminating my contract. Ed and I have become good friends and I want him to continue to represent me. He had negotiated my $180,000 contract this season along with the fringe benefits like my furnished apartment, the use of the dealer's car from Quay Buick, and round-trip airfare from Los Angeles for Barbara and the kids. I knew I would have to take a big cut just to manage, but I was resigned to it. For openers, Ed and I had $80,000 in mind but we were willing to back off to $70,000 for a two-year contract. Before we talked numbers, I asked about two years.

"No way," Phil said. "It's against club policy."

"It's not against club policy for *you* to have a two-year contract as general manager," Ed said. "It wasn't against club policy for the Perry brothers to have two-year contracts."

"It's not club policy, Phil," I said. "It's your policy."

"If a one-year contract is good enough for Walter Alston," Phil said, "it should be good enough for Frank."

"What's your offer," Ed asked, "for one year?"

"We were thinking," Phil said, "of $75,000."

That was a pleasant shock. I had expected them to start somewhere between $50,000 and $65,000.

"How about $80,000?" Ed replied.

"That's no problem," Phil said.

I suddenly was among the highest-paid managers, up there with Alston, Ralph Houk, Dick Williams, Earl Weaver, and Gene Mauch. I don't know exactly what they make but I'm told they're all in the $80,000 bracket, give or take a few dollars. Then we began talking about the numbers if I also was the dh. Ed mentioned $200,000, plus the fringes, plus bonus clauses as manager based on attendance, where we finish, and won-lost percentage. They wanted to think that over, but I got the impression that Ted and Phil didn't have any strong objections. I did better in Ted's office than my ball club did in our twi-night doubleheader. We got to .500 by beating the Orioles in the opener, 7–1, with Dave LaRoche saving Dennis Eckersley's 12th win. But then we lost, 6–5, in thirteen innings. Charlie Spikes hit a two-run homer to give Jackie Brown a 2–1 lead, but in the thirteenth he misjudged Ken Singleton's liner to left field that set up their winning rally.

Charlie has had a difficult year. He got off bad and never really got going. But he's willing to listen. He took my suggestion to hold the bat straight up instead of parallel to the ground. He should be playing every day, but I've had to platoon him with Oscar and he understands. He's not a complainer. Things just seem to happen to Charlie Spikes, like misjudging that ball tonight.

Cleveland, Thursday, September 11

Forget about second place. We're now 9 games behind the Orioles after a 10–2 loss tonight. But we had a little excitement. Rico drilled a single off Jim Palmer's ankles in the fourth and Jim didn't like it. Pitchers never like it when you hit the ball back at them. They think you're aiming at them. You're really not, yet one of the basic theories of hitting is to try to hit the ball back through the pitcher's box. By the time Rico got to first, Jim was yelling at him and Rico was yelling back.

"Next time I bat," Rico shouted, "we see who is the better man."

Next time, Rico lined out to right but in the ninth he hit a shot over the leftfield fence for his 17th homer. That's my kind of hitter, somebody who's a better hitter when he's angry. I also had an angry pitcher. Larry Anderson, brought up from Oklahoma City last week, relieved Roric Harrison in the seventh, but after the Orioles got three hits off him in the eighth he threw a fastball up and in that Ken Singleton resented. Singleton put on a good act. He seemed to be telling himself, *I better take a couple of steps toward the mound . . . I better stop now because I don't see any of my teammates joining me . . . here come a few, I better take a few more steps . . . all right, that's far enough, they might think I really mean it . . . well, maybe a few more steps to make it look good . . . oh, oh, here comes Boog over from first base, I better stop before he takes me seriously.* But by then Singleton had almost everybody laughing at him.

"I wanted a piece of Anderson," he told the writers later. "But with Boog there, I suddenly realized we are going for a pennant. It would be dumb to get hurt."

Singleton isn't dumb, because the Orioles are still alive. They're 5 behind the Red Sox with more than two weeks left. We're 3 behind the Yankees with a 3-game series in New York beginning tomorrow night. We need a sweep.

New York, Friday, September 12

Tonight's rain-out created a twi-night doubleheader tomorrow. If we win both, we would be only one game behind the Yankees who obviously are concerned about protecting third place. They've announced Catfish Hunter as their starter Sunday with only two days' rest. Billy Martin likes to say, "Only first place is important," but he must think third place is important.

When the season started, the Yankees thought they had a shot at the pennant with Catfish Hunter and Bobby Bonds, but it hasn't worked out that way. Through no fault of Hunter and Bonds, because each has had a good year. Hunter is 21–13 with a 2.58 earned-run average and 28 complete games. Bonds has hit 26 homers and driven in 74 runs with a .268 average despite a bad knee. But the Yankees have had some injuries and some disappointments, especially Jim Mason and Sandy Alomar, their double-play combination. They don't want to be embarrassed anymore by having us drop them into fourth place. By using Hunter against us Sunday, they also will be able to start him next Friday night in Cleveland in the opener of a four-game series.

I'd probably do the same thing if I had Catfish Hunter available. He's some pitcher.

When he was a twenty-year-old righthander with the A's in Kansas City in 1966, the Orioles used to laugh at him because he was a junkball pitcher. He depended on offspeed stuff and his breaking ball. We couldn't understand a guy that age throwing junk. But in 1967, the year before the A's moved to Oakland, he started throwing more fastballs and hard sliders. That was the beginning of Catfish Hunter developing into a real pitcher. He's never been overpowering like Jim Palmer, and he doesn't have a real good breaking ball like Bert Blyleven, but he doesn't walk many people. He challenges you into swinging that bat. He moves the ball around with something on every pitch. He's a control pitcher but he's not the type that nibbles. He comes right at you. Even with two strikes and no balls, you better be ready to hit because the next pitch is going to be a strike. He knows the corners.

I'm flattered that the Yankees are starting him with two days' rest against us but I wish they weren't.

New York, Saturday, September 13

As we were getting into our uniforms for the doubleheader, I had a meeting with my coaches.

"I'm coming back as manager," I said, "and I want all of you back, if you want to return."

Almost like a chorus, they said, "Yeah, sure." I told them to talk to Phil about their contracts. Tom McCraw might have a problem because he wants to play next year, but I don't see how he can fit on our roster as a first baseman and pinch hitter. Being both a coach and a player, as he was early this season, makes it difficult for him to be ready. We also have a logjam at first base with Boog and Rico there. I want more balance next season. I'll be looking for a more useful player, maybe an infielder or an extra catcher who can also play other positions. But as a coach, Tom has been an excellent batting instructor. He's really helped Frank Duffy this year. He and Duffy got to be good friends last season before I got here and they're really close now. Next year I hope Tom also works with the other hitters as much. Harvey Haddix and Jeff Torborg have done a good job with the pitchers, especially in developing Dennis Eckersley and Rick Waits, straightening out Jim Bibby, and helping Dave LaRoche come into his own as a reliever. Dave Garcia has been a good third-base coach and a good example for the players. I wish each of the players did his job as completely and as efficiently as Dave Garcia does his.

In the doubleheader, Fritz pitched a five-hitter as we beat the Yankees in the opener, 7–1, his ninth in a row. But then we lost, 4–3, to drop 3 games behind them again. Tomorrow maybe Catfish Hunter won't have his control with only two days' rest.

New York, Sunday, September 14

Catfish wasn't as quick as he usually is. I thought we should have hit him better than we did. But he still pitched a typical Catfish game. He didn't beat himself. He left after seven innings but he got credit for the 6–2 win that I protested. George Maloney, the third-base umpire, called time with the ball still alive. Instead of getting one out, I thought we should have had a double play to end the first inning. Bobby Bonds was on third and Sandy Alomar on second when Thurman Munson grounded to Rick Waits, who trapped Bonds in a rundown.

We worked the rundown correctly, for a change, Alan Ashby running Bonds back to third. But by then, Alomar had come down to third and Ashby tagged him first. Bonds wandered off the base and Ashby tagged him but Maloney disallowed the double play.

"I called time," Maloney told me.

"The ball wasn't dead," I said.

"I wanted to stop the confusion."

But an umpire has no right to stop the flow of a play as long as the ball is alive. If the ball is dead, it's different. But the ball was still alive. That's why I protested. Some people didn't think it made any difference because the Yankees didn't score in that inning. But it made a big difference. If it's a double play, Graig Nettles leads off the second inning instead of following Munson in the first inning. That changes the entire complexion of the game. The loss dropped us 4 games out of third place and 3 games under the .500 mark. I know my protest is useless. I also know I'm right.

I guess T. J. O'Hays's arm hasn't come around. This was our only trip to New York that I didn't hear from him.

Detroit, Monday, September 15

Off-day here. I let a few players go back to Cleveland from New York last night, but it's a quick flight across Lake Erie and we don't play here until tomorrow night. I thought about spending the off-day in Cleveland, but as the manager I should be with my ball club. Like when I joined the Indians last year, I couldn't believe how Ken Aspromonte would let the players wander off on an off-day and how he would wander off himself. My first week, we had an off-day in Milwaukee during a road trip but Aspro and half the team didn't travel to Milwaukee with the rest of the ball club. That's asking for trouble.

Detroit, Tuesday, September 16

One of our radio-TV sponsors, Stroh's brewery, had a luncheon for the ball club at their plant. I didn't make it mandatory but about a dozen ballplayers went there with me. We had steaks, we met the executives, and we were given a tour of the brewery. I just wish it could have been arranged for yesterday when we were off. But we beat the Tigers tonight, 9–2, and the Yankees lost. We're only 3 games out of third place again. George Hendrick hit a three-run homer, Oscar Gamble hit a two-run homer, and Dennis Eckersley got his 13th win. I brought in Tom Buskey in the ninth, much to the kid's surprise. As soon as I got to the mound, he gave me a hard look.

"You're not taking me out, are you?"

I waved to the umpires to bring in Buskey and that really annoyed him.

"You got to be kidding," he said.

He's a great kid. He's not cocky but he is a competitor. He believes in his own ability. You don't always see that in young players now. He had so-so stuff tonight but he had a four-hit shutout until the ninth, when I took him out after two more hits. Winning with so-so stuff is the sign of a good pitcher.

Detroit, Wednesday, September 17

Damn it, we lost to the Tigers tonight, 4–0, to drop 4 games behind the Yankees and 3 games under the .500 mark. If we can't beat the Tigers, let's forget about third place. Roric Harrison got knocked out in the third. The Duke was getting his pitches high. He doesn't throw hard enough to get away with that. He's got to keep his stuff low. Joe Coleman kept his low and moved it around.

But to me, Coleman's catcher deserved the credit for the shutout. Terry Humphrey was the difference between the Joe Coleman we saw earlier this season and the Joe Coleman we saw tonight. That's why I consider an experienced catcher who's a good handler of pitchers to be one of our most important needs next year. Most fans don't understand how a good catcher helps a pitcher. John Roseboro was the best catcher I've seen. I didn't see that much of Roy Campanella and Yogi Berra when I was younger. I haven't seen that much of Johnny Bench because I've been in the American League most of the time since he came up. But of all the catchers I've known well, John Roseboro did the most things when he was the Dodgers' catcher. He knew the hitters' strengths and weaknesses. He knew how to set up a hitter. As a hitter, I always felt that it was a battle between me and John Roseboro, not me and the pitcher. When he gave a sign, the pitcher rarely shook him off. That's what I want—a catcher who controls the pitchers. Too many pitchers control the catcher now. You even see a young pitcher shaking off the catcher's signs. That didn't happen when John Roseboro was catching. He also was a good hitter and a tough catcher. He wasn't afraid to stick his body in there to block the plate when he had to. But most of all, John Roseboro was the kind of catcher I'd like to have.

I hadn't even wanted to discuss tonight's loss but I'm not giving up on third place. And my ballplayers better not give up.

Detroit, Thursday, September 18

We bounced back with a 2–1 win over the Tigers as Boog drove in both runs with his 24th homer and a sacrifice fly. Tom Buskey saved Jim Bibby's 5th victory since the trade by striking out Bill Freehan on three hard sliders for the final out. Dave LaRoche had pitched well but I couldn't let him pitch to Freehan in Tiger Stadium, the best ball park in the league for hitters. The ball just jumps out. I was hoping that the Tigers' manager, Ralph Houk, wouldn't go to Gates Brown as a pinch hitter for Freehan, and I was surprised when he didn't. Just as important was Duane Kuiper's diving stop of Dan Meyer's ground single. If the ball had gone into the outfield, the tying run would have scored. But that extra speed is why Duane Kuiper is my second baseman.

We've still got a shot at third place. We're 3½ games behind the Yankees and now we're going home for a 4-game series with them. We need a sweep. They've got Catfish ready for tomorrow night, but we've got Fritz ready.

Cleveland, Friday, September 19

Fritz won his 10th in a row, with help from both Buskey and LaRoche, and we beat Catfish tonight, 3–2, to pull within 2½ games of third place and 1 game of the .500 mark. We got all our runs in the third when Rico singled, Buddy singled, Ashby doubled, and Duffy singled. The only runs off Fritz came on two homers by Bobby Bonds, in the first and sixth.

Fritz has shown me he's a real pro, a great guy to have on the ball club. He's going great now but he's the same guy as when he was going bad earlier. Just give him the ball, that's all he asks. I wish I could give him the ball again tomorrow and again in both games of Sunday's doubleheader. But at least we'll throw our fans at them. Our fans were louder than ever tonight. There were only about 9,000 but they sounded like 90,000 the way they were yelling. Considering our bad start, the Cleveland fans have been great. It doesn't look like we'll draw a million, but with a good start we would have drawn well over a million. In a way, I'm glad we're finishing strong instead of starting strong. Through the years, the Indians have had a history of getting off good and folding. The trouble is, some fans don't take our strong finish seriously.

"It doesn't mean anything," I've heard people say. "The pressure's off now."

I don't buy that. The pressure is never off, especially when we're trying to catch the Yankees for third place. But unless you put a good start and a good finish together, you can't please everybody. If you get off to a good start and fold, they say you choked. If you get off to a bad start and then come on, they say it doesn't mean anything. But if I had a choice, I'd prefer the way it happened. For the front office, a good start is better for attendance. But for a manager, I think it's better for a ball club to come on after a bad start. It shows character and determination. It also shows that the ball club has something going for next season.

With an opportunity to move within 1½ games of third place tomorrow, Phil is on me to put myself in the lineup.

"You should be hitting against a lefthander like Rudy May," he said. "Put a little Novocaine in your shoulder. You'll be all right. You might win the game with one swing. Your shoulder will hold up."

Phil suddenly knows more about my shoulder than I do.

Cleveland, Saturday, September 20

We had 10,000 fans today but they didn't help. We lost to the Yankees, 4–1, wasting another chance to get to the .500 mark. The manager was the dh, at least the first two times around, but that didn't help either. I went along with Phil's suggestion to have Novocaine injected into my shoulder so I could hit against Rudy May, but I flied out to center, then took a called third strike. Now that the Novocaine has worn off, the shoulder hurts more than ever.

Don Hood pitched well, but not well enough. We might have had a big inning in the sixth but Larry McCoy, the plate umpire, killed us with a bad call. Trailing, 3–0, we had the bases loaded with one out when Rico topped a grounder to Chris Chambliss at first base. I was surprised when Chambliss tried for a force at home instead of making the easy play himself at first, because Frank Duffy had a good jump coming down from third. Duffy slid, beating the throw to Thurman Munson, but McCoy called him out. The manager argued that one strenuously.

"How could you call him out?" I yelled.

"The throw beat him," McCoy answered.

"But he was on his way up from the slide before Munson got the ball."

"The throw beat him," McCoy said.

I'm told that the TV replay clearly showed that Duffy had beaten the throw. That's when the TV replay should be used to monitor an umpire's decision. If that call had occurred early in the season, I'm sure I would have yelled loud and long and been ejected. But by now I've developed much more self-control. I've also learned that you can't win arguing with an umpire. Let him know that you think he missed the call and let it go at that. Maybe his conscience will bother him and he'll give you the benefit of the doubt next time. It seemed to work that way four pitches later when George Hendrick checked his swing on a 2-and-1 pitch. McCoy called it a ball and Billy Martin was all over him. Rudy May went on to walk George, forcing in Duane Kuiper with the only run we got that inning.

Not that I want an umpire to even up after a bad call. I'd rather have him make the correct call the first time, no matter which team it favors. Evening up creates more problems than it solves.

Cleveland, Sunday, September 21

We needed a sweep of the Yankees to move to within 2½ games of third place and to reach the .500 mark. We got a split.

Rick Waits won the opener, 3–2, with Rico getting four hits and Dave LaRoche getting his 17th save, tying the club record that Tom Buskey set last year. But we lost the second game, 11–5, because Dennis Eckersley didn't have it. That was my fault, not his. I started the kid with my heart instead of my head. The kid had a cold in Detroit, where the Tigers' team doctor gave him a penicillin shot. But his hands and feet became swollen, with a rash that looked like he had the hives—a bad reaction to the penicillin. I didn't want to start him today but he came into my office to show me that the swelling and the rash had pretty much disappeared.

"I'm all right," the kid insisted. "I want to pitch."

His competitive urge sold me. I love that, especially in young players. But his competitive urge wasn't enough. In the third Sandy Alomar and Roy White hit back-to-back homers to put the Yankees ahead, 3–1, and we were never in the game after that. I had to take him out in the fourth. He didn't give me an argument this time.

Our trainer, Jim Warfield, deserves a lot of credit for getting ballplayers back after an injury or an ailment. But next year I want to be more fully informed about how doctors treat my ballplayers.

I'm not going to tell a doctor what to do, but I want to know what they're going to do *before* they do it, not after. Sometimes a pitcher might be given a cortisone shot when he's scheduled to pitch the next day. Now he can't pitch for two or three days. If the shot can be delayed, I would prefer to wait until after he was scheduled to pitch. That way, the two or three days he has to miss because of the shot would be part of his normal rest.

Cleveland, Monday, September 22

We had a team meeting to vote on our third-place bonus shares—if we finish third. It won't come to much, maybe $350 for a full share. And realistically, most of the ballplayers, even the manager, doubted that third place will materialize now that we failed to sweep the Yankee series. Maybe that's why everybody was generous in tossing full shares around. If we were voting on real World Series shares, which last year came to more than $22,000 for the A's and nearly $16,000 for the Dodgers, the ballplayers would have been more strict and less liberal. When it's big money, it's different. I remember the Orioles in 1970 when I couldn't convince enough players to award even $200 to Don Baylor, who had joined us in September.

"It comes to less than $10 a man," I said. "This kid is going to help us someday."

"The ball club called him up to look at him," Eddie Watts said. "We didn't need him."

About the only crackdown in our meeting developed over the ballplayers who were with us early in the season. Gaylord and Jim Perry and Dick Bosman were cut out, although Bos will be getting an A's share. But maybe the thought of the extra $350 inspired us tonight. We rallied to beat the Brewers, 7–6, on Oscar Gamble's two-run pinch-single in the ninth for Tom Buskey's fifth win. Tom deserved it after holding the money meeting. He recently succeeded Buddy Bell as our player rep. But we had a scare just before Oscar's winning hit when Rico was beaned by Tom Murphy, the Brewers' reliever. His helmet saved him. He walked off the field but he was groggy.

"I'm dizzy," he told me. "The left side of my face is numb. I can't hear much out of my left ear."

He went for X-rays as a precaution. But the doctors don't think it's serious. I hope not. Rico has had enough problems—tuberculosis, shoulder separations, a bad knee. He's one of the big reasons we're now only 2½ games out of third place, after the Yankees lost. We're also only 1 game under the .500 mark again. But we almost blew it because of a missed sign. Alan Ashby missed a suicide-squeeze sign in the eighth and George Hendrick, running on the pitch, was an easy out at the plate.

"What happened?" I asked Alan later.

"No excuse," he said. "I missed it."

For his honesty, I won't fine him. But his mistake kept the score at 5–5, and then George Scott hit a homer in the ninth to put the Brewers ahead before Duane Kuiper walked and Boog singled to get our winning rally going. After the game Phil came down to tell me that he and Ed Keating had settled my contracts for next season—$80,000 as the manager, $200,000 if my shoulder lets me be the dh. Plus the fringe benefits and the manager's bonus arrangements that could earn me nearly $250,000 if we win the World Series.

"We're announcing it tomorrow morning," Phil said. "Try to get to my office by nine."

"Nine o'clock," I said. "You know I never get up until noon. I'll never make it."

Phil just puffed on his pipe and walked out. He knows I'll be there.

Cleveland, Tuesday, September 23

I tried but I was still about 20 minutes late. Not that I was missed. By the time I got to Phil's office, he had read the ball club's mimeographed announcement that I had been rehired with a one-year contract. That's all it was—an announcement, not really a news conference. Only about four writers were there, including Russ Schneider, but Bob Sudyk was back at his office. He's still not talking to me. After a while a photographer, a TV camera crew, and a radio newsman with a tape recorder showed up. I had some fun with the radio guy.

"If you were Phil Seghi," he asked me, "would you have rehired Frank Robinson?"

"If I was Phil Seghi," I said, "there is no way I would rehire Frank Robinson as the manager of the Cleveland Indians."

"Why?"

"The Indians finished fourth last year and they'll finish fourth again this year. The Indians did nothing the first half of the season. We started to win a few ball games now. But that's like being on a banana peel, sliding around and going no place. It just goes to show you again about *those people*. They can't handle responsibility."

I couldn't help comparing the casual scene surrounding today's announcement with the mob scene at the big news conference last year when I was hired—the commissioner, the president of the American League, sportswriters from all over, several TV cameras.

I like it better this way. I'm just another manager now, a manager who has been rehired because his bosses thought he had done a good job. To me, being rehired is more important than being hired last year. And now that I was rehired, I was back in Phil's office with my coaches in the afternoon to go over the ball club for next year. My coaches and I feel that a good catcher is our primary need, then a big hitter who can be depended on to drive in 100 runs. Johnny Bench would be ideal as both the catcher and the rbi man. But the Reds aren't about to trade him. Another catcher who might do both is Joe Ferguson if the Dodgers made him available. Phil feels that pitching is our big need, then an infielder who can play shortstop when Duffy needs a rest. I think Phil wishes Johnny Ellis was catching more. Before and after my trouble with Ellis developed, Phil kept talking about how Ellis had hit .291 and knocked in 59 runs last year.

"But that was last year," I told Phil several times. "He was able to get away with anything last year. He did whatever he wanted."

Tom McCraw had told me that Dave Duncan would go to Ellis and tell him, "If you catch all the time, you'll get tired and you won't be able to hit. You better ask the manager to put you at first base." Duncan knew that if Ellis was playing first, he would be catching. McCraw knew about it because that was Ken Aspromonte's explanation for taking him off first base and putting Ellis there. Ellis also was able to take early batting practice without any supervision. I wanted it supervised and he couldn't accept that.

"Ellis is like Gaylord, always making little comments here and there, little digs," I often told Phil. "He's not good for the ball club."

In our meeting today, Phil got to talking about Ellis again, about how he couldn't be *that* bad for the ball club. Phil even wondered why he hadn't been catching more lately.

"He's still got his hamstring," I told him.

"He's not on my injury report," Phil said.

"He's on mine," I said. "And he's also told me that he can't play yet."

My quietest coach, Dave Garcia, spoke up.

"Ellis is a bad person to have on your ball club," Dave said. "He'll come off the trainer's table and tell Tom McCraw he can't play, then he'll walk over to me and he'll say, 'I can play, I'm ready.' That type of thing."

"If he's healthy," I said, "I'd be using him."

I was really annoyed. After the meeting, I went downstairs and checked my injury reports. Somehow he had been left off the last report. I took all the injury reports with Ellis's name on them and went back upstairs to Phil's office.

"Here, here, here," I said, showing him the sheets. "Ellis, Ellis, Ellis."

Phil believed me now. I was just disappointed that he thought I hadn't been using John for personal reasons. Overall my relationship with Phil has been smooth. It's not perfect. Nothing's perfect. Ever since we got Jim Bibby and Jackie Brown in the Gaylord deal, Phil has been wondering why they didn't pitch more often. In the meeting today, he was talking about Jackie, saying, "We've got a pitcher who won 13 games last year, why isn't he pitching more?" As he was talking, he was staring at the coaches.

"Don't look at the coaches," I said. "Look at me. I'm the manager. I'm the one who's not using him."

I hadn't used Jackie that much because when we got him he wasn't the pitcher I had hit against last year. His curveball wasn't the same. But in the bullpen Jeff Torborg got him to drop to a three-quarter overhand motion on his curveball and got him to keep his shoulder closed longer. Jeff also helped Bibby get straightened out. Bibby and Brown each will be better next year, but I'm not going to use Bibby like the Rangers did when he won 19 and lost 19 last year. I would rather have him with a 17–9 record.

As smooth as my overall relationship with Phil has been, next year I want to be told more about what's going on in the front office. I want to know more about the farm system. I want to know more about what players we're drafting.

Like the day we drafted Rick Cerone, the kid catcher from Seton Hall, nobody asked me to sit in. Nobody showed me a list of prospects. Nobody even told me we had drafted Cerone until one of the writers mentioned it to me. Nobody told me he was coming in for a workout before he reported to Oklahoma City until Jeff told me the kid was in the clubhouse. Nobody brought him into my office to introduce him to me. Nobody told me he was going on the road with us for a few days. Nobody told me he went to Oklahoma City until after he left. Maybe next year I'll be told things like that.

Instead, it seems like I'm always told things that I could care less about, like Eric Raich being in the American League final of Joe Garagiola's bubble-gum blowing contest before tonight's game.

Eric blew a 17-inch bubble but Kurt Bevacqua of the Brewers won with a 17½-inch bubble to qualify for the World Series blowoff against the National League winner. I'm just as pleased. When my players go to the World Series, they all will go. To play in it.

And tonight we beat the Brewers, 4–3, in the ninth on George Hendrick's 24th homer. Boog had hit his 26th in the third for our other three runs. Roric Harrison pitched well into the eighth but George's homer gave Dave LaRoche his fifth win.

George has had a strange season. He's got 24 homers and 86 runs batted in with a .264 average. Not bad, but I'm beginning to think that outsiders have expected too much from him.

I've heard people say that George should hit .320, drive in 110 runs, hit 35 homers. Since he hasn't, he hasn't fulfilled his potential. But maybe George just doesn't have that much potential. I saw Vada Pinson go through that. He was supposed to be "the next .400 hitter" and unless he hit .350, he wasn't fulfilling his potential. But if Vada Pinson gets 3,000 hits, I wonder if people will think he fulfilled his potential. George might be the same type. He's not a .264 hitter, I know that. He should be up around .280 at least. With his casual style, he's never going to look like a hustler. George is just going to be George, nobody's ever going to change him. I've been told, "If he doesn't play for you, he won't play for anybody." But he has played for me. And he's played when he was hurt. Once he had a bad leg but he knew Boog had a bad shoulder.

"I want to stay in," George told me, "because Boog is out. We can't both be out."

George has played for me. He just hasn't played like some people expected him to play. Maybe those people were expecting too much of him, and maybe I was too. But that homer tonight was sweet. We're now only 2 games behind the Yankees, who got rained out. We're at the .500 mark with a 77–77 record, and we've got another game with the Brewers tomorrow night, our last at home. We've got Fritz ready to win that one.

Cleveland, Wednesday, September 24

Third place just isn't meant to be. Fritz had won 10 in a row but the Brewers jumped on him for two in the first, then George Scott hit a three-run homer in the second and we were on the way to a 10–3 loss. It dropped us 2½ games behind the Yankees, who got rained out again. It also dropped us 1 game under the .500 mark before we finish with 4 in Boston, beginning tomorrow night. If we had won tonight, a split in the Red Sox series would give us an 80–79 record. Now we've got to win 3. But we've handled the Red Sox all season, even if they are about to clinch the AL East title.

Our loss tonight ended our home season on a sour note. We had opened with a crowd of 56,000 but we didn't have even 6,000 tonight. The season total was 977,039, disappointing to Ted Bonda and the other owners.

I'm told the ball club will lose about $500,000 this year.

But he never made a big issue out of attendance with me. He mentioned it only once, in connection with our radio-TV contract. The higher we finish this season, the higher the rights sell for next season. But we made history tonight. We had a bat girl, seventeen-year-old Marcie McGee, the first girl to play on an Ohio high school varsity. I knew most of the players would be on their best behavior but I also knew they might forget she was there.

"You might hear some bad language," I warned her.

"I've probably heard worse in school," she said.

Even so, I asked Marcie to sit on a chair next to our dugout when the Brewers were up. Some players hardly noticed her. About the fifth inning Rico, who wasn't playing and who had been sitting at the other end of the dugout, suddenly stared at her as if she were a ghost.

"That's a girl," he said. "That's girl."

After that Rico stared at her every few minutes and shook his head.

"I don't believe it," he would say. "I don't believe it."

But like all of us, he realized that Marcie was doing a good job. She really hustled to pick up the bats and retrieve the batting helmets. Our bat boy, Mike Moulder, didn't appreciate Marcie taking his job, especially since it was his last game. He'll be going to college next year. Somebody suggested to me that Mike could sit in the radio booth tonight but I wanted him around in case Marcie had any problems.

"You sit in the dugout," I told him. "You're part of this ball club."

Mike liked that. And he deserved it. He did a good job all season.

In another bit of history, I might have seen Hank Aaron swing a bat for the last time. I hope so. He got two singles but he's hitting .231 and he hit only 12 homers this season—745 for his career. He looks like a guy who's through. His hand-speed at forty-one just isn't as quick as it used to be. He sits on the fastball now. When he gets a breaking ball, he doesn't react the way he used to. Not playing the outfield, just being the dh, his body isn't as sharp as it used to be. It shows in his bat. On a fastball, you can see the old Hank, but on a breaking ball he looks bad. I hope I know enough to stop playing before I look bad.

As for the national impact of my rehiring, I got one congratulatory telegram—from a high school teammate, Joe Jacobs, who lives in Los Angeles now. What a difference a year makes.

Boston, Thursday, September 25

All season none of my ballplayers had challenged my rule that "moustaches are fine, but no other facial hair will be permitted." I noticed last night that Jim Bibby had a heavy stubble but I assumed that he just hadn't shaved. On the plane from Cleveland today, the stubble was thicker.

"By the time we get to the ball park," I told him, "I want that off."

"Just three more days," he said. "Can't I keep it for just three more days? It'll give me a good start on my winter beard."

"I want it shaved off."

"I don't have a razor."

"Then buy one," I said.

But we never got to Fenway Park tonight. Hurricane Eloise rained us out early, creating a twi-night doubleheader tomorrow. For the Red Sox, the magic number is 4 to clinch the AL East, meaning any combination of 4 Red Sox victories and Oriole defeats. For us, the magic number also is 4, meaning if we sweep the series we'll surely finish above the .500 mark and we'll still have a chance to finish third.

Boston, Friday, September 26

We got wiped out of both finishing third and finishing above .500 when we lost a doubleheader to the Red Sox tonight. Luis Tiant shut us out on four hits, 4–0, then Reggie Cleveland shut us out on five hits, 4–0.

Maybe the guys enjoyed themselves too much last night after the rain-out. Whatever the reason, we were flat. Tiant outpitched Dennis Eckersley, who finished with a 13–7 record and a 2.59 earned-run average. The kid gets my vote as the rookie pitcher of the year. Tiant was Tiant, pitching from all angles for his 18th win. In his windup he looks at center field or up at the sky, sometimes at both. That windup fools some hitters because they're watching his head instead of the ball. But his head doesn't deliver the ball, his right hand does.

"Watch his hand," I kept reminding our hitters. "Not his head."

But that's easier said than done, especially when Luis has his best stuff. To show how smart he is, Tiant was keeping the ball lower than usual to create grounders and prevent fly balls into the fog that rolled into Fenway Park from right field. The fog was so bad that the outfielders sometimes couldn't see fly balls. George told me that he couldn't always see the batter from right field. Oscar got a headache squinting in left field to pick up the ball. I complained to Bill Haller, the plate umpire, about the fog but he referred me to Marty Springstead, the crew chief.

"I can see the ball," Marty said.

"But you're not in the outfield," I said. "You're at first base."

"It's the same for both teams."

When it's raining, it's the same for both teams but the umpires stop the game.

Boston, Saturday, September 27

Before today's game I called some players into my office, one by one, to talk about next year.

I told Buddy Bell I wanted him to trim down to between 195 and 190 and to firm up. He was about 202 most of the season. But less weight will make it easier on his knee. He's still not convinced his knee is all right. He takes bp and infield without it being wrapped but then he has it wrapped before the game starts. Even so, he finished well. His average is up around .270, with 58 runs batted in and 10 homers. Not bad considering his poor start. As we talked, he apologized for telling me in June that he couldn't play for me.

"I'm glad," he said, "you didn't take me seriously."

"I did take you seriously," I said. "I didn't get mad at you but I took you seriously."

"Well," he said, "I've enjoyed playing for you."

I also talked to Boog and Charlie Spikes about their weight. Boog is up around 270 but I want him at 255, which he can carry.

"I'll watch myself," he said.

Charlie is up to 246 but I want him at 220.

"I'll be 218," he assured me.

I told Charlie I was sorry I hadn't played him more but that we had too many outfielders.

"No promises," I said, "but we'll try to clear that up."

I congratulated Rico on his great year—.308 with 64 runs batted in and 18 homers in fewer than 400 at-bats. He seems to be over his beaning.

"I can play," he said.

"Relax," I told him.

I talked to Don Hood about how he can be an important pitcher. I talked to Duane Kuiper about how playing winter ball in Venezuela can help him be a better second baseman and a better leadoff man next season.

"Don't go down there for a vacation," I said. "Go down there and work on your drag bunting and your stealing. Polish your tools."

I talked to Jim Bibby about how he had come along in the last few weeks and that I expected him to be a big winner next season. And then I realized that he hadn't shaved off that growth of beard. I had forgotten about it last night. I hadn't even seen him last night. He went down to the bullpen early. Maybe to hide.

"You didn't shave it off, did you?" I said.

"No," he said, shrugging and looking away.

"You're just going to defy me on it?" I said.

"I'm not defying you," he said. "I just want a beard for the winter and I want to get it started."

"I told you to shave it off."

"Then do what you have to do."

That's a ballplayer's way of saying, if you want to fine me, fine me. He probably thought I wouldn't fine him because the last paychecks have been prepared. I knew that Mike Seghi, our traveling secretary and Phil's son, would know about the checks.

"Have the checks been made out?" I asked Mike.

"They've been run through the computer," he said. "Why?"

"I want to fine one player."

"We can run his check back through the computer."

"No problem?"

"No," he said.

"Then take $300 out of Bibby's check."

"$300?" he said.

"$300," I said.

I had to do it. I knew the other ballplayers had seen him and if I didn't fine him, some of them might be tempted to test me next year. I don't enjoy taking a player's money but sometimes I have to, especially when a player challenges a rule. I don't think of it as me fining a player. To me, the player fines himself. He knows the rules. If he doesn't go by the rules, he's fining himself. He should have more pride than that. Speaking of pride, we got our pride as a team back today when Rick Waits stopped the Red Sox, 5–2, to become the only lefthanded starter to win in Fenway Park all year. If the Red Sox had won, they would have clinched the AL East— and they had the champagne on ice. As it turned out, they clinched anyway because the Yankees swept a doubleheader from the Orioles, but they had to wait nearly three hours after our game to celebrate.

We had a team party too. With the more than $500 in our Kangaroo Kourt kitty, we blew it on drinks and food in one of the Sheraton Boston's meeting rooms. No curfew tonight.

Boston, Sunday, September 28

The season's over. We creamed the Red Sox, 11–4, as Alan Ashby hit a grand slam and Joe Lis hit a two-run homer. We led both leagues in homers with 153, but we hit 91 with the bases empty. Nobody enjoys a homer more than I do but if they don't come at the right time they are not that important. Not getting the big hit at the right time is one reason why we finished with a 79–80 record. If we had played those three games with the Twins that got rained out four weeks ago, we probably would have been over the .500 mark. But at least we were better than last year's 77–85 record. And after the game I had a brief meeting.

"I appreciate everything you've done for me," I told my ballplayers. "Thanks for making my first season a success. Thanks for having such a great attitude in turning things around. Next year we can do what the Red Sox did this year."

They clapped and yelled and that's what I want them to think about all winter—winning next year. On the way into my office off the visitors' clubhouse, I noticed a big sign above Johnny Ellis's locker. "Thanks for the Memories—Jonathan E." He knows he'll be gone. He even left before the game. When we got to Fenway Park, he asked me if he could leave during the last few innings.

"What for?" I said.

"My wife's here," he said. "We'd like to get an early start."

"Leave now then."

"No, that's all right," he said. "I'll stay around for most of the game."

But when the game started, he wasn't in the dugout.

"He took off," somebody told me. "He's gone home."

That's a typical Johnny Ellis move. If I had refused to let him go early, he would have been upset. But after telling me he would stay around, he left without letting me know. Learning about Johnny Ellis was part of my education as a manager. So was learning what it was like to suffer through a slow start. But the most enjoyable part, the most satisfying part, was watching the ballplayers get themselves together, watching kids like Eckersley and Manning and Kuiper prove they're major-leaguers, watching Boog and Rico and Fritz come back strong, watching LaRoche and Buskey do it out of the bullpen, watching Buddy and Oscar come out of their slumps, watching Duffy improve as a hitter, watching George play well enough to make the All-Star game, watching Alan Ashby develop, and watching the manager learn how to manage. I learned that the manager has to give in sometimes, that the manager has to change his thinking in order to do what will work for his ball club. I learned that the manager can't be stubborn with his ballplayers or with the umpires.

The manager also learned in recent weeks that baseball people think the Cleveland Indians have a team that should be a contender next year.

By baseball people, I'm thinking of Don Zimmer, the Red Sox coach, telling me two weeks ago that he hoped they had clinched first place before we arrived for this final weekend series. I'm thinking of Ralph Houk, the Tigers' manager, telling me, "Your ball club is on the way." I'm thinking of umpires Nestor Chylak and Bill Kunkel telling me the same thing. And most of all I'm thinking of picking up the dugout phone today when it rang in the seventh inning and hearing the voice of Darrell Johnson, the Red Sox manager.

"I just want to tell you, Frank," he said, "that for the last two-thirds of the season, you were the best manager in the league."

I really appreciated that. Some year, maybe next year, I'll be the best manager in the league for three-thirds of the season.

Epilogue:
Only the
Beginning

Bel Air

I'm home now, with a scar on my left shoulder. After taking in the first five games of the World Series, I went to Lutheran Medical Center in Cleveland where Dr. Earl Brightman repaired my torn shoulder tendon and removed several bone spurs. About ten days after the operation I was playing tennis, using my right hand both to toss the ball up and serve. I'm not ready to challenge Jimmy Connors, but it keeps me in shape. I want to be the dh next season. I want those 72 more hits for 3,000 and those 17 more home runs for 600. But most of all, I want to help my ball club win. If the Cleveland Indians were to win the AL East and go on to win the World Series, I wouldn't care if I ever got another hit or another homer. I'm more of a manager now than a player. I'm thinking more like a manager than a player. I'm thinking more about how to improve the team than I am about how to improve myself as a ballplayer. My bad shoulder was a blessing in disguise. It forced me to be virtually a full-time manager. I couldn't depend on my bat to make up for my mistakes.

I also learned to appreciate how important a manager is to his ball club, beginning with writing out the lineup. My mistakes probably held the ball club back at times, but after I blew my stack in Minnesota I think I was really in command. And a manager has to be in command.

The day of the World Series opener, I walked into Fenway Park and Herb Fitzgibbon of the commissioner's office took me aside.

"Ted Bonda phoned," Herb said. "Ted had a call from some guy who threatened to shoot you if Ted didn't fire you as manager."

That guy doesn't have to worry. Ted Bonda will fire me someday. All managers except Walter Alston get fired sooner or later. But until then, I'll turn the Cleveland Indians into a winner. The first year was only the beginning.

I'll be tougher next season. There will be a curfew all the way. I'll also try to have more of a set lineup. I remember Phil telling me in late August, "I understand you've had eighty-nine different lineups so far. I think I'll only give you nine players next year." That was his way of telling me to use a set lineup. And he was right. I'll also know how to handle myself with the umpires. Near the end of the season we were far behind in a game and an umpire gave us a bad call. His explanation was, "What difference does it make?" It makes a big difference. But as proof that I've cooled it, I don't even remember which umpire it was who said that. Honest.

Cleveland Indians, 1975 Season

Pitcher	IP	H	SO	BB	W	L	ERA
Andersen	5.2	4	4	2	0	0	4.76
Beene	46.2	63	20	25	1	0	6.94
Bibby	112.2	99	62	50	5	9	3.20
Bosman	28.2	33	11	8	0	2	4.08
Brown	69.1	72	41	29	1	2	4.28
Buskey	77	69	29	29	5	3	2.57
Eckersley	186.2	147	152	90	13	7	2.60
Harrison	126	137	52	46	7	7	4.79
Hood	135.1	136	51	57	6	10	4.39
Kern	71.2	60	55	45	1	2	3.77
LaRoche	82.1	61	94	57	5	3	2.19
Odom	10.1	4	10	8	1	0	2.61
Perry, G.	121.2	120	85	34	6	9	3.55
Perry, J.	37.2	46	11	18	1	6	6.69
Peterson	146.1	154	47	40	14	8	3.94
Raich	92.2	118	34	31	7	8	5.54
Reynolds	9.2	11	5	3	0	2	4.66
Strickland	4.2	4	3	2	0	0	1.93
Waits	70.1	57	34	25	6	2	2.94

American League, 1975

EAST	W	L	Pct.	GB
Boston	95	65	.594	—
Baltimore	90	69	.566	4½
New York	83	77	.519	12
Cleveland	79	80	.497	15½
Milwaukee	68	94	.420	28
Detroit	57	102	.358	37½

WEST	W	L	Pct.	GB
Oakland	98	64	.605	—
Kansas City	91	71	.562	7
Texas	79	83	.488	19
Minnesota	76	83	.478	20½
Chicago	75	86	.466	22½
California	72	89	.447	25½

Cleveland Indians, 1975 Season

Batter	Avg.	G	AB	R	H	HR	RBI
Ashby	.224	90	254	32	57	5	32
Bell	.271	153	553	66	150	10	59
Berry	.200	25	40	6	8	0	1
Brohamer	.244	69	217	15	53	6	16
Carty	.308	118	383	57	118	18	64
Cerone	.250	7	12	1	3	0	0
Crosby	.234	61	128	12	30	0	7
Duffy	.243	146	482	44	117	1	47
Ellis	.230	92	296	22	68	7	32
Gamble	.261	121	348	60	91	15	45
Hendrick	.258	145	561	82	145	24	86
Kuiper	.292	90	346	42	101	0	25
Lee	.130	13	23	3	3	0	0
Lis	.308	9	13	4	4	2	8
Lowenstein	.242	91	265	37	64	12	33
Manning	.285	120	480	69	137	3	35
McCraw	.275	23	51	7	14	2	5
Powell	.297	134	435	64	129	27	86
Robinson	.237	49	118	19	28	9	24
Smith	.125	8	8	0	1	0	2
Spikes	.229	111	345	41	79	11	33
Sudakis	.196	20	46	4	9	1	3
DH Hitters	.255	—	591	86	151	30	91
PH Hitters	.330	—	103	11	34	3	28

FRANK

United Press International photo

Frank Robinson and his wife, Barbara, the day the Indians announced the hiring of major-league baseball's first black manager.

United Press International photo

Arriving in Tucson for spring training, he and general manager Phil Seghi display his Indian uniform.

Before the exhibition opener, he and Giants manager Wes Westrum meet with umpires Lou DiMuro and Hank Morgenweck.

Framed under Dennis Eckersley's windup, he inspects the rookie pitcher warming up with coach Jeff Torborg.

TOpposite:
The day before the season opener in Cleveland, exhorting his players from behind the batting cage.

Opposite:

In the on-deck circle before his first time at bat on opening day, he keeps his hands warm and his concentration cool.

This swing (above and below) produced the historic homer that contributed to a 5–3 opening day victory over the Yankees.

Crossing the plate, slapping palms with George Hendrick while ignored by Yankee catcher Thurman Munson.

Opposite:

The satisfied smile of a winning manager on opening day. The victory "meant more" to him than the famous homer off Doc Medich.

Above:
At the time of Hank Aaron's first appearance with the Milwaukee Brewers in Cleveland, Robinson and Aaron had, combined, 1,308 homers.

E Left:
Enjoying a moment with Roy Campanella while receiving the Image Award of the Edwin Gould Services for Children.

The day after the "bumping" incident, he avoids a confrontation with umpire Jerry Neudecker as he comes to bat.

A year's difference—the casual announcement with Phil Seghi of his rehiring as the Indians' manager for 1976.